Dewey *on* Democracy

Dewey
on
Democracy

WILLIAM R. CASPARY

CORNELL UNIVERSITY PRESS

ITHACA AND LONDON

First published 2000 by Cornell University Press

Printed in the United States of America

Cornell University Press strives to use environmentally responsible suppliers and materials to the fullest extent possible in the publishing of its books. Such materials include vegetable-based, low-VOC inks and acid-free papers that are recycled, totally chlorine-free, or partly composed of nonwood fibers. Books that bear the logo of the FSC (Forest Stewardship Council) use paper taken from forests that have been inspected and certified as meeting the highest standards for environmental and social responsibility. For further information, visit our website at www.cornellpress.cornell.edu.

Library of Congress Cataloging-in-Publication Data

Caspary, William R., 1937–
    Dewey on democracy / William R. Caspary.
        p.   cm.
    Includes bibliographical references and index.
    ISBN 0-8014-3705-9 (cloth)
        1. Dewey, John, 1859–1952—Contributions in political science.
    2. Dewey, John, 1859–1952—Contributions in democracy.   I. Title.

JC251.D48 C37 2000
320.5'092—dc21   99-054584

Cloth printing   10 9 8 7 6 5 4 3 2 1

This book is dedicated to the memory of George Kraft,
dear friend, colleague, teacher, and activist,
who relished life
and was an inspiration to all
whose lives were touched by his

Contents

Acknowledgments

I was introduced to the ideas of John Dewey by Richard Bernstein's book *Praxis and Action* (1971). Jonathon Moreno helped me find my way to Dewey's writings. Miranda Duncan and the late James Laue taught me about conflict-resolution. Washington University provided two sabbaticals; during the first this book was launched and during the second, completed. From the outset of this book project, colleagues and friends provided abundant stimulation, support, and invaluable critical feedback. Jane Loevinger's advice got me started. Thanks to John Rensenbrinck, Jeff Fishel, Dan Liston, and David Hadas for reading early versions. James Bohman and George Shulman painstakingly read and provided me with insightful comments on early versions of these chapters. Arthur Wirth gave me much encouragement and inspired by example. Ralph Page, editor of *Educational Theory*, where earlier, substantially different versions of Chapters 4 and 5 were published, was unfailingly supportive. Mary Ann Dzubak and Tim Lensmire were generous and encouraging readers. John Forester, Jack Knight, Larry May, Mark Warren, and Carl Wellman each commented on a particular chapter and pointed out issues requiring further thought. Thanks to Richard Bernstein for his helpful comments on the final manuscript. All of these people contributed greatly to this book but are in no way responsible for its errors, or for its particular emphases and interpretations.

Sonia Friedman taught me about the ethical deliberations of women facing decisions about abortion, and about much else as well. The Applied Psychoanalysis Study Group in St. Louis was a model of intellectual community and provided much stimulation and support. The students in my Dewey seminar and our democratic classroom experiments contributed ideas, challenges, and evidence of their capacity for participation. Seminar participants Sandra Lubezky, Karen Ho, and Donna Jeffe were especially helpful. Many other colleagues and friends, more than I can thank here, contributed indirectly to this effort. Thanks are due, especially, to the late John Holt, David Hadas, the late Robert Boguslaw, Susan Wynne, Mark Berger, Marshall Rosenberg, Ron Robbins, Jan Eigner, George and Peggy Kraft, and George Shulman. Thanks to my wife, Rima, the joy of my life! Janet Rensing offered good humor as well as hard work in typing parts of this manuscript. Marquita and Thelma Daniels of La Patisserie provided the coffee and good vibrations that fueled most of this writing.

A Note on Sources

For the readers' ease of access, citations of Dewey's books, with the exception of *Ethics*, are to original editions or Dewey's own substantially revised or augmented editions, available in libraries and often in paperback reprints. Citations of *Ethics*, and of Dewey's articles, are to the critical edition, *The Collected Works of John Dewey, 1882–1953*, edited by Jo Ann Boydston (Carbondale: Southern Illinois University Press, 1969–1991), and published as *The Early Works: 1882–1898* (EW), *The Middle Works: 1899–1924* (MW), and *The Later Works: 1925–1953* (LW).

For ease of identification, the most common and important sources are indicated by an abbreviation: e.g., *The Public and Its Problems* (PP), "Science and Society" (SS), *The Later Works, Volume 10* (LW10). A list of abbreviations is included just before the notes at the end of this volume.

Other less prominent writings to which individual attention should be called are cited by their date of publication. These sources can be looked up by date in the chronological list of works by John Dewey in the References section: e.g., looking up (1928b) and (1936), one will find, respectively, "Progressive Education and the Science of Education" and "Authority and Social Change."

Finally, articles which are cited only for one or two brief points are identified simply by their location in the critical edition: for example, (MW15:154).

Dewey *on* Democracy

Introduction

Renewal of Interest in Dewey's
Thought and Democratic Theory

Interest in the philosophy of John Dewey has been revived in the last fifteen years, bringing renewed enthusiasm and fresh insight to his work. Democratic theory has also seen vigorous activity during this period. This book stands at the intersection of these two traditions. During much of his career, Dewey was a dominating presence in the fields of political theory, philosophy, and education, but his influence went into eclipse following World War II. In the era of McCarthyism, Dewey was portrayed as dangerously radical. At the same time, the domination of the analytic and logical positivist approaches in philosophy made Dewey seem obsolete. But in the 1980s, with rising challenges to the analytic approach in philosophy (from postempiricists, feminists, neo-Hegelians, neo-Kantians, and postmodernists) and a renewed search for a strong democratic perspective in political theory, interest in Dewey was rekindled. By this time, political theorists interested in continental critical theory and European Marxism had assimilated these traditions sufficiently to permit reconsideration of approaches originating in the United States, and more directly concerned with democracy. Democratic revolutions in Eastern Europe have swelled this trend but are far too recent to account for its origins. From this perspective, Dewey appears as a major contributor to the emerging theory of participatory democracy.

In light of postempiricist and postanalytic perspectives, philosophers and social scientists could see that Dewey was no less sophisticated than those who had pursued highly formalized or narrowly specialized analytic and empirical studies. Instead, he carved out a completely different path, or, if you will, a different paradigm. Far from having left Dewey behind, we may just now be catching up with him. In Richard Rorty's words, Dewey was "waiting at the end of the dialectical road which analytic philosophy traveled" (1982:xviii). Able to recognize and appreciate Dewey's basic outlook, we can now search in his work for answers to current problems in democratic theory.

To rediscover and embrace Dewey as a theorist of participatory democracy, however, is also to revive old criticisms and doubts. Do Dewey's twin commitments to science and democracy take sufficient account of the limits of science, the disenchantment and dehumanization attendant on rationalization, and the darker side of human nature? Does Dewey overlook the fact that political deliberation is embedded in institutions shaped by power and wealth? Does he, in his attack on dualisms, evade genuine contradictions and offer facile solutions? Is he simply a naive liberal optimist, pursuing the obsolete agenda of the eighteenth-century enlightenment? The Dewey revival has helped gain recognition of the depth and power of Dewey's thought, and dispel some of the misrepresentation and denigration that prevailed in earlier years. Again and again, however, several recent comments on Dewey's democratic thought begin by celebrating him as an early and still-inspirational participatory democrat, only to conclude that he offers little guidance toward solving the current dilemmas and impasses of democracy.[1]

Is it possible that Dewey built his theory better than has been recognized thus far? Both the easy dismissals of Dewey and those conveying more thoughtful, reluctant disappointments may be too hasty. Are these conclusions a result of viewing his thought through a late twentieth-century mood of despair, or of reading our own meanings into his terms? Do we tend, for example, to interpret his usage of "science" to mean positivism, despite his explicit critique of positivism and elaboration of his sharply different Pragmatist approach? Is Dewey's unwavering commitment to participatory democracy more an expression of courage and vision in the face of obstacles than of naiveté and denial? Does Dewey's liberalism—his self-designation as a liberal, his critique of Marxism-Leninism, and his stress on social intelligence and cooperation—blind us to another side of his thought—a vigorous critique of the disproportionate influence of wealth, power, and privilege and a call for political contestation against it? Is Dewey's failure to provide a concrete political strategy mitigated by his provision of the tools for constructing one? The thesis of this book is that Dewey anticipates many of our objections and provides us with satisfying answers.

Far from being only of historical interest, Dewey's writings beckon us to new discoveries and new adventures in the pursuit of democracy. His answers are sometimes fragmentary, however, requiring us to reassemble and elucidate them. And like any great thinker, Dewey is not entirely consistent. In his writings, for example, technocratic themes with elitist implications clash with strong ideas on participatory democracy and dreams of consensus clash with a lively awareness of ongoing conflict. Here, I present Dewey in his most democratic mood—particularly his recognition of conflict as an inescapable condition of democratic politics—and explore the theoretical implications of these orientations. This being an exercise in political theory, not biography or intellectual history, it seems appropriate to explore one fruitful strand of a thinker's views rather than strive for a comprehensive, balanced account of his entire life's work.

With globalization of commerce and the end of the cold war, democratic theorists are extending their analysis beyond established industrialized democracies and beyond the nation-state. Influenced by the tragedy of World War I, Dewey, too, writes about democracy on a global scale. To keep the analysis compact, however, I have eschewed this broad a perspective here. It is assumed that analysis at the national level is needed to lay the groundwork for discussing democracy on a global scale.

I propose that Dewey's philosophical Pragmatism and his democratic politics, alike, revolve around a central theme of conflict and conflict-resolution. Though it may not be stated overtly, this theme lies just below the surface of his writings. It emerges most explicitly and centrally in Dewey's theory of ethical deliberation, which is concerned with the harmonization of conflicting tendencies within the individual and the group. Dewey sees harmonization/resolution as occurring through inquiry, leading to novel discoveries that transform the conflict situation. The process of inquiry which results in innovative solutions that restore harmony to problematic situations is precisely how Dewey characterizes scientific activity. This characterization of inquiry helps us to understand why Dewey viewed ethical deliberation as similar methodologically to scientific investigation. Once the idea of conflict-resolution is seen to pervade Dewey's philosophy, one is alerted to the scattered but crucial references to it in his political writings. In Dewey's work, conflict-resolution emerges not merely as another political technique, but as a constitutive element of the very meaning of democracy. The contrast then becomes clear between Dewey's account of democratic discourse and those of liberal democratic theory, Jurgen Habermas's discourse theory, and communitarian theory.

Sources

Dewey's best known and most intensive engagement with political theory is presented in his 1927 book, *The Public and Its Problems* (PP). By itself, however, that work is insufficient to convey his view of democracy, for three reasons. First, it contains numerous but oblique references to his thought on philosophical issues concerning science, ethics, language, psychology, and esthetics. Second, Dewey's theory of conflict and conflict-resolution is not presented in *The Public and Its Problems*, although it is discussed in his other texts and is crucial to his entire philosophy and political theory. Third, *The Public and Its Problems* is but one of his four important books on political theory, including *Individualism Old and New* (ION 1930), *Liberalism and Social Action* (LSA 1935), and *Freedom and Culture* (FC 1939), each of which adds new elements to the picture even as it repeats familiar Deweyan themes. To this corpus must be added substantial observations on politics presented in books on other topics, especially *Democracy and Education* (DE 1915), *Reconstruction in Philosophy* (RPh 1920; 2d ed. 1948), *Human Nature and Conduct* (HNC 1922; Modern Library ed. 1930), and *Ethics* (E rev. ed. 1932). Dewey also made important additions to his theory through articles and lectures. Some of these are gathered in *Problems of Men* (1946), including "Democracy and Educational Administration" (DEA 1937), which presents concisely and forcefully the idea of participatory democracy and suggests how democracy can be implemented in the workplace as well as in government. Dewey's essay "The Economic Basis of the New Society" (EBNS 1939) is his most focused statement on workplace democracy and full employment. Another important article, written at the outset of World War II, is "Creative Democracy" (CD 1939). Here Dewey clarifies his views on public discourse and conflict-resolution, and on democracy as an attribute not only of governmental structures, but also of community and personal life (CD:225). Finally, there are Dewey's topical articles, written not for posterity but as contributions to the politics of the day. By his own admission, Dewey was not a particularly astute observer and strategist of electoral politics. Nonetheless, used circumspectly, these sources lend clarification to Dewey's more abstract formulations on this subject. To sum up, Dewey wrote four books on politics, a number of philosophical articles and chapters, and occasional observations on the concrete issues and strategies of the day. A full appreciation of his political thought requires consideration of the full range of these sources. Since Dewey's thought on politics is deeply integrated with his views on science, ethics, the self, and other topics, additional sources must be consulted to aid in interpreting the political ones. Dewey's account of human experience, which he termed metaphysics, is largely presumed rather than presented here; it has been thoroughly and insightfully analyzed by others (R. Bernstein 1966, 1971; Boisvert 1988).

In addition to this large corpus of primary sources, Dewey's political theory has been the subject of extensive scholarly commentary in recent years (Campbell 1995; Hickman 1990; Kaufman-Osborn 1991; Rockefeller 1991; Ryan 1995; Shusterman 1994a, 1994b; Smiley 1990; West 1989; Westbrook 1991). Other writers have drawn strongly on Dewey's democratic thought in pursuing their original work (Bellah et al. 1991; Yankelovich 1991). Much of Dewey's thinking has been placed in the intellectual and political setting of his own time, and recovered and clarified for ours. Links of Dewey's political theory to his esthetic, metaphysical, and educational views have been delineated. It is widely agreed among recent commentators that Dewey was a participatory democrat and a social democrat (e.g., Kloppenberg 1986). Earlier nonscholarly views that assimilate Dewey into mainstream New Deal liberalism have been corrected. It is now agreed that Dewey, despite his emphasis on the relation of theory to practice, offered few concrete suggestions for political action or governmental structures. In the introductory section of Chapter 1, some of this established ground is retraced. I have quoted primary sources extensively to present Dewey's more familiar views in his own voice. My principal goal in this book, however, is to break new ground.

There is considerable disagreement on the prominent role in democratic life which Dewey proposed for the spirit and methods of science in democratic life. Some critics see this as a blot on an otherwise worthwhile theory (Damico 1978; Rorty 1995). Others celebrate Dewey's experimental rather than dogmatic orientation but do not analyze sufficiently what he meant by "experiment" in natural and social science and in political life. In this volume, I emphasize the striking difference between Dewey's understanding of science and mainstream conceptions.

With this in mind, Dewey's views on the importance of the scientific spirit for democracy are given a fresh interpretation. With regard to natural science and social science, reference is made particularly to *Reconstruction in Philosophy* (1920), *Experience and Nature* (EN 1925; rev. ed. 1929), *The Quest for Certainty* (QC 1929), and *Logic: The Theory of Inquiry* (LTI 1938), as well as the essays "Science and Society" (SS 1931), "Social Science and Social Control" (SSSC 1931), "Progressive Education and the Science of Education" (PESE 1928), and "Liberating the Social Scientist" (LSS 1947), and "Introduction" to the second edition of *Reconstruction in Philosophy* (1948). Among commentators, Ian Hacking (1983) is particularly insightful, and Larry Hickman (1990, 1998) has written on Dewey's experimentalism.

Relatively little has been written on Dewey's theory of ethical deliberation and conflict-resolution, and the way these play out in his theory of political discourse. In this book, I emphasize these topics and their consequences for democratic theory. This discussion draws especially upon Dewey's two major mature books on ethical theory, *Human Nature and Conduct* (1922) and the completely revised *Ethics* (E 1932). Additional material is found in the chapters on ethics in *Reconstruction in Philosophy*, and *The Quest for Certainty*, and in the late monograph *The Theory of Valuation* (1939). I refer to *Art as Experience* (AE 1934) for Dewey's thoughts on moral imagination. *Experience and Nature* is the source for Dewey's ideas on the element of critique in moral reflection. On the nature of the self, Dewey's major statement is *Human Nature and Conduct*, but important material on the self and language may also be found in *Experience and Nature*. Dewey's brief but crucial insight on the transformation of self attendant upon inquiry is found in the late essay, "Experience, Knowledge and Value: A Rejoinder" (EKV 1939). Dewey's thought on intrapersonal conflict-resolution is presented in terms of harmonization in ethical deliberation in *Human Nature and Conduct* (Part III, Section 3). His account of intergroup conflict-resolution appears in his later political writings (LSA, FC, CD). Dewey anticipated the pioneering work of Mary Parker Follett (1924; 1942; Davis 1989) and perhaps influenced it. Today's developed conflict-resolution theory and practice (e.g., Moore 1996) provides retrospective insight into Dewey's account.

The sources mentioned above are, with one exception, from 1920 or later and represent Dewey's mature views—that is, views he developed when he was over age 60 and had experienced and reflected on World War I and its aftermath. I have made no attempt here to trace the evolution of his mature positions from their earlier precursors, as Dewey's biographers and some commentators have already carried out this task (Edel and Flowers, 1985; Rockefeller 1991; Ryan 1995; Sleeper 1986; Westbrook 1991). I do, however, make occasional references to his pre-1920 work, especially *Democracy and Education* (1915) and *Essays on Experimental Logic* (EEL 1916).

Overview

In the first chapter I review Dewey's account of participatory democracy and sketch a "politics of transition," involving the intertwining of political action and political discourse. My summary of Dewey's philosophical Pragmatism introduces the themes of conflict and conflict-resolution. I present Dewey's conception of community, and note the role of conflict-resolution in instituting community. I discuss Dewey's account of the procedures and outcomes of conflict-resolution and supplement this with material from today's professional practice of mediation. The section concludes with an introduction of Dewey's concept of "social intelligence." In the next four chapters, grouped in pairs, I explicate in detail Dewey's account of science and of ethics, providing the basis for his theory of social intelligence, and hence, conflict-resolution. Chapters 2 and 3 present, respectively, Dewey's account of natural science and his recommendations for social science. The implications of Dewey's democratic experimentalism are explored in concrete detail. Chapters 4 and 5 discuss, respectively, individual ethical deliberation and public deliberation and ethical theory. Here I develop a basis for understanding Dewey's account of public deliberation. Finally, Chapter 6 considers Dewey's strategy for activist progressive politics. Dewey's perspective on building progressive political movements for a more democratic society is illustrated with examples from recent social movements. I bring together the broad themes of the book in my concluding statement on a Deweyan politics of transition.

1 Participatory Democracy, Pragmatism, and Conflict-Resolution

Participatory Democracy: Situating Dewey's Thought

Dewey is, above all, a participatory democracy theorist, as Westbrook (1991), and others, have convincingly argued.[1] Though stated half a century earlier, Dewey's views resemble the formulations of participatory democracy developed since the term was used in the Port Huron Statement by Students for a Democratic Society (1962).[2] His views have affinities too, with communitarian and civic republican ideas of participation, civic education, and civic virtue.[3] Dewey's ideal is a high level of citizen participation in public discussion and decision making: "a responsible share according to capacity in shaping the aims and policies of the groups to which one belongs" (PP:147). Access to participation is to be free and equal, "without respect to race, sex, class or economic status" (RPh:186). Such participation is to be voluntary: "in service of a freedom which is cooperative and a cooperation which is voluntary" (1939b:368).

Dewey espouses "democratic methods in all social relationships . . . educational institutions . . . industry and business" (DEA:225). "The principle holds as much of one form of association, say in industry and commerce, as it does in government" (RPh:209). Indeed, if workers "have no part in making plans or formulating policies" this will "render their minds unfit for accepting the intellectual responsibilities involved in political self-government" (E:353). Furthermore, "the struggle for democracy has to be maintained on as many fronts as culture has aspects:

8

political, economic, international, educational, scientific and artistic, religious" (FC:173). "Shaping the aims and policies" of these groups would depend on public discussion according to "democratic methods, methods of consultation, persuasion, negotiation, communication, cooperative intelligence" (FC:175)—although final decisions could be made by representative bodies. "Democratic method is . . . public discussion carried on . . . in legislative halls . . . in the press, private conversations and public assemblies" (FC:128). Seyla Benhabib recently articulated a related conception, "a plurality of modes of association in which all those affected can have the right to articulate their point of view" (1996:73). Dewey envisions vital dialogue that includes elements of empirical investigation, interpretation, critique, narrative, ethical deliberation, conflict, and conflict-resolution. Such discussion, however, is continuous with political contestation, not isolated in a separate, ideal discursive space. Dewey is neither naive about the quality of public discussion today, nor dismissive of its achievements; his concern is with its future potential.

Dewey believes such public discussion would lead to the discovery of common interests, not simply to bargaining over private interests. "Popular government is educative. It forces a recognition that there are common interests" (PP:207). "Conflicting claims are to be settled in the interest of the widest possible contribution to the interest of all" (LSA:79). Common interests are more than merely a sum of compatible private interests, or a compromise. Dewey envisions "form[s] of experience which [are] augmented and confirmed by being shared" (RPh:205; also PP:27, 54). "The positive import of 'common good' is suggested by the idea of sharing, participating—an idea involved in the very idea of community" (E:345). Schooling should prepare students to discover common interests (DE:98).

In emphasizing common interests, Dewey does not deny conflict (cf. Warren 1996:243, 267), but instead stresses constructive resolution. Conflict is ubiquitous. "It might even be admitted that a society in which there was no opposition of interests would be sunk in a condition of hopeless lethargy" (FC:87). "The very heart of political democracy is adjudication [sic] of social differences by an exchange of views" (1944: 273). Dewey is not referring here to adjudication in the courts, but to public discussion moving toward, though never entirely achieving, consensus. In other words, "the very heart of political democracy" is conflict-resolution. The theme of conflict-resolution is emphasized in this volume as being central to Dewey's vision. Though at times Dewey appears to neglect political conflict, over the course of his works there are numerous references to it. I believe Dewey's entire philosophy revolves around conflict-resolution and therefore is equal to the challenges of a dynamic, diverse, democratic society.

For Dewey, participation in decision making does not imply constantly redeciding every detail. Society operates largely by conventional practices, just as individuals operate by habit (PP:159–162; HNC:75–83). This lends efficiency to activity, leaving intelligence free for application to problematic situations. The goal is not to eliminate custom and habit, but to revise them from time to time as needs and values change. We require flexible, intelligent habits, not constant reinvention of our behavior (HNC:72). Intensive participation is needed on occasion to decide on changes in customary practices in response to a changing environment or changing values. Once a decision is reached, outcomes need to be monitored, but intensive deliberation is no longer required. As Deborah Meier (1995) puts it, reflecting on the experience of a democratically organized school faculty: "we learned not to discuss everything—at least not all the time. This has actually meant more time for discussing those issues that concern us most" (26).

Dewey, like all participatory democrats, hypothesizes that participation in public deliberation, in itself, would be educative. The more the involvement in public affairs, the more knowledgeable and skillful participation would become. "Full education comes only when there is a responsible share . . . in shaping the aims and policies of the social groups to which he belongs" (RPh:209; also ION:132–133). Participation would not merely draw on citizens' abilities as presently manifested, but would "liberate" and "release" capacities not even anticipated under current social arrangements (RPh:209; DEA:220). This, in turn, would contribute to wiser public decisions and improved implementation. "The best guarantee of collective efficiency and power is liberation and use of the diversity of individual capacities in initiative, planning, foresight, vigor and endurance" (RPh:209). Like democratic theorists of many stripes, Dewey views local communities as schools of democracy which prepare citizens for effective participation in the more complex and mediated national political discussion (PP:211–214, 218). Conversely, Dewey recognizes that the educative effect of national political discourse helps in overcoming parochialism and stasis in local communities (PP:212, 216; 139). Finally, formal, mediated conflict-resolution, as will be seen, can be especially educative.

The educative effect of democratic participation, in Dewey's view, goes beyond skills and knowledge to involve moral development, and thus, personal transformation (Rosenthal 1986:191). "The formation of a self new in some respect or some degree is, then, involved in every genuine act of inquiry . . . in the distinctively moral situation [the emphasis] falls upon the reconstruction of the self as the distinctively demanded means" (EKV:70). "All inquiry and discovery . . . implicate an individual still to make . . . for to arrive at a new truth is to alter. The old self is put off and the new self is only forming" (EN:245). Ethical deliberation involves precisely this kind of inquiry. "Morals means growth of conduct in meaning; . . . expansion in meaning which is consequent upon observations of the conditions and outcome of conduct. It is all one with growing. . . . Morals is education. It is learning the meaning of what we are about" (HNC:280). There is an affinity between Dewey's account of the formation of a new self, and the perpective of Benhabib's (1996) perspectives on "moral transformative discourse," Jürgen Habermas's ideas on moral development (1979, 1990), and John Stuart Mill's moral "perfectionism" (Nino 1995:97–100). For Dewey, moral development is far more than a movement toward impartiality, autonomy, or the sovereignty of reason and will. It involves moral imagination, empathy, care, and the articulation, integration, and expansion of the meanings that constitute the self (HNC 280, 283, 293; EN 411; see also Belenky et al. 1986). For some, however, the notion of transformative discourse raises the specters of coerciveness and utopianism (Knight and Johnson 1994). Dewey emphasizes, however, that inquiry and attendant change in the self are voluntary, and are natural responses for anyone engaged in and with one's world. He would agree with Benhabib's assurance that participation in discourse and inquiry "does not entail dedifferentiation, value homogeneity, or even value reeducation" (1992:53).

Considerations about moral development are crucial aspects of Dewey's overall argument—not in and of themselves, but in conjunction with other crucial ideas about theory and practice, conflict-resolution, discovery and justification, and cooperative community life. In Dewey's view, dialogue occurs not in a vacuum, but in the practice of political coordination and contestation over specific issues and conflicts. Dewey offers no conception of political discourse unsullied by particular interests, such as one finds in Rousseau and, as Hanna Pitkin (1981) argues, in Hannah Arendt. Thus, social movements, which articulate interests and struggle for the power to place issues on the public agenda, are crucial to Dewey's theory of democracy and democratic discourse. Dewey's linking of practice and discourse, however, does not preclude the creation of special spaces, such as mediated conflict-resolution, which allow discussion at some remove from political struggle. Dewey also encourages the introduction of rigorous scholarship and research, or reflective and nonpartisan analysis, into the public debate—although these pursuits are never entirely free of interests and particular standpoints. Benhabib takes a position close to Dewey's: "The relationships between 'discourse' and 'action' is [sic] complex. . . . Discourses involve a certain 'bracketing' of the constraints of action; they represent a momentary pause of deliberation amid the intensity of engaged conflict and disagreement. [Yet] they themselves reach back upon contexts of action" (1986:316).

Like civic republicans, Dewey hypothesizes that a decent approximation to equal participation can only take place where disparities in wealth are kept within a reasonable range. One of the chief obstacles to participation and reasonable discussion, in Dewey's view, is the social class structure which enables economic elites to dominate politics. "Our institutions, democratic in form, tend to favor in substance a privileged plutocracy" (LSA:85). Wealthy people and large corporations own and control the mass media, use contributions to candidates to influence elections, have privileged access to government offices, and withhold investment or shift capital abroad (FC:148; PP:180, 182). Political organizing and action against this unjust distribution of power is essential for the transition to participatory democracy (FC:162; LSA:91). "Most political issues of the present arise out of . . . the distribution of wealth and income, the ownership and control of property" (E:356). "Political action and thought will be confused and insincere as long as the importance of economic issues in political life is kept from view" (E:357).

Dewey envisions national and local communities so organized that the self-realization of each individual would contribute to conditions that foster the self-realization of others. "The democratic idea in its generic social sense . . . demands liberation of the potentialities of members of a group in harmony with the interest and goods which are common" (PP:147). Though typically found among communitarians, this idea also resembles John Rawls's notion of social union, and of democratic society as a social union of social unions. "It is only in active cooperation with others that one's powers reach fruition. Only in a social union is the individual complete" (Rawls 1971:525n). While discussing personal flourishing, Dewey stresses the interdependence of actively participating individuals seeking a fulfilled life: "only when individuals have initiative, independence of judgment, flexibility, fullness of experience, can they act so as to enrich the lives of others and only in this way can a truly common welfare be built up" (E:348). Whether such a condition can be realized on a large scale—in the "Great Community," is, for Dewey, an empirical question to be settled by social experimentation. It can neither be established nor rejected a priori. "The democratic ideal [of mutually enhancing individuality] poses, rather than solves, the great problem. . . . Like every true ideal, it signifies something to be done rather than something already given . . . Because it is something to be accomplished by human planning and arrangement, it involves constant meeting and solving of problems—that is to say the desired harmony never is brought about in a way which meets and forestalls all future developments" (E:350). This theme of experimentalism in Dewey's theory suggests that, in Rawls's terms, this is a "theory of transition" (1993:17–18). This is discussed shortly.

Given Dewey's ideal of democracy as involving mutually enhancing self-realization, the question arises: would this not lead to a "politics of virtue"—a unitary state in which conformity is the price of harmony? Donald Moon, among others, raises this question about participatory democracy and communitarianism (Moon 1993a:5). Moon critiques an imagined "form of social life in which the conditions creating estrangement and opposition have been overcome, a life in which the free self-realization of each person enhances the self-realization of others, thereby eliminating the need for authority to make and coercion to enforce, social norms" (6). Moon's mention of mutual self-realization suggests Dewey's position. On closer examination, however, the politics of virtue is drastically at odds with Dewey's vision of participatory democracy. Mutual self-realization does not require the elimination of opposition; indeed, it is through working out conflicts with one another that citizens contribute to each other's learning and development. Nor does mutual self-realization eliminate the need for law and law-enforcement, although these functions would be rendered more responsive (E:227). Self-realization, in Dewey's view, is not "free," if that means unconstrained by social obligation. Nor does Dewey go to the other extreme, and advocate the submergence of the self in a social whole. It is the creative interaction and tension between individual and society that Dewey proposes: "the full development of individuals in their distinctive individuality, not the sacrifice of them to some alleged vague larger good" (E:348). Dewey's account of multiple common interests, arrived at through deliberation and political struggle, must be distinguished from Rousseau's idea of a single a priori general will, with its decidedly illiberal overtones (PP:54). Dewey is not advocating a unitary state (MW15: 154). He celebrates diversity and advocates civil liberties protections for dissenting speech, and for cultures and lifestyles apart from the mainstream. He defines his problem as developing community in the "Great Society," in modern, complex and diverse social and economic organization, and never confuses this with the small homogenous local community (PP; cf. Shulman 1983). The issue of potential, though unintended, coerciveness can still be raised, however. Dewey's answer to this is that community and civic virtue are achieved by choice of facilitative institutions, not by demands upon individual behavior (cf. Sandel 1996). Dewey rejects the notion that experts or majorities "know better than others what is good for them" (E:251). Instead, "social conditions should be such that all individuals can exercise their own initiative, in a social medium which will develop their personal capacities" (251; also 366; EBNS:318). Institutional design is always partial, contestable, and experimental—perhaps somewhere between Karl Popper's piecemeal social engineering and grand schemes of state planning. Dewey seeks not a planned society, but a planning society (EBNS:321).

The fact that diversity in a complex society presents challenges to democracy does not tempt Dewey to seek a homogeneous community. Diverse subcultures bring more resources to solving social problems (RPh:209), just as genetic variation is a storehouse of potential solutions to problems posed by changing physical environments. Diversity is also cherished for its potential to enrich life experience, and add fresh perspectives to our complex reality (E:366; also Young 1996). Democracy, then, would involve the "breaking down of those barriers of class, race, and national territory which keeps men from perceiving the full import of their activity" (DE:87). "To cooperate by giving differences a chance to show themselves . . . is a means of enriching ones own life experience . . . [this] is inherent in the democratic personal way of life" (CD:228). Common democratic culture must not be achieved by the suppression of differences. On the assimilation of immigrants, Dewey writes: "the consolidation has occurred so rapidly and ruthlessly that much of value has been lost which different peoples might have contributed" (PP:115; also MW2:85). Dewey is not, however, a believer in preserving subcultures in some alleged pristine state. "No form of life does or can stand still" (LW11:182). To freeze a culture at some point in its continuous process of change is to induce its stagnation and eventual demise. People in vigorous interchange will, indeed, be influenced by one another. Unique subcultures would not be suppressed, but neither

would they be preserved in museum-like isolation. A common democratic culture would develop, cutting across, but not superseding individual subcultures (Ryan 1995:172).

Rejecting the unitary community and state, Dewey embraces pluralism and civil libertarianism. He firmly identifies himself both as a participatory democrat and as a liberal (see LSA). Perhaps the recent indi-
cations of a rapprochement in the liberalism-communitarianism debate
make room for understanding such a combined position (Galston 1994:
733; Ryan 1993). Dewey's liberalism has several features. It includes representative institutions; participation is not identical with direct democracy. Dewey is a pluralist. He celebrates diversity both for the freedom it offers to individuals, and for the learning opportunities each
group offers to the others. "A progressive society counts individual variations [of class, race, and nationality] as precious since it finds in them
the means of its own growth . . . the play of diverse gifts and interests"
(DE:305). Dewey was a civil libertarian—indeed, he was a founding
member of the American Civil Liberties Union (LW11:372–375; Ryan
1995:169). His commitment to freedom of speech and other basic rights
is emphatic. "Free inquiry and freedom of publication and discussion
must be encouraged and not merely grudgingly tolerated" (E:329).
Dewey views basic rights as instrumental, indeed essential, to democratic government and to individual self-realization. He rejects the idea,
however, that there are natural rights, or that rights are given by intuition or reason—that there are fixed standards for human morality that
arise outside of experience. Though certainly a liberal, Dewey is clearly
not a classic liberal, but rather, a modern liberal, or progressive, or social
democrat who sees a key role for government in regulation, social insurance, and planning (see EENS, LSA; also Kloppenberg 1986). Dewey
contributes an important theoretical statement, *Liberalism and Social
Action*, identifying these two strands of liberalism and tracing their history. Having looked at some broad features of Dewey's participatory
democratic and liberal approach, let us examine further the conflict-
resolution theme in his work. This is discussed in relation to Rawls's
liberal democratic theory.

Politics of Transition and Conflict-Resolution

Dewey's experimentalism suggests that his theory of participatory democracy is centered on the problem of "transition" (Rawls 1993:17–18),

not on a constitutionalist or contractarian account of what that democracy must be. The emphasis on transition requires Dewey to go further
than Rawls, by indicating "how to get there from here"—suggesting the
program and organization of a democratic movement for social transformation which can operate despite a less than fully democratic society.
A theory of transition requires less, however, than Rawls attempts by
way of formal demonstration of the stability of an imagined, ideal democratic order. In Dewey's pragmatist view, the question of stability can
only be settled experimentally, not deductively (E:350). Theory can anticipate the outcome of experiments but not preclude unsuspected variables, and outcomes. Dewey asks both less and more of citizens than
does Rawls. In Rawls's ideal theory, all citizens—except a marginalized
minority—must hold reasonable comprehensive doctrines. Dewey sees
citizens entering into fruitful discussion without prior agreement on
what constitutes justice or reasonableness. But Dewey expects that participation in public discourse will be transformative—educative in a
profound way that leads the parties to greater reasonableness. In short,
Rawls asks whether a society characterized by "reasonable pluralism"
will be stable, and Dewey asks whether there is a politics of transition
that can begin with unreasonable pluralism and arrive at what Rawls envisions as the starting point.

Not all forms of life and systems of belief—racist views and practices,
for example—are equally compatible with democratic community.
Dewey writes: "our anti-democratic heritage of Negro slavery has left us
with habits of intolerance toward the colored race—habits which belie
profession of democratic loyalty" (1941:277). This does not imply, however, that racist views—unreasonable comprehensive doctrines—must
be excluded from the democratic conversation. On the contrary, it is
Dewey's thesis that full discussion would, eventually, dispel such views.
He calls for "open and public communication in which prejudices have
the opportunity to erase each other" (1950:86); "discussion in which
there takes place purification and pooling of the net results of the experiences of multitudes of people" (1941:276). If this seems naive, it must
be emphasized that Dewey is referring to much fuller and freer dialogue
than exists at present: to dialogue in the context of political struggle;
and what amounts to dialogue facilitated by formal, mediated conflict-
resolution. He envisages not instant changes but evolution that may
take decades or generations (FC:176; 1936:145).

Rawls's questions about "stability" and the "well-ordered society,"
are linked to his deductive constitutionalist and contractarian approach.

In their strict, formal sense, they do not apply to Dewey's experimentalist theory of transition. Informally, however, as questions about the workability of pluralistic democracy (1993:xvi–xxvii), they challenge Dewey to offer ways in which society might deal fairly with passionate cultural and ideological conflict. To answer this question is to return to Dewey's conflict-resolution approach. This approach begins by opening up dialogue between opposed groups, even those engaged in bitter conflict (CD:228). What is crucial, however, beyond the respectful exchange of views, is inquiry and discovery which uncover novel solutions. Innovative courses of action create unsuspected common interests, and transform conditions which generate conflict. Dewey predicts that such conflict-resolution would enable diverse groups in society to preserve their distinctiveness, yet come to constructive accommodation with one another, thereby creating a common political culture. Shared principles would be the product of such dialogue, not its precondition. To understand Dewey's ideas on conflict, conflict-resolution, and community requires that we take a step back to examine Dewey's philosophical Pragmatist conception of human experience and human community.

Dewey's Pragmatism: Living in Community, Resolving Conflict

There is a conventional account of modernity that defines it as the hegemony of positivism in science, of bureaucracy in politics, and of industrialism in the economy. The hegemony of positivism is broken only by the emergence, after World War II, of postempiricist philosophy of science, feminist thought, and poststructuralism. The result is a recent dramatic shift in academic theory from the strategic, and the empirical, viewed naively as objective, to the interpretive and subjective. There is a shift toward concern with the construction of identity and away from empirical investigation of policies and institutions. Finally, there is a crisis of relativism, as the old presumed certainties of objectivism are undermined, and theory must proceed without foundations. But, like all narratives, this account of modernity distorts as well as illuminates. The thought of recent centuries has never been homogeneous. There have always been nonpositivist and antipositivist strands of modern thought, and Dewey's Pragmatism is one of them. Dewey embraces both the interpretive and the empirical, both engagement in the world and reflection, both the esthetic and the practical. Dewey's thought shares the emancipatory aspirations of the enlightenment, but not the mechanistic and atomistic view of human beings, nor the positivist account of knowledge and science. Dewey's thought condemns objectivism but does not slide into relativism and skepticism (R. Bernstein 1983). He seeks to substitute the security of reflectively settled practices, which survive critique and are tested in experience,[4] for the illusion of certainty.

Dewey's point of departure is that of human engagement in and with the world—people living immersed in a dynamic natural and social environment. People act in the world, and are impacted upon by the world. "Man is within nature, not a little god outside" (EN:434). Humans transform their natural and social environments, rather than merely adapting to existing conditions, and are themselves transformed in the process. Dewey uses the term, "experience" in this context of engagement in and transactions with the world. Thus experience is not something characteristic of a mind separated from, but rather seeking contact with, an external world (RPh:123). Humans are social beings, and their experiences occur within a social matrix. The possibility of experience of any degree of complexity depends upon language, which is a product of humans in communities coordinating their activities.

Dewey observes, following William James, that experience alternates between "perchings and flights" (EN:400)—between states of completion and harmony, on the one hand, and situations of change, disequilibrium, conflict, need, threat, and challenge, on the other. The term, "esthetic," in Dewey's usage, refers to moments of felt consummation, integration, and equilibrium (EN:80). Thus the esthetic aspect is crucial to our conceptions of the good (AE:17–18; E:168; EN:xi–xii). The term, "practical," refers to moments of felt disharmony, of conflict or need or threat, and are perceived as problems that demand action, and demand thought to guide the action (RPh:66; MW4:71, 125–142). "Practical," is employed by Dewey—as by Habermas—in its classical sense—to encompass both ends and means, the ethical as well as the empirical. Furthermore, Dewey treats the "ethical" as involving both the good and the right, and he uses "moral" and "ethical" interchangeably. Though conceptually distinct, esthetic and practical aspects of experience are intertwined in Dewey's theory of ethics. Furthermore, science has its esthetic moments, art has its moments of practical problem-solving, and both are present in everyday living (AE:30, 38, 55). Indeed, at the deepest level, Dewey perceives those working in science, ethics, and art as grappling with problematic situations, resolving conflict, and achieving consummation (LW2:107).

In everyday practice we encounter familiar conditions for which we have a repertoire of routine, approved responses (EEL:196–197; MW3: 37; HNC:279; E,1908:195; also Kekes 1989). To put it in different words, throughout the day we deal with "established situations" (Boguslaw 1965). It is also a ubiquitous feature of life to be faced with situations of greater or lesser novelty, "emergent situations" (Boguslaw 1965), for which we have no settled response. In Dewey's terms: "Practical activity deals with individualized and unique situations which are never exactly duplicable and about which, accordingly, no complete assurance is possible" (QC:6, also 207; RPh:168; EKV:69). In these instances, we often have to puzzle over what to do—over both what is good or right to do, and by what means to achieve it. Pragmatism, while acknowledging the background of established situations and settled responses, finds its challenge in understanding how human beings respond, and how we might respond more effectively, to emergent situations. In contrast, much of mainstream epistemology and philosophy of science are concerned with analysis of established situations, and much of mainstream social science is concerned with bringing unruly experience under the sway of established situations. Bearing in mind this difference in emphasis may help us avoid the "talking past one another" that often occurs in discussions of Dewey's thought.

All situations are constituted by interpretations; they are not brute facts and are not given by unsituated "objective" observation. Interpretations employ intersubjective symbols provided by language, and incorporate shared cultural perspectives, yet also reflect the particular desires and purposes of the individual facing the particular situation. Emergent situations are characterized by "discordance, dissen[sion], conflict"— conflict over how they are to be understood and over the appropriate response; conflict within and between persons, and between persons and obstacles in the environment (EEL:11). The active, engaged person's response to conflict is inquiry, both empirical and ethical, with the goal of discovering harmonious solutions. "The ultimate end and test of all inquiry is the transformation of a problematic situation which involves confusion and conflict into a unified one" (LTI:491). In conflicts of interpretation, resolution accompanies discovery of a unified course of action. Science and ethics, both of which involve inquiry, are all about conflict and its resolution. On the subject of science, Dewey writes: "It is of the nature of science not so much to tolerate as to welcome diversity of opinion, while it insists that inquiry brings the evidence . . . to bear to effect a consensus . . . and even then to hold the conclusion subject to . . . new inquiries" (FC:102). And on the matter of ethics, he states: "Reflective morality emerges when men are confronted with situations in which different desires promise opposed goods and in which incompatible courses of action seem to be morally justified. Only such a conflict of good ends and of standards and rules of right and wrong calls forth a personal inquiry into the basis of morals" (E:164). Politics, operating in the sphere of the practical, like science and ethics, also revolves around conflict and its resolution. "As [associations] develop in number and importance," they pose the task of "preventing and settling conflicts" (RPh:203).

How does inquiry lead to a harmonious solution? In one type of case, there are two clearly delineated alternatives and an agreement on what constitutes decisive evidence or argument for one over the other. Inquiry, then, is a matter of finding the necessary empirical evidence, or making a logical inference from principles. This is close to what Kuhn (1970) calls "normal science," directed at established situations. Much of political theory is concerned with this sort of evidence and argumentation. More interesting for Dewey, however, are those emergent situations in which inquiry is devoted to novel discovery. Discoveries can reframe a problematic situation, eliminating a seeming conflict between opposed theories. Discoveries can reveal new mechanisms and policies through which all of the interests at stake can be accommodated. Dewey celebrates "the method—and spirit—of science as inquiry, which is perforce discovery" (RPh:xxxiii). Discoveries can also open up new realms of thought and action, rendering the original questions, and the theories associated with them, obsolete. "Intellectual progress usually occurs through sheer abandonment of questions . . . We do not solve them: we get over them (1910:14; also RPh:xvi). Thus conflict is resolved by inquiry, leading to empirical and ethical discoveries that transform the meanings of situations, creating a harmony between formerly opposed theories, interests, and courses of action. Hans Joas (1993) and Sandra Rosenthal (1986) are among the few commentators to recognize the role of creativity in Pragmatist philosophy. "Pragmatist ethics . . . is not only interested in the application of pregiven normative rules, but in the construction of new possibilities for moral action . . . [in] the creative character of the solution of moral problems (Joas 1993:253). Since, for Dewey, the self is made up of meanings, inquiry results in a "new self in a new world" (EKV:70; EN:245; Gouinlock 1972:237–244). Encountering conflict and resolving it, then, are central features of practice, of the engaged life. Hence, conflict-resolution is at the core of science, ethics, and democratic politics—not simply one social technique among many. This thesis, asserted baldly here, is developed at length in subsequent chapters. I devote much of this book to a detailed account of Dewey's theory of inquiry in science and ethics.

Here is the crux of Dewey's Pragmatism. Conflict is resolved by, if you will, paradigm shifts. These occur not through deductive reasoning based on given premises, or inductive generalization from agreed-upon instances internal to paradigms, but through open-ended inquiry, leading to transformation of the situation and, correlatively, the self. This is what sets Dewey's approach to democratic discourse apart from the "public reason" of Rawls (1993), the "argumentative validation" of Habermas (1996), and the "justify[ing] . . . by giving reasons" of Amy Gutmann and Dennis Thompson (1996:52); as well as the open-ended public conversation of Benjamin Barber (1984) or the interpretive approach of Charles Taylor (1985) or Robert Bellah et al. (1985).

Nor is Dewey trapped within the framework of assumptions and values of a particular form of life, a problem attributed to communitarianism and to Rorty's liberalism. Like other postfoundationalists, Dewey proceeds from existing principles in ethics and science, but his emphasis on discovery frees Deweyan discourse to transcend its starting point. Dewey's employment of critique and of inter-cultural dialogue contribute to Pragmatism's ability to move beyond its initial framework (PhC:83; AE:332–336).

Thus far, inquiry and conflict-resolution have been presented somewhat abstractly. It is now time to view these processes in context. Dewey's idea of community must first be introduced.

Community and Communication

For Dewey, human community, like individuality, involves action in the world. Common action, whether a primitive hunt or a modern election, requires extensive coordination of individuals' activities. This coordination requires communication, and more than minimal communication requires language (PP:152). Thus, working out modes of coordination involves "personal participation in the development of a shared culture" (ION:34; also 85). Common symbols and common purposes develop in tandem. "Wants and impulses are then attached to common

meanings . . . converting a conjoint activity into a community of interest and endeavor" (PP:153). Coordination of action in each new emergent situation necessitates the creation of new symbols. Language is
thereby enriched, and this increases the potential for future coordination. "Symbols in turn depend upon and promote communication"
(153). Communication is not incidental to social life, it is constitutive
of it. "Society not only continues to exist . . . *by* communication, but it
may fairly be said to exist . . . *in* communication" (DE:4). "Communication through speech, oral and written, is the familiar and constant
feature of social life. We tend accordingly, to regard it as just one phenomenon among others of what we must in any case accept without
question. We pass over the fact that it is the foundation and source of all
activities and relations that are distinctive of . . . union of human beings
with one another" (AE:334–335).

The establishment of language makes possible more than mere sig-
naling among individuals in order to coordinate activities. It allows for
the identification, formulation, and consideration of problems. It makes
possible joint inquiry to discover and invent plans of action which solve
those problems. It enables us to recollect and learn from past experience,
and deploy this knowledge in devising responses to anticipated problems. Chronicling the past, and inquiry and problem-solving for the future become forms of joint action in their own right and become intrinsically satisfying as well as instrumentally effective. Communication
and community are not limited to the realm of the practical, but involve
consummation as well as instrumental action (EN:183, 202). Common
activity is extended in time; it has a history which is grasped, appreci-
ated, and preserved through narrative. Language has its own esthetic
qualities of symmetry, vividness, and novelty. Language lends itself to
song, story, drama—out of which ritual grows (EN:183–184). Common
symbols become objects of affection as well as instruments of deliberate coordination. Cooperative problem solving becomes pleasurable in
its own right (EN:184). Communication moves over into communion,
which appears to be one of the most exalted forms of consummation,
one of the most highly valued human goods (EN:184, 202). These two
aspects, coordination and communion, jointly constitute community.
For Dewey, "no amount of aggregated collective action of itself constitutes a community. . . . Human associations . . . develop into [commu-
nities] in a human sense only as their consequences, being known, are
esteemed and sought for" (PP:151–152). Several recent interpretations

of Dewey's thought (T. Alexander 1995; Campbell 1998; Boisvert 1998), share this account of community, but conflict—as a vital and constant feature of community life—has received less attention.

Conflict

Not every individual or group in a community will understand a problematic situation in the same way or bring the same purposes and values to it (MW15:32; QC:218; ION:166). Coordination requires dealing with conflict. As evident in his writings which span many decades, Dewey recognized that conflict is a constant feature of social experience. Very early, in 1894, Dewey states: "The elimination of conflict is . . . a hopeless and self-contradictory ideal" (EW4:210; Westbrook 1991:80). In 1916, he continues: "The energy of the world is plural . . . there are different centers of force and they . . . come into conflict, they clash" (MW10:212). In 1920, reflecting on the group theory of politics Dewey states, "As associations develop in number and importance, the state tends to become more and more a regulator and adjuster among them . . . preventing and settling conflicts" (RPh:203). Dewey critiques the view of society as an organism precisely because it gives too little attention to conflict (RPh:190–191). In 1922, Dewey notes that "conflict [of diametrically opposed values] occurs between propertied classes and those who depend upon daily wage; between men and women; between old and young" (HNC:83). In 1927, Dewey asserts that there will always be conflict: "Things do not attain such fulfillment" that "the pulls and responses of different groups [always] reinforce each other and their values [always] accord" (PP:148). In 1932, Dewey notes the conflict between personal wants and duties. What is right will "conflict with what the individual judges to be his good" (E:218). In fact, he presents an extended account of the types of social conflict (E:324–328). In 1935, Dewey accepts the Marxian view of the ubiquity of conflict—though rejecting class struggle as the solution. "Of course there are conflicting interests; otherwise there would be no social problems" (LSA:79). In 1939, Dewey again acknowledges that, "the strife of interests, parties, and factions . . . is a common human one . . . affecting all alike" (FC:72). "Recognition of class conflicts as facts . . . provided a needed correction to the early nineteenth-century notion of universal harmony and universal interdependence" (FC:86). "Uniformity of belief is possible only when a dictator has power" (FC:128). Also in 1939, reflecting on the threat of fascism, Dewey writes that in a democracy, conflicts "are bound to arise" (CD:243).

Conflict is not a negative condition to be deplored and evaded; it can be a stimulus to thought and problem solving. "Men go on thinking only because of practical friction or strain somewhere, . . . thinking is essentially the solution of tension" (EW4:210). "Conflict is the gadfly of thought . . . instigates to invention. . . . a *sine qua non* of reflection and ingenuity" (HNC:300). "The disparities and conflicts that give rise to problems are not something to be dreaded . . . they are something to be grappled with . . . converted into the enjoyment that attends the free working of the mind" (ION:162). "It might even be admitted that a society in which there was no opposition of interests would be sunk in a condition of hopeless lethargy" (FC:87). "The habit of amicable cooperation—which may include, as in sport, rivalry and competition— is itself a priceless addition to life" (CD:243). "The very heart of political democracy is adjudication of social differences by discussion and exchange of views" (1944:273). If conflict is a potential stimulus to the creative thought and problem solving that build community, it can also lead to escalation and polarization that destroy community. Dewey's account of conflict-resolution, presented below, addresses that threat.

Dewey provides two approaches to the role of conflict in complex society. Any form of human life—whether revolving around religious worship, playing a game, conducting warfare, keeping domestic animals, or pursuing an esoteric hobby—develops a set of symbols, meanings, and emotional investments linked to its particular common activities. In complex, pluralistic society, forms of life proliferate and grow isolated from each other. The symbols and common meanings that create a sense of community within one form of life may also become barriers that exclude others who are not participants. "For segregated classes develop their own customs" (HNC:82). "Civilization is uncivil because human beings are divided into non-communicating sects, races, nations, classes, and cliques" (AE:336). As each group develops parochial interests and makes claims on resources, conflicts arise between them. To overcome these barriers and conflicts, groups must "interact flexibly and fully in connection with other groups" (PP:147). As they attempt to resolve conflict between them, and coordinate joint action, the participants forge new common symbols. A broader sense of community is recreated. Imagining such coordination occurring repeatedly among different groups in the contemporary United States, Dewey writes: "Communication can alone create a great community," because, "our Babel is not one of tongues but of the signs and symbols without which shared experience is impossible" (PP: 142; also AE: 335).

Furthermore, in interdependent society, private transactions between a few parties have ramifications affecting other groups not directly involved. In his best-known writing in political theory, Dewey defines a public as those people and groups who are indirectly affected by some transaction, and who become conscious of their diverse interests with regard to it (PP: 126). That is, the public is made up of stakeholders in a conflict situation. The task of the public is to find policies that regulate the transaction in the interest of the great majority of the stakeholders (LSA: 79)—a mutually satisfactory, or win-win solution.

In well-established communities, conflict is often settled by compromise. But what builds community is conflict-resolution in the strongest sense, which Dewey refers to as creating a common interest, as a unification. In a politics of transition to participatory democracy, therefore, strong resolution is a theoretically central and crucial term. Other theorists sometimes use the word "resolution" in a weaker sense, as mere compromise, compulsory arbitration, or in reference to moral argumentation only (Habermas 1996: 139–141; Gutmann and Thompson 1996: 17). Let us now proceed to Dewey's account of conflict-resolution.

Conflict-Resolution

There are a number of aspects of public conflict-resolution, in Dewey's view, including interest articulation, communication, moving from fixed ends to underlying interests, and inquiry to discover novel courses of action that institute common purposes. Let us examine each of these aspects.

First, interests must be articulated and placed on the agenda (FC: 128). Adversarial processes may have an important role in interest articulation (FC: 73). Stakeholders in a conflict must become aware of their interests, purposes, and normative values, and communicate them to others. This self-awareness includes a large narrative and interpretive component, and involves thick description and sensitivity to context (see Ch. 4; also, Smiley 1990; Young 1996: 127; Mansbridge 1996). The very act of communicating one's interests decenters one's view of them. "Try the experiment of communicating, with fullness and accuracy, some experience to another, especially if it be somewhat complicated,

and you will find your own attitude toward your experience changing. . . .
The experience has to be formulated in order to be communicated
[which] requires getting outside of it, seeing it as another would see it"
(DE:5–6).

Second, stakeholders have to listen respectfully to the interests and
concerns of others (DE:5; AE:336). Dewey would have us "treat those
who disagree—even profoundly—with us as those from whom we may
learn" (CD:243). Conflict-resolution depends on "conducting disputes,
controversies and conflicts as cooperative undertakings in which both
parties learn by giving the other a chance to express itself" (CD:243;
also, E:329; DE:5, 344). "Each contributes something distinctive from
his own store of knowledge, ability, taste, while receiving at the same
time elements of value contributed by others. . . . enjoyment of new
meanings, new values. . . . The ideas of one are corrected and changed by
what others say" (E:345). This account resembles Gadamer's (1975) notion of the merger of horizons in conversation. In today's language of
conflict-resolution: "The ability to see the situation as the other side
sees it . . . is one of the most important skills a negotiator can possess"
(Fisher and Ury 1981:23–24). Motivation for listening comes from the
need to settle a conflict; altruism is not a prerequisite. Respectful listening may have to be initiated by one side, without expectation of reciprocation in the short term, but with the long-term goal of building trust
and inviting reciprocation.

Third, the parties to the conflict will have to identify their broad
underlying interests, and let go of narrow "fixed ends." "Fixed ends inevitably lead thought into the bog of disputes that cannot be settled" (RPh:
166; also 181; HNC:223–237, 287; ION:164–165; MW4:37). When fixed
ends—in today's conflict-resolution parlance, "positions"—are mutually exclusive, broader interests may, nonetheless, overlap (Fisher and
Ury 1981:Ch. 1). Identification of broader interests permits inquiry into
new means of satisfaction, and vice-versa. Conflicts among narrow goals
become open to resolution "in the light of more inclusive interests than
are represented by either of them separately" (LSA:79); "some more comprehensive" point of view from which the divergencies may be brought
together" (MW9:336; J. Campbell 1998:36). Fixed ends suppress the free
exercise of creativity in inquiry, discovery, and invention, upon which
conflict-resolution depends (MW4:37).

Fourth, conflict-resolution involves discovery and invention of new
modes of action and new meanings, which establish common goals.

Dewey advocates "organized cooperative inquiry" to find novel integrative solutions (LSA:71). He calls for "far reaching experiments in construction of a new social order," and "bold imaginative ventures in invention and construction" (LSA:43, 74). Dewey proposes "social invention" and "invention . . . in human affairs" (HNC:147–8; RPh:xxx). It is here that social science, like natural science—as inquiry, as a powerful engine of discovery—becomes crucial for resolving social conflict and building community. In conflict-resolution terminology, this involves brainstorming and integrative problem solving (Moore 1996:257–258; Fisher and Ury 1981:Ch. 4). In today's language of game theory, this inquiry generates win-win solutions, by transforming fixed-sum games into variable sum or mixed motive games.

Finally, satisfactory completion of public conflict-resolution requires explicit agreements on courses of action, procedures for implementation, and monitoring procedures. These agreements must be carried out, evaluated, clarified and adapted through further negotiation. To sum up, conflict-resolution, in a strong sense, depends on mutual learning through respectful communication, and on creative inquiry to discovery novel options which institute common interests. With this introduction to Dewey's theory, let us explore various features and potentialities of conflict-resolution. Limitations on these potentialities are explored in a later section.

Conflict-Resolution Explored

Today there is a modest but growing movement for mediation and conflict-resolution, which, at its best, holds out the promise articulated by Dewey, and which offers illustrations for Dewey's theory. Conflict-resolution practices have become codified (Moore 1996), and a research literature on their effectiveness is reported in mediation and negotiation journals. Academic centers conduct research and train practitioners. Trained and certified mediators, and citizen mediators on community mediation boards, conduct thousands of negotiations yearly on business conflicts, environmental disputes, contested divorces, and landlord-tenant conflicts. Local governments and federal agencies may be involved, along with giant corporations and major public interest groups. Conflict-resolution and mediation have been introduced in schools, the workplace, universities, churches, the business world, governments, and in international diplomacy. Let us examine the rules and principles for the conduct of mediated conflict-resolution, and compare these with principles of deliberative and discursive democracy.

Conflict-Resolution Process and Deliberative Democracy

The spirit of conflict-resolution as proposed by Dewey, and the rules of today's conflict-resolution practice, require equal participation by all parties. In this they resemble aspects of the Habermasian ideal speech situation (Benhabib 1986:285). Equal opportunity—to initiate proposals, challenge arguments, and express perceptions and desires—is enforced by an impartial mediator. Conflict-resolution involves, in John S. Dryzek's terms, "formal or informal canons of reasoned discourse. Such canons might rule out threat, concealment of information, delaying tactics, embarrassment of another party" (1990:44). Furthermore, Dewey states, participants in discourse should, "meet one another on a plane of knowledge and trained intelligence as nearly equal as possible" (E:329). If one party lacks knowledge or communication skills, it is the prerogative of the mediator to redress the balance with information resources and skills training (Laue and Cormick 1978). Dryzek reports a prenegotiation inquiry in which the facilitator "created a public space in which ordinary [citizens] could develop, express, and share their views . . . his staff provided information and educational materials" (1990:127). The mediator can also enforce equality by insisting that each side demonstrate understanding of the other's statements, even though the representatives of one side may be less articulate or lacking in "cultural capital." This is done by requiring listeners to restate a speaker's message, in their own words, to the satisfaction of that speaker (C. Rogers 1951). According to Dryzek, "mediation contains intimations of discursive politics in the form of both a search for reasoned consensus and understanding of the legitimate, if different, interest of other parties" (1990: 46). At its best, it qualifies as an "incipient discursive design" (46).

Lawrence Susskind and Jeffrey Cruikshank suggest that the criteria of validity for conflict-resolution should be based on the fairness of the procedure (1987:21–25). Judgments concerning substantive outcomes are too likely to involve irreconcilable perspectives. This position resembles Rawls's principle of justice as fairness, and his rejection of comprehensive doctrines as the basis of public reason (1993:60–62, 243). The resemblance to Habermas's procedural approach to justice is also marked (1996:296). Roger Fisher and William Ury add a criterion of presenting one's negotiating position in terms of legitimate principles (1981:86, 92–94), reminiscent of Rawls (1993:217). In common ground discussions, which are a particular variant of conflict-resolution, there is an agreement that the core values and interests in conflict are not on the table for discussion. Neither side will attempt to convert the other. Instead they will search for goals and policies, outside the core area, on which they agree. This is reminiscent of Rawls's restriction on public reason as compared to private belief, and liberal theories of "conversational restraint" (Moon 1993a:76, quoting Bruce Ackerman). The difference is that, in common ground dialogue, the restriction is voluntary; it is mutually agreed upon, by particular individuals, for a specific time, place, and purpose.

It seems, then, that mediated conflict-resolution provides a democratic public sphere, in Habermas's terms, and something resembling an exercise of public reason, in Rawls's terms. Conflict-resolution, however, seeks creative solutions to achieve mutual satisfaction, not adjudication of the merits of prior positions. Novel solutions can institute new value positions, so conflict-resolution is not confined to the horizons of past traditions. Conflict-resolution is situation-specific, thus context-sensitive, not universal—though cumulative experience leads to generalizations. Conflict-resolution, depending upon mutually agreeable solutions, is voluntary and experimental; its legitimacy is emergent, not established *a priori*. Conflict-resolution is intertwined with political action and struggle. Though creating a protected space with fair procedures, it cannot substitute for or free itself from politics and power, as discussed below. Let us turn now from the procedural to the substantive features of conflict-resolution, by considering illustrative examples of mutually satisfactory solutions.

Examples of Successful Conflict-Resolution

A sense of the concrete meaning of win-win solutions can be obtained by reviewing some exemplary cases of conflict-resolution, one from post-World War II Europe, and others from the United States today (see also Ostrom 1990). One example is the settlement of the conflict between France and Germany over the Saarland after World War II. Initially, the French insisted that possessing the Saarland was essential to their security, while Germany insisted that this was part of its national home-

land. Both countries wanted the economic benefit of this resource-rich
territory. Later, within the integrative framework of the European Coal
and Steel Community, it was agreed that the security interests of France,
the territorial integrity of Germany, and the economic interests of both
could be served while returning the Saarland to Germany. Another example is illustrated by a progressive political coalition in a U.S. city,
in which labor groups have learned to work with homosexual-rights
groups, despite initial antipathy. By joining forces with each other, and
other progressive groups, they were able to elect state legislators who
pledged to vote yes on each group's issues but could not have been
elected without the support of both groups. Third, in disputes over wilderness areas with endangered species, the U.S. government has bro-
kered land swaps by which private companies give up environmentally
sensitive holdings in exchange for parcels of land with equivalent resource value but less ecological significance (*New York Times*, Dec. 6,
1996, A18:4). Fourth, in a dispute over building an incinerator for toxic
waste disposal, both parties agreed to abide by the results of an experiment. A pilot project incinerator was to be built and closely monitored
for toxic emissions. The application for a full-scale incinerator plan was
to be withdrawn if emissions from the model exceeded agreed-upon limits (Susskind and Cruikshank 1987:160). Fifth, on the abortion issue,
some pro-life and pro-choice advocates have found common ground on
the need to prevent teenage pregnancies, make adoption more available,
and improve prenatal and maternal health care. Abiding respect and
friendship have developed among representatives of these bitterly opposed groups (Arbogast 1994; Kelly 1994). On a smaller scale, neighborhood mediation boards have found ways to resolve landlord-tenant disputes and quarrels among neighbors over property upkeep, pet behavior,
noise, and other areas of contention (Schwerin 1995). While less dramatic in their substantive results and mechanisms of resolution than
some of the examples mentioned, neighborhood mediation allows thousands of individuals to participate directly in the conflict-resolution
process. Resolution rates are high, and this is largely due to adversaries
coming to understand each others' point of view. In each of the above
examples, conflict-resolution has been transformative to some extent.
The parties, agreeing to work together, changed their perceptions of
each other, and of collaboration generally. These concrete examples suggest that win-win solutions are available in a wide variety of specific
cases, often where irreconcilable conflict might be expected. For further

clarification of both the procedural and substantive aspects of conflict-resolution, a comparison with adjudication by the courts is helpful.

Comparison with Adjudication

"A cured body or mind is in no sense the same thing as a healthy growing mind or body," Dewey writes, "any more than winning a law suit is the same thing as cooperative social relationships" (MW15:43). Dewey would agree with Michael Walzer that many conflict settlements can be based upon "the value of mutual accommodation in a pluralist society," not upon "rights [adjudicated by courts] which are best reserved for more important matters" (1996:54). Dewey would add that the meanings of rights and of justice are, themselves, articulated and developed in the course of creative resolution of conflict. As Ury, Jeanne Brett and Stephen Goldberg put it, "reconciling interests" is an approach that "tends to generate a higher level of mutual satisfaction with outcomes than [going to court for] determining rights" (1988:14). In principle, and often in practice, judicial solutions are based on universal tenets and judgments of right and wrong; they retrospectively assign blame and punishment, rather than prospectively creating fresh solutions; they deal with the narrow conflict at hand, rather than broadening the agenda to find mutually agreeable trade-offs. Thus a court judgment often exacerbates conflict, resulting in further litigation and power struggles. Ury, Brett and Goldberg further observe that conflict-resolution "can resolve the problem underlying the dispute." "Often the real problem is something else" than the manifest contractual or rights issue that is brought to the court (13). This point, similar to Dewey's rejection of "fixed ends" (RPh:145–146, 166, 181), highlights a key distinction between conflict-resolution and most accounts of deliberative democracy, which assume that the manifest issue is the actual one, requiring reasons for extant proposals. Having explored both the procedural and substantive sides of conflict-resolution, let us turn to the theoretical question of legitimacy.

Legitimacy of Conflict-Resolution

Mediated conflict-resolution is not a governmental institution with coercive powers. When mediation is court-mandated, parties who do not

reach voluntary agreement can return to the courts. Thus the legitimacy
of conflict-resolution need not be established *a priori*, but will emerge
experimentally. If, as their experience with conflict-resolution increases,
more and more people and groups make uncoerced choices to enter into
formal mediation, it will become a reflectively settled practice. Hypothetical grounds for such legitimation, however, can be anticipated theoretically. Participant satisfaction with conflict-resolution appears to
rest on two pillars: procedural fairness and mutually satisfactory substantive outcomes. The first basis of legitimacy, fair procedures, has been
discussed above, from a theoretical standpoint. It remains to be seen if
participants actually find the procedures fair in practice. Let us now examine the second basis, mutually satisfactory outcomes.

Even the fairest procedures will not become legitimate if the substantive results fail to satisfy. Will the practice of conflict-resolution, as it
evolves, reliably produce creative solutions that fulfill the interests
of both parties? We can approach this question theoretically by asking
whether there are both specific and general forms of social organization
and policy that meet the mutual satisfaction criterion. Dewey asks this
question in its strongest form, not just for small, homogeneous communities, but for the "Great Society" with its diverse groups, complex interdependence, and mediated communication. Dewey begins with a general orientation: "Different people are going to have different ideals and
beliefs but . . . we have enough common work, common responsibility,
and common interest and sympathy so that in spite of these other distinctions we can go on working together" (MW15:154). Numerous examples of successful conflict-resolution have already been presented.
General theoretical reasons for the existence of such solutions will now
be examined. Dewey explores major axes of conflict in complex society,
and identifies the bases for resolving them.

Types of Conflict and Bases of Resolution

The clash of interests between elites and masses is a fundamental axis
of conflict in American society (E:325–327). Several bases can be identified for finding common interests despite this cleavage. Hierarchical management suppresses motivation and creativity in workers. The
increased productivity resulting from collaborative labor-management
relations could be distributed to benefit all (Ury, Brett and Goldberg
1988). According to empirical observations, "integrative bargaining" in

recent contract negotiations exists alongside of cases where management finds it advantageous, in the current economic environment, to
bargain adversarially (Walton, Cutcher-Gershenfeld and McKersie 1994:
308–313). More broadly, in an interdependent society, elites cannot
completely insulate themselves from the misfortunes of the least well-
off. The problems of the poor and excluded—epidemic diseases, drugs,
violent crime, deterioration of urban centers—threaten the quality of
life for all. Though often unrecognized, the life experience of elites is
distorted by the isolated and defensive position required to maintain
their status (H. Putnam 1992:189). "All special privilege narrows the
outlook of those who possess it. . . . induces a standpat and reactionary
attitude . . . Intellectual blindness . . . distorted ideas and ideals" (E:347–
348; also Memmi 1965). That elites as well as the less-advantaged suffer from class division—so that a basis for common interest exists—
does not mean that this is easily made conscious, much less enthusias-
tically embraced. It does mean that there are grounds for committing
oneself to long-term political struggle, social inquiry, education, and
conflict-resolution on behalf of articulating and eventually realizing this
potential.

Conflicts over scarce resources are a ubiquitous feature of social life.
There are society-wide distributional conflicts over sharing the burden
of taxation, defining property rights, and determining access to basic services from transportation to medical care. Much of political philosophy
is devoted to ascertaining principles of fair distribution, or fair procedures for choosing those principles. Dewey, rather than dividing a fixed
amount, seeks a win-win solution by increasing the stock of goods. He
advocates "providing the objective political, economic, and social conditions which will enable the greatest possible number because of their
own endeavors to have a full and generous share in the values of living"
(E:251–252). He proposes inquiry to find forms of economic organization, not marred by exploitation and waste, which fully utilize available
productive resources and create new ones (as discussed in Chapters 3
and 5).

Today's conflict-resolution theorist-practitioners have written extensively on distributional conflicts among groups. However difficult they
seem, these conflicts over material resources are, in practice, easier to
resolve than conflicts over rights or ideology (Ury, Brett and Goldberg
1988; Susskind and Cruikshank 1987). The parties have a stake in resolution, to avoid greater losses from ongoing conflict and stalemate.
Technological or organizational means of expanding productivity may

provide gains that can be divided between the parties. Enlarging the agenda opens new possibilities for resolution. Several resources may be included that are differently valued by the two parties, allowing for trade-offs (Susskind and Cruikshank 1987:180). When carrying out business requires a continuing relationship between the parties, maintaining the quality of the interaction may be counted as a good. Third parties, who have other resources to trade and a stake in keeping the peace, can also be included. Third parties can invest in developing more of the goods that are in conflict. They can make side payments to compensate one side for losses incurred in a solution that benefits the others.

In extreme cases of, say, environmental conflict, the only possible resolution of a distributional conflict involves the demise of a business firm, an occupation, or a whole way of life. This can lead to violent clashes, as in struggles over old growth forests. But such transitions may be inevitable due to resource depletion or changing technology. Government agencies may assist in transitions to new occupations and ways of life, by providing information, capital, and job retraining. Creative inquiry can suggest new occupations and enterprises that do not disperse the existing community, and which make use of its capabilities and express its values. An example is retraining loggers for watershed reclamation projects. In Sweden, the "active manpower policy" of the government, "by socializing the risk" of displacing workers, removes a major obstacle to phasing out declining and/or environmentally destructive industries (Esping-Anderson 1985:229–230).

Third, conflicts over morality often seem irreconcilable. Not only are tenets diametrically opposed, but what counts as reasons for the two sides may implicate incommensurable paradigms. Consider today's struggle between the religious right wing and the mainstream. There appears to be no ground for dialogue between biblical literalists who seek a theocracy, and scientific empiricists who uphold separation of church and state. The ideas of the former would not be considered "reasonable comprehensive doctrines" by Rawls, and would be excluded from the democratic conversation, according to his theory (Rawls 1993:xvii, 64n). Though dialogue for its own sake is unlikely between members of the religious right and the mainstream, the exigencies of practice may bring it about—in meetings of school boards, church-governing bodies, Republican Party committees, state legislatures, and Congress. In such dialogues, common ground can be found on concrete issues—safety and civility in schools, violence in entertainment, unemployment, and teenage pregnancy. When religious conservatives enter into public life and find themselves in the minority, they experience cross-pressures. They face choices between participation and coalition-building, or doctrinal purity and ineffectiveness. Many, but by no means all, will choose the latter course. Whether their mainstream counterparts dialogue with them respectfully, or demonize or treat them contemptuously will have some effect on their choices in the long run (Carter 1993). Dewey's full response to the daunting problem of resolving morality conflicts requires a review of his entire ethical theory, which is undertaken in Chapters 4 and 5. Here, I present his approach in brief: First, there is never only one value at stake, so trade-offs are inevitable. Second, moving from ethical "fixed ends" to broader ethical interests opens unsuspected potential for mutuality. Third, creative inquiry expands the possibilities of moral understanding and action. In Chapter 5, the common ground process applied to the conflict over legal abortion is used to illustrate this approach.

One morality issue—rights—has preoccupied political theory. This conflict, too, seems like a zero-sum game. Dewey sees present society pitting groups against each other, but he envisages a democratic community in which defending the rights of any group enhances the rights and fulfillments of all. Dewey stresses resolving each particular rights conflict in its context, arguing that universalistic abstract determinations will not succeed. His approach alerts us to the presence of distributional and identity issues in what appear to be solely questions of rights. It highlights the interaction of political struggle with ethical discourse, and the tension between particularity and universality. Rights conflicts are further considered in Chapter 5.

Fourth, an evident source of social conflict in today's world, is antagonism over group identity. Identity politics becomes a zero-sum game, in which recognition must be wrested from another (Connolly 1991). For Dewey, this situation is a response to particular conditions, not a timeless feature of individuality or society. In a world of insecurity, where commodities are unequally distributed, recognition, too, becomes a scarce resource. Respect goes to economic elites and is withheld from other groups, which then fight against one another for recognition. The search for group identity and the claims for group pride become essentialist and exclusive. Thus the "quest for certainty," in response to insecurity, that Dewey identifies in epistemology and ethics is played out in the domain of identity. Conversely, when there is sufficient economic security, opportunity, respect, and challenge, identity becomes both more secure and more flexible. As one ventures into new realms of occupation, social encounter, and academic study, and receives recognition for one's efforts, one's selfhood is augmented and redirected. Dewey identifies recognition as a requirement for human identity-formation (LW5:239; 1927a:22). Recognition of one's identity by others, increases one's capacity to provide recognition to others. Diversity becomes a resource, with each group enriched by learning from the others. What had been a win-lose conflict is transformed into a cooperative encounter (Burton 1987). This mutuality is central to what Dewey understands as the democratic way of life (CD:228; E:350; FC:127, 162).

To sum up, Dewey and today's conflict-resolution thinkers identify bases for resolution of conflicts along each of these major cleavages in today's society. They emphasize, however, that settled conclusions can only come from experimentation. Along with these potentialities, reflection can also identify constraints in practice and in principle on the fairness and success of conflict-resolution.

Limitations of Conflict-Resolution

If the potential of conflict-resolution is to be realized, there must be scrupulous attention to its limitations, real and imagined, so that strategies can be devised to deal with them. Limitations discussed include: tragic conflicts, co-optation, power disparities, objections to entering mediation, and the risks of engaging in dialogue with adversaries. At the conclusion of this chapter, a conflict-resolution paradox is presented.

Dewey's view is not utopian. His account of conflict-resolution does not imply that every conflict—now, or even in an anticipated great community—can be resolved to everyone's satisfaction. Distributional conflicts would never be eliminated. The health of Americans, for example, could be greatly increased by lifestyle changes, health education, and preventive programs (1937b:337). But at the margins, there would always be conflict about when to pursue heroic treatment measures. Inferences from prevailing ethical principles, adjudication by the courts, and legislative horse-trading remain as inescapable processes for distributing benefits and losses in these cases. Public interests and matters of rights, interpreted by representative assemblies and courts, must be enforced. Groups and individuals must, from time to time, accept compromises, sacrifices, and defeats in political contestation (PP:31). This raises a classic question of democratic theory—the procedural conditions of legitimacy for institutions enforcing such solutions (Habermas 1996; Rawls 1993; J. Cohen 1996; Mansbridge 1996). Dewey is not unconcerned with this legitimacy question and contributes theoretical explorations concerning principles for just decisions (PP: 67, 181, 208; also see E). But, in Dewey's view, it is crucial that the continuing tension, due to the imperfect resolution of these conflicts, be contained within a broadened range of collaborative efforts and mutually satisfactory solutions. If sacrifices must ultimately be made, it is far easier to do so on behalf of a community toward which one feels identification, loyalty, and a profound debt of gratitude (RPh: 210; HNC: 330; *A Common Faith* [ACF]: 85–86). Dewey hypothesizes that in a society approaching a condition where the good of each contributes to the good of all, people will cherish the maintenance of community and construct the legitimate institutions most conducive to that end. "We are not concerned, therefore, to set forth counsels as to advisable improvements in the political forms of democracy. . . . The problem lies deeper . . . the search for the conditions under which the Great Society may become the Great Community. When these conditions are brought into being they will make their own forms" (PP: 147). It is toward the transition to such community that Dewey directs his major efforts, and conflict-resolution, in a strong sense, is a major instrument for such a transition. Let us now examine a class of conflicts that have been labeled "tragic conflicts," and consider Dewey's response.

Tragic Conflict

Many conflicts are insoluble in practice, at a given time. These are called "tragic conflicts" insofar as failure of resolution leads the weaker party to accept a less than satisfactory outcome (Hook 1974; Moon 1993a: 10–11, 63; Rorty 1995: 91; Nussbaum 1990; Williams 1973). In democratic societies, the weaker parties can accept their losses in tragic conflicts, because they believe that the process is fair, and/or their own time will come in the future (PP: 208). The concept of tragic conflict, however, can be misleading. It is easy to slide from the restricted usage— unresolvable at present, in practice—to the a-historical notion of irreconcilable in principle (Silver 1994). This becomes a rationalization for avoiding the hard work of inquiry and political action. A conflict can easily be misjudged as tragic if we mistake positions for interests. A conflict can be taken out of context, overlooking social changes that could resolve it or reduce its salience (Silver 1994:51). A diagnosis of tragic conflict also tempts us to discount people's capacity to rise to challenges and respond in fresh ways. It overlooks the extent to which human limitations are culturally imposed rather than inherent. The judgment of tragic conflict is a poor heuristic for ongoing inquiry into the sources of and resolution of social tensions.

A virtue of the notion of tragic conflict, on the other hand, is that it counters the Rousseauian, or Leninist, or theocratic temptation to coerce settlements—out of belief that all conflicts have solutions, and that one's theory, or science, or faith will reveal them. Dewey, himself, is critical of Rousseau, and of Leninism and its pseudo-scientific claims (FC:96). The whole thrust of his Pragmatism, his experimentalism, is that the appropriate settlement of a conflict cannot be known *a priori*. Would Dewey nonetheless be tempted to force people to the negotiation table, if not to dictate the outcome? It is the exigencies of practice, the severity of unresolved conflict, the costs of stalemate, in Dewey's view, that will push parties to negotiate, not coercion from authorities. And it is guarantees of confidentiality, fair rules of discussion, and cooperative search for mutually satisfactory solutions that will attract parties to the table. If the experiment succeeds, there will be positive incentives to repeat it, refine it, and extend its scope. Dewey calls for "cooperation which is voluntary" (1939b:368).

Co-optation: Conflict-Resolution and Power

The idea of conflict-resolution has gained some visibility and even cachet. The terms "win-win solution" and "common ground" are found in the jargon of management consultants and journalists, and on the tongues of politicians. Claims to be seeking common ground are used to cover opposite intentions. What passes for conflict-resolution is often little more than splitting the difference. At its worst, a settlement is imposed on a weaker party in the guise of a mutual agreement. If the transformative potential of conflict-resolution is to be realized, as the theoretical and practical basis for fulfillment of democracy, then these tendencies must be criticized and genuine creative problem-solving advocated. The biggest threat of co-optation comes where disparities in power are wide.

Conflict-resolution may strive toward an ideal of discourse undistorted by power. But in a politics of transition, it must operate within the constraints of actual power disparities, even as it works to create a world in which these are reduced. The range within which win-win solutions are sought is bounded by negative power—the material penalties each side can impose on the other for making unsatisfactory offers. It is also constrained, more subtly, by constructive power, operating through the dominant discourse which permits only certain options and rationales to be articulated. The mediator has some limited options for ameliorating power disparities. With regard to coercive power based on material resources and cultural capital, the mediator can provide prenegotiation training and information to the weaker parties, and demand a respectful hearing from the stronger parties. The mediator can also help the weaker parties to identify their best alternative to a negotiated solution, and counsel them to withdraw from negotiations if, due to power imbalances, they cannot improve on that alternative (Fisher and Ury 1981: 101–111). But power disparities cannot be eliminated and must be dealt with outside of negotiations, through political action. Social movements, which mobilize power for disadvantaged groups and demand a respectful hearing, are required. A public interest group confronting a large corporation has to generate its own power through mobilizing grassroots membership, winning sympathizers in the larger public, and engaging in protests, boycotts, electoral politics, litigation, and lobbying. Social movements and conflict-resolution are intertwined; any attempt to treat them in isolation does justice to neither.

The process of conflict-resolution is also not immune to constructive power—the dominance of a particular form of discourse which constructs identities as well as limits the articulation of options. Even a skilled and sensitive mediator, trained in intercultural dialogue, may fail to recognize, much less break through, such constraints. The struggle against this form of power, too, must take place outside of negotiations, through cultural critique and contestation and through the development of countercultures and subcultural identities, or, in Mansbridge's terms, "deliberative enclaves of resistance" (1996:47, 57–59). Recent theorists have broadened the conceptualization of power to include "power to" and "power with" (Boyte 1989; Lappé and DuBois 1994). Political mobilization and social invention can increase competence, generate resources, and foster coalitions, contributing to these forms of power within a stakeholding group. Collaborative inquiry and problem solving in the process of conflict-resolution also contribute directly to such creative power for all parties involved.

Objections to Entering Mediation

As conflict-resolution services become more available, professionals report people's reluctance to enter mediation. In this adversarial and litigious culture, the preference for legal and political combat continues, despite the high costs. This circumstance is attributable in part to habit, and to caution about new alternatives. Some objections are based on misunderstandings. Conflict-resolution is seen as compromising away one's interests, despite the presentation of mediation as an alternative to both concession and domination (Fisher and Ury 1981). Similarly, conflict-resolution is perceived as idealistic, whereas people in general are self-interested. This attitude overlooks the central role of interests in conflict-resolution, the creative effort to find solutions that satisfy the interests of all stakeholders. These obstacles owing to habit, caution, and misunderstanding can be overcome gradually by education and positive experience. A concern about power disparities is one reason for reluctance to use mediation. Women may be fearful, sometimes with justification, that the advantages men hold in patriarchal society will carry over into the practices and discourses of divorce mediation. Mediators and those who study their work critically must detect and overcome these biases.

A crucial objection is that conflict-resolution demands not just accommodation of interests, but disclosure and reconciliation of feelings and beliefs. It is seen as invasive and manipulative, a threat to privacy and identity. In this view, coexistence and peace can be achieved out of mutual respect among worthy adversaries. It does not require that they agree on beliefs or become friends. Conflict-resolution can, indeed, operate in this agonistic fashion. In many distributional conflicts, self-disclosure, interpersonal encounter, and belief change are not relevant, and such is the case for some conflicts over rights and ideologies as well. If personal risk does become relevant, according to the principles of conflict-resolution, the decision to take such risks is voluntary and subject to informed consent. People are likely to take on that risk only when they assess the cost of not doing so as very high, and when the process has strong protections for privacy and against manipulation. An example can clarify the conditions under which such choices are made, and the positive outcomes that are possible.

Risk and Growth

In the following case, as in many others, the prior conceptions and values are deeply rooted, but the vicissitudes of life confront the actors with drastic choices that make reconsideration imperative. Thorough documentation makes this example of conflict-resolution useful, although, as it happens, mediation was not employed. In the book *Beyond Acceptance: Parents of Lesbians and Gays Talk About Their Experiences*, the authors draw upon interviews to present the ethical dilemma of parents whose son or daughter has just come out to them as gay or lesbian (Griffin, Wirth and Wirth 1986). For the sake of brevity, a composite from a number of actual cases is presented here:

A young man has told his parents that he is homosexual and that he has felt this way since he was very young. He has formed a satisfying, intimate relationship with a man. He is deeply convinced that he can live this life openly with integrity. All that remains is to be accepted by his parents for who he is. The parents' initial reaction is a welter of negative and contradictory thoughts and feelings (Griffin, Wirth and Wirth 1986: 1–16). They experience revulsion, denial, and determination to change him. They wish never to see him again, but feel intense pain at losing him. They sense that they've done something horribly wrong as parents. Their religious beliefs proclaim that their son has chosen a life of sin and condemned himself to eternal punishment. Another thought is that he will never give them a grandchild. They also wish to spare him the pain he will endure at the hands of an intolerant society. Forgetting him for the moment, they imagine fearfully what friends and neighbors will think of them. In the ensuing days, they will anguish over all of these feelings and wishes. They will talk, plead, listen, and argue with their son. Eventually, they will make a decision that amounts to accepting or rejecting him.

These parents do manage to accept their son as he is. What is more, they reach a deeper relationship with him. "If we can share this kind of thing, then there's very little else [he] can't tell me. Or that I couldn't tell [him]" (Griffin, Wirth and Wirth 1986:162). In the son's view, "We have come to see and largely heal the rifts that separated us in the years of my childhood and adolescence. . . . This newfound honesty led us . . . back to each other" (187). Despite the initial shock and the ongoing loss of cherished hopes, the parents find themselves changed in positive ways. "Accepting differences in [my child] helps me to be kinder to myself, to accept my own differences" (158). "I found that prejudice, though hard to give up, was an enormous burden" (157). At first it seems they face an either/or choice between their son and their religious faith. But they come to a new understanding of God's love and commandments. They continue to honor human care, love, and fidelity, while accepting that these can be expressed in a wider range of sexual relationships. Recognizing the prejudices their son will face leads these parents outward to involvement in political and social action for homosexual rights (187). Thus their decision to reconcile is not mere renunciation or accommodation. It is the choice of a deeper intimacy and respect for their son; a new self-understanding and self-acceptance; a renewed and more reflective religious faith; and a new engagement with the public sphere. This case exemplifies what Dewey means by transformation of self consequent upon inquiry—inquiry which arises from the exigencies of life in a changing society. It suggests that, when extreme circumstances demand it, people are capable of deep self-examination, dialogue, and change. Conversely, in less extreme situations, such vulnerability of the self is not demanded. Let us turn now to one more limitation which might be called a conflict-resolution paradox.

Conflict-Resolution Paradox

There are indeed many bases in principle for win-win solutions to crucial social conflicts, but the most integrative ones may be on such a large scale as to present daunting problems. An economic system featuring full employment and worker ownership and control might prove highly integrative for society as a whole, greatly reducing social problems attendant on joblessness, powerlessness, and worker alienation. But discussion of such a drastic change, much less negotiated consensus on it, is nowhere on the horizon. Piecemeal settlements are far easier to negotiate, but likely to leave major tensions unresolved. This might be called a "conflict-resolution paradox." A Deweyan approach to the conflict-resolution paradox is to work from both ends simultaneously. Modest local-level conflict-resolution can be directed at teaching skills and fostering the process, moving toward conflict-resolution as a goal in itself, as well as a means. Democratic firms, progressive schools, and democratically organized political groups can prefigure general schemes of collaborative community. Theoretical efforts, such as Dewey's own, can lay the groundwork in philosophy, social theory, and psychology for envisioning collaborative community on a large scale. If, as this discussion suggests, there are no insuperable obstacles to the conduct of strong conflict-resolution and community building, what resources, according to Dewey's analysis, are required to realize these possibilities?

Conclusion: Social Intelligence

The building of democratic community, through the resolution of conflict, depends on discovery and invention of unanticipated win-win solutions. Above all, this requires methods of creative inquiry, which Dewey sees exemplified in the natural sciences, viewed as a powerful engine for discovery of new ideas. Capacity to solve problems involving physical and biological processes has increased exponentially from generation to generation. Capacity to solve social problems, however, has lagged far behind (LW8:93). If we understand the natural sciences as oriented to discovery, and apply this lesson to the social sciences, social problem-solving capacity would dramatically increase (see SS, SSSC). To resolve social conflict, however, we must devise innovative ethical options—new insights into what is just and what is conducive to human flourishing. Methods, skills, and knowledge for ethical deliberation are also needed. The four chapters of this book which discuss science and ethics (Chapters 2–5) present the philosophical groundwork for Dewey's belief in the creative power of conflict-resolution—his belief in "social intelligence."

Dewey's term, social intelligence, refers to methods of creative inquiry in science and ethics, and the innovative options they produce. The words "social" and "intelligence" are used advisedly. What is at issue for Dewey is the ability to solve problems, and common parlance attributes this to individual intelligence. But our actual problem-solving capacity depends on our mastery of intellectual tools discovered by others and available as cultural resources. "Effective intelligence is not an original innate endowment. No matter what the differences in native intelligence (allowing, for the moment, that intelligence can be native), the actuality of mind is dependent upon the knowledge from the past . . . embodied in the utensils, devices and technologies" (PP:209, also 158;

HNC:314; LW6:46–47; FC:52; *How We Think* [HWT]:112). A high school student today can solve mathematical problems that would have been out of the reach of Newton, the inventor of the calculus.

The understanding that intelligence is social has two major consequences for democratic theory. First, intelligence can expand with each generation, keeping pace with the problems generated by an increasingly large, interdependent, and complex society. Second, intelligence is available to all citizens, given adequate education and dissemination of ideas. "Given a social medium in whose institutions the available knowledge, ideas and art of humanity were incarnate . . . the average individual would rise to undreamed heights of social and political intelligence" (FC:69–70). This is Dewey's answer to the "democratic realists" who believe that the complexity of issues makes citizen participation in decision making an unrealizable dream.

2 Natural Science

Dewey stakes the viability of his theory of democracy on his account of social intelligence. And social intelligence depends on science—on the method, spirit, and findings of natural science, and the development of social science. Dewey's optimistic outlook on science could easily be taken for an anachronism, lingering naive Victorian optimism, or an endorsement of the mainstream social science of today. It is easy, therefore, to celebrate Dewey's democratic commitments but reject his insistence on science. "Dewey's preoccupation with scientific method is a central weakness of his entire political theory" (Damico quoted in Sleeper 1986: 213). Likewise, Timothy Kaufman-Osborn (1991) writes of Dewey's "scientistic excesses," although he allows that Dewey's views on science "may be interpreted in more or less charitable ways" (1991:xii; also Smiley 1990, Manicas 1989). These recent statements echo critiques that Dewey heard throughout his career (e.g., Randolph Bourne 1917:59; Lewis Mumford and Mortimer Adler, reported in Westbrook 1991:514–523). These critiques, however, mistakenly attribute to Dewey mainstream philosophical views of science. To clear the air, one might drop the term "science" altogether, and use Dewey's terms, "inquiry" and "social intelligence." But Dewey seeks to rescue the actual history and practice of science from positivist misunderstandings. Thus his emphasis on "science" is maintained here.

Dewey sees the ethical and the empirical as deeply and continuously intertwined. It is possible, however, to bracket the ethical considerations while developing an account of empirical inquiry. (I return to the relation of science to ethics at the end of this chapter.) Similarly, in the following presentation, issues of justification are separated from those of discovery and are treated later. Let us begin by placing Dewey's effort in theoretical context. First, several perspectives are considered from other schools of philosophy which can now illuminate Dewey's approach to science in ways that were not possible when positivism and analytical philosophy dominated thinking in the U.S. Second, Dewey's approach is clarified by examining the role of epistemology in the philosophy of science tradition, and Dewey's critique of it. Third, postempiricist approaches to the issue of discovery in science are touched upon. This discussion sets the stage for an explication of Dewey's views on discovery.

Historical Setting

A glance at historical origins immediately establishes differences between Dewey's approach and positivism. Positivism is a direct descendent of Cartesian dualism, of the British empiricist tradition with its psychological atomism, and of the Kantian solution to Humean skepticism. Dewey's thought is rooted in philosophical schools that arose in opposition to those sources—Hegel's critique of "sense certainty," Charles Peirce's Pragmatism, and William James's functional psychology (Hegel 1977:58–67). Continental schools of thought, contemporaneous with Dewey's mature work, also contest atomistic empiricism: gestalt psychology, phenomenology, and critical theory. Wittgenstein's later thought concerning language games and forms of life also undermines positivism and inspires postempiricism. Though not an influence on Dewey, the existence of these schools demonstrates that positivism and modernity are not synonymous—that there were alternative modern views of science and of knowledge. In this broad context, it is perhaps easier to recognize that, already in the first decade of the twentieth-century, Dewey could be espousing a view of science sharply at odds with Comtean and Machian positivism and with their forerunners, British empiricism, Cartesianism, and Kantianism.

In the late twentieth-century it is not the positivism of Auguste Comte and Ernst Mach that is at issue so much as the more sophisticated logical empiricism of the Vienna Circle. Though inspired directly by Mach, this school depends upon the modern logic of Gottlob Frege and Bertrand Russell, substituting logical atomism for psychological atomism. This shift presents no special problem for Dewey's critique. His views on formalist logic, articulated in his critique of Rudolph Lotze, and later, of Bertrand Russell, amount to a critique of Frege and the logical positivists (Sleeper 1986:5, 64–65, 79, 111).

In Dewey's view, what has passed for philosophy of science in the Anglo-American tradition, and in Kantian and neo-Kantian philosophy, is primarily concerned with epistemology, not science. Having accepted a dualism of mind and matter, subject and object, philosophers set out to solve the resultant question of how the subject-object gap could be bridged—how anything at all could be known about "external" reality (MW3:118–120; MW4:138; QC:85). Since science provides thoroughly settled understandings of physical nature—the nearest thing to indubitable knowledge of reality—it is called into service. Since epistemology bends science to purposes not its own, it is to be expected that the resultant "philosophy of science" is concerned with neither the practice, nor the history of science (QC:85–86). How scientists come to know some particular thing is not the issue here but rather "rational reconstruction" or transcendental analysis of the conditions of possibility of knowing—the ground or foundation of knowing, itself. Epistemology is not motivated by the interest in discovery that is the "lifeblood of science," not drawn prospectively to the adventure of the search for new knowledge, or the urgencies of solving extant problems and puzzles (EN:52). It is instead, retrospective, concerned with justification of past achievements—which scientists, themselves, are eager to transcend. Dewey, like Wittgenstein, Heidegger, and the postempiricists, views this quest for foundations—this effort to overcome a presumed subject-object dualism—as pursuit of a pseudo-problem (EN:75–76). He wishes to "emancipate philosophy from all the epistemological puzzles that now perplex it," thereby freeing us to discover new knowledge of human affairs (RPh:123).[1]

In the U.S. at mid-century, the verve and technical sophistication of logical positivism and British analytical philosophy swept away all that came before them, and Dewey's views seemed archaic and naive. Alternative views found in continental philosophy were also forgotten or excluded. Thus the postempiricism of the 1950s and 1960s, which challenged the views of the Vienna Circle, seemed to be an unprecedented innovation (Feyerabend 1970; N. Hanson 1958; Kuhn 1970; Polanyi 1962; Quine 1961; Toulmin 1970). We now have the advantage of the postempiricist perspective, a renewed engagement with continental philosophy, and a new body of history of late nineteenth- and early twentieth-century philosophy. We can look back and recognize that

strong alternatives to positivism coexisted with the rise of logical positivism, and we can place Dewey's views among them (McCarthy 1992:
243). Seen in this light, it is clearer that taking critique of positivism as
critique of Dewey utterly misses the mark. Conversely, rereading Dewey's work in light of today's postempiricist insights will uncover important elements of his view of science missed by previous generations.

Like the postempiricists, Dewey is aware that observations are
theory-laden and that standards for judging science emerge within science (LTI:6, 140, 113, 138, 246; QC:107, 256, 277). He uses the term
"scientific revolution" (RPh:xvii; QC:94–95) and criticizes the notion
of scientific progress as accumulation (RPh:xvi). He is deeply sensitive
to the time-bound and context-bound nature of knowledge, and the corrigibility of even our best established theories. "There is no belief so
settled as not be exposed to further inquiry" (LTI:8; also 140–141; RPh:
145). Richard Rorty (1979:39, 166) has drawn our attention to Dewey's
critique of the "spectator theory of knowledge" (QC:23, 196, 213, 245)
and the correspondence theory of knowledge (EN:283).

Like Norwood Russel Hanson, Michael Polanyi, and Thomas Kuhn,
Dewey emphasizes discovery and criticizes the disjunction between discovery and justification—such as appears in logical positivist thought
and in Karl Popper's "logic of scientific discovery" (1959, 1965). Dewey
rejects "a sharp distinction . . . between genesis as psychological and validity which is logical" (EN:379; also, EEL:154–155; Sleeper 1986:5).
Scientific conjectures come into the world with considerable epistemic
value, and settled theories are only conjectures rendered highly plausible by their subsequent contributions. In Werner Heisenberg's words,
"At the very moment of its first appearance . . . the correct closed theory possesses an enormous persuasive power . . . long before . . . many
experiments [have] confirmed it" (1983:328). The scientific values, fruitfulness and unification, identified by Thomas Kuhn (1970) apply equally
to fresh conjectures and well-established theories. Paul Feyerabend
(1970), Kuhn (1970, 1977), Imre Lakatos (1970), and Michael Polanyi
(1962) critique the positivist notion of a crucial experiment presumed
to justify a theory conclusively, thereby setting it apart from a conjec-
ture. Such experiments are often technically possible only long after the
theory is either well-accepted or obsolete. Even when such experiments
are timely, the results are challenged—only in retrospect are they seen
as crucial. Dewey's discussion on the role of imaginative conjectures
(1926:10) is related to that of Georg Polya (1954), Hanson (1958), and

Polanyi (1962). But, like Ian Hacking (1983), experimentation by deliberate intervention in natural and social processes is Dewey's central theme.[2]

The following review of Dewey's thoughts on discovery is organized around his concepts of discovery, prospective orientation, intervention, exploratory experimentation, practice, and significance; and Hacking's concept, "the creation of phenomena." I next consider the issue of justification. Far from neglecting justification, Dewey, profoundly reconfigures our understanding of it. After discussing these topics, Dewey's views on the scientific community, "social intelligence," and the relationship between science and values are explored.

Discovery

For Dewey "the lifeblood of modern science is discovery" (EN:52). Discovery proceeds by means of exploratory experiments and daring hypotheses (EEL:208; 1926:10; QC:138, 310). Dewey celebrates "the method and spirit of science as inquiry which is perforce discovery," with the result that, "old intellectual attitudes and conclusions are unceasingly yielding to the new" (RPh:xxxiii). He claims that, among natural scientists themselves, it "is taken for granted," that science is about "discovery . . . uncovering the new and leaving behind the old" (RPh:xxx). Dewey approvingly refers to Francis Bacon, who "had an exceedingly slight opinion of the amount of truth already existent and a lively sense of the extent and importance of truth still to be attained" (RPh:31). Three centuries after Bacon, physical science has matured and can boast an impressive body of settled findings, so Dewey applies this sense of truth-yet-to-be-attained to human affairs (LTI:77, 487, 492). He expects that each discovery will soon be replaced by a deeper one, a falsifying one, or a revolutionary one. There is a "continuum of inquiry" in which each investigation grows out of previous ones and prepares the way for future ones (LTI:8–11, 140, 246). The continuum is cross-sectional as well as longitudinal. All specific inquiries are related to ones in neighboring fields, with the ultimate goal being unification into a coherent account of our complex existential situation (LTI:316). Thus specialization to the point of isolation is a danger to significant discovery and the growth of knowledge (LTI:508; PP:168–171). But, Dewey also rejects the notion of science as simply cumulative. Dewey endorses the view of Darlington: "'fundamental discoveries . . . always entail the destruction or disintegration of old knowledge before the new can be created'" (RPh:xvi).

Dewey's emphasis on discovery implies an orientation toward the future, the prospective. "While the content of knowledge is what . . . is taken as finished and hence settled, the reference of knowledge is future, or prospective. For knowledge furnishes the means of understanding . . . what is still going on and what is to be done" (DE:341). "A logic of discovery . . . looks to the future" (RPh:33). This prospective orientation is accompanied by a sense that knowledge is in process, not static. "Continued progress in knowledge is the only way to protect old knowledge from degeneration" (RPh:33–34). "In modern science systematized knowledge exists in practice for the sake of stimulating, guiding, and checking further inquiries" (EN:152). Dewey contrasts acting to produce "new arrangements of things," with observing "some antecedent state of things" (QC:136). "The object of knowledge is prospective and eventual, being the result of . . . operations which redispose what was antecedently existent" (QC:181, also 184–186, 200, 296).

In contrast to Dewey's prospective orientation, the central orientation of logical positivism is retrospective: the "rational reconstruction" of established scientific achievements. Dewey does not address the logical positivists directly. Instead, he takes classical Greek science as the epitome of the retrospective outlook, preoccupied with "antecedent properties of reality" as opposed to properties that can be newly created/discovered through experiment (QC:57). This emphasis on the future, the prospective, is also a leit-motif that appears in Dewey's writing on esthetics, language, politics, ethics, and education (DE:151, 341; EN:179, 365; HNC:19, 316; PP:156; E:172, 304). It is related to Dewey's concern with practice, consequences, process, and continuity. "We live not in a settled world" (DE:151). Like existentialists, Dewey is aware of the uncertainty and risk of a prospective orientation. "Looking ahead, toward the eventual, toward consequences, creates uneasiness and fear. It disturbs the sense of rest that is attached to the ideas of fixed truth already in existence" (RPh:159). The scientific community is striking in its ability to compensate for insecurity by anticipating the rewards of discovery. Dewey strives to bring this optimism about discovery to social inquiry and political discourse.

The hallmark of the prospective orientation, the promotion of discovery, is intervention. "If a . . . physicist or chemist wants to know something, the last thing he does is merely contemplate. He does not look, in however earnest and prolonged a way, upon the object . . . He proceeds to do something to bring some energy to bear upon the substance to see how it reacts; he places it under unusual conditions in order to induce some change" (RPh:113). The scientist is active, intervening in nature, not passively observing it. Although observation plays a role, the spectator metaphor is an utter misconception of the process of inquiry in science, and indeed, is a poor account even of everyday perception. "The rudimentary prototype of experimental doing for the sake of knowing is found in ordinary procedures. When we are trying to make out the nature of a confused [sic] and unfamiliar object [we do not merely look at it]. We perform various acts with a view to establishing a new relationship to it, such as will bring to light new qualities. We . . . rattle and shake it, thump, push, and press it" (QC:87). The object does not reveal itself to our gaze. It remains mysterious, until we intervene. "The object as it is experienced prior to the introduction of these changes baffles us. The intent of these acts is to make changes which will elicit some previously unperceived qualities . . . shake loose some property which as it stands blinds or misleads us" (QC:87). Phenomena are not simply there on the surface of things to be observed—or even to be disentangled, through statistical modeling, from one another and from the background. Creation and transformation must be induced by deliberate intervention.

Dewey writes that "physical science did not develop because inquirers piled up a mass of facts about observed phenomena. It came into being when men intentionally experimented on the basis of ideas and hypotheses . . . [to] disclose new observations . . . and [bring] to light significant phenomena" (SSSC:66). Scientists are not content with simply observing phenomena as they happen to arise and become available to inspection in the ordinary course of living. "Active experimentation must force the apparent facts of nature into forms different from those in which they familiarly present themselves" (RPh:32). Experiment contrives to produce particular elusive phenomena reliably, on demand. But more than this, experiment arranges new conjunctions of forces to produce configurations that don't occur naturally at all! "Nature is now to be acted upon "so as to transform it into new objects" (QC:100). This can be illustrated with examples from the early history of research on electricity.[3]

The study of electricity began with the common experience that amber rubbed with cloth attracted small objects. William Gilbert experimented with other materials and found that the same effect could be pro-

duced in ways never before seen—for example, by rubbing glass. Francis
Hauksbee produced this effect more powerfully and reliably with an apparatus that rotated a glass cylinder rapidly against a fabric pad. In Dewey's terms, experimental apparatus, such as Hauksbee's, has "the purposes of . . . introduction of a much greater range of variations" (QC:87).
Stephen Gray used Hauksbee's generator and discovered, serendipitously, the hitherto unknown phenomenon of conduction of electricity.[4]
Experimenters continued during the eighteenth-century to disclose new
features of electricity, using the Leyden jar and other apparatus. A dramatic turn of events was Alesandro Volta's discovery of the "electric
pile," today's electric battery. With his pile, Volta produced continuous
electric current. More than isolating and enhancing an elusive natural
phenomenon, Volta had created something that does not occur naturally
at all. As Dewey puts it, "science . . . confers upon things traits and potentialities which did not previously belong to them" (EN:381). Later,
Michael Faraday discovered the influence of electricity upon magnetism, which led to the electromagnetic generation of electricity—in
much the same form as used today. This generation of continuous alternating current electricity, through the influence of magnets on rotating
coils of wire, is another phenomenon not occurring naturally. The twentieth-century produced the cyclotron, the laser, and a host of other devices which create new phenomena. We can find similar examples in
other sciences, the most obvious being the production of new elements,
heavier than uranium, not found to occur in the natural world.

In Hacking's words, "to experiment is to create, produce, refine and
stabilize phenomena. . . . Phenomena [are not] plentiful in nature . . .
[they] are hard to produce in any stable way. That is why I spoke of creating and not merely discovering phenomena" (Hacking 1983:230). One
may concede that this "creation of phenomena" is an intriguing curiosity of the scientific enterprise, and a source of useful technology, but
question its philosophical significance. Dewey answers, "scientific principles and laws do not lie on the surface of nature. They are hidden and
must be wrested from nature" (RPh:32). The scientist proceeds, therefore, by "the construction of a new empirical situation in which objects
are differently related to one another" (QC:86).

Emphasizing discovery raises the issue of significance. An epistemol-
ogist, concerned with truth *per se*, is interested in the truth of any fact
at all. A scientist, however, is not interested in discovering just any item
of new knowledge. In the scientific community, some questions are rec-

ognized as important, others as trivial. Scientists are interested in solving problems that impede the development of their field and in filling in the major building blocks of theory. "One seeks to bring "to light significant phenomena" (SSSC:66); "to discriminate significant from trivial facts" (SS:62). Significance is seen by Dewey, and by the postempiricists, in terms of scope, fruitfulness, and unification. Dewey uses terms like "scope and depth," "fruitful," "large and generous ideas," "integration," "interrelations," and "intelligible wholes" (QC:310–311; SSSC:65). "The astronomer, biologist, chemist, may attain systematic wholes, at least for a time, within his own field" (QC:312). Scientists "bind facts together in systems of increasing temporal-spatial extent . . . [and] range of applicability" (RPh:xv). Fruitfulness, as an instrument for further inquiry and discovery, is an important criterion (RPh:33–34). In selecting scientific problems, in the further selection that comes at each turning point in a research program, the scientific values of scope, fruitfulness, and unification—significance—are important guides. This consideration of scientific values forms the basis for discussion of human values and science at the end of this chapter.

The theme of discovery carries over into Dewey's account of the origin of science in the practical arts, and his view of the tacit knowing that characterizes these arts. Examining artisanship and other practical know-how, in Dewey's view, is crucial for understanding how immature scientific disciplines like the social sciences can be founded and developed.

The Practical Arts and Tacit Knowing

Dewey finds it instructive to inquire into the earliest origins of science—not just its advanced form in the twentieth-century, its maturity after the scientific revolution of the seventeenth-century, or even its premodern form in classical Greece. He concludes that no science starts with a blank slate. Deliberate experimental efforts build on regularities already discovered in the skilled pursuit of the practical arts. "The accumulated results of the observations and procedures of farmers, navigators, builders, furnished matter of fact information about natural events" (EN:125). "We inherit the discrimination and skill of the good carpenter, pilot, physician, captain at arms" (EN:354). Tools are developed in "conformity to the efficacious resistances and adaptations of natural materials. . . . Accumulation and transmission of information are products" (EN: 122). In this way, we gain "a store of practical wisdom useful in conducting the affairs of life" (354).

Through the efforts of many generations, practitioners of practical arts learn how to produce useful objects and results—through trial and error, intuitive insight, use of metaphor and imagery, serendipity, and perhaps informal theorizing and deduction. In the process, they produce regularities heretofore unavailable through passive observation; in short, they create phenomena. Dewey continues, "It may be supposed that primitive astronomy . . . grew out of the practical necessities of agriculture . . . [that] the practical needs of medicine . . . [led to] the growth of physiological and anatomical knowledge" (LTI:72). Recently, ethnobotanists have developed great respect for the knowledge that native healers and artisans possess about local flora and their medicinal and chemical properties. The contemporary, highly developed physical sciences may have little use for such information and insight. But the social sciences, in their current state of development, may have much to learn from the practical arts of leadership, teaching, diplomacy, and management.

Dewey goes so far as to say that all existing sciences have emerged from practical arts. "That the sciences were born of the arts . . . is, I suppose, an admitted fact" (EN: 128). In the scholarly field of history of science in the second half of the twentieth-century, there has been a revolt against the received view that science developed from artisanship during the Renaissance. It has been pointed out that by the time of Copernicus, astronomy was a theoretical mathematical science practiced by scholars (Hall 1959). This is not, however, a refutation of Dewey, who is referring to the origins of astronomy among early agricultural civilizations. In any case, to view Dewey's hypothesis as suggestive for the social sciences, does not necessitate that this be true of every science in every historical period.

Dewey proposes that new sciences—especially social sciences—must develop from practical arts: "There cannot be a science of an art until the art has itself made some advance . . . If we do have a reasonable amount of technique, then it is by deliberately using what we know that we shall develop a dependable body of social knowledge" (SSSC:67). This view contradicts a commonly held belief—"The assumption is generally made that we must be able to predict before we can plan and control. Here again, the reverse is the case. . . . We should take measures to bring the event to pass. And I would add that only then can we genuinely forecast the future in social matters" (SSSC:67). We must create new phenomena before we can understand the underlying regularities that enable us to predict.

Two contrasting points of view can be articulated concerning the relationship of the practical arts to science. One view identifies the practical arts with those who are slaves to tradition, mindlessly following rules, and using random trial and error as the only source of change (EN:120). This stands in marked contrast to the enormous sweep and power of abstract scientific ideas and the power of deliberate scientific research methods (Bledstein 1976:88). The goal, then, is to free society from the constraints of the practical arts, much as we would be free from superstition, and to start from scratch on a scientific basis. Hence the rush in the nineteenth-century to professionalize medicine and engineering, and later, social work and psychology (88). This approach continues to be influential in the social sciences today. This resonates with the logical positivist position that a pure scientific language can and should be created, purged of the imprecision and contextuality of ordinary language.

An alternative view, akin to Dewey's, rests on two key tenets. First, much more respect is due to the practical arts, to which we owe much that is fine, not only in material artifacts, but also in leadership and other social arts. Second, there is an inescapable element of practical art even in the most highly refined work in the natural sciences (Polanyi 1962)— not only the arts of the laboratory, but even the art of understanding and creatively deploying the precise abstractions of higher mathematics. Echoing Polanyi, Kuhn stresses that science cannot be reduced to a set of explicit rules, but contains a large element of tacit knowing, acquired from apprenticeship and from the contemplation of exemplary scientific achievements—paradigms (Kuhn 1970:187–191). Gilbert Ryle's (1949) identifying and affirming of "knowing how" in contrast to "knowing that" is yet another recognition of the contribution of practical arts to significant knowledge. Hubert Dreyfus and Stuart Dreyfus (1986), and Joseph Rouse (1987) have applied Heidegger's conception of practical knowing to the one sphere he mistakenly excluded from that account— the sciences. Meanwhile, the ideal of pure scientific language freed of the taint of natural language was finally being recognized as unworkable by its chief exponent, Rudolph Carnap. Mary Hesse (1980), using the Duhem-Quine network thesis, makes the case that scientific language is rooted in natural language. This is akin to Edmund Husserl's thesis that scientific inquiry is rooted in, not separate from, the life-world. Ludwig Wittgenstein's linking of language games to forms of life leads to a similar perspective. These developments were anticipated by Dewey in his early critique of formalism in logic (Sleeper 1986:5). A number of recent schools of thought converge, then, on the recognition, anticipated by Dewey, of practical arts as sources of valuable knowledge—indeed, as the underpinning of all knowledge.

Not only the origins, then, but the ongoing operations of science are grounded in skills and inarticulate knowings. Dewey, and more recently, Polanyi and others have sought to clarify the status of this mode of knowing that is different from the more widely discussed explicit knowing characteristic of settled scientific findings.

Tacit Knowing

Polanyi, seeking to articulate his conception of practical skill and associated inarticulate knowledge, employed the term, "tacit knowing" (1966). Polanyi traces his conception to the gestalt psychologists with their distinctions between focal and peripheral perception, figure and ground. Dewey presents a very similar view, rooted in the ideas of William James, who, given his study of psychology and philosophy in Germany, may have shared a common intellectual ancestry with the gestaltists. Dewey asserts that knowledge can be "implicit" as well as explicit (HWT:280). "The carpenter, the physician, and the politician know [largely] with their habits, not with their consciousness" (HNC:182). Indeed, Dewey, asserts this of "the scientific man and the philosopher" as well (HWT:182)! Even our most explicit and settled knowledge could not exist without an immense background of tacit understanding, "a vast penumbra of vague, unfigured things, a setting which is taken for granted and not at all explicitly presented" (HWT:182). "We continually engage in an immense multitude of immediate organic selections, rejections, welcomings . . . of the most minute, vibratingly delicate nature. We are not aware of . . . most of these acts . . . yet . . . even our most highly intellectualized operations depend upon them as a 'fringe' by which to guide our inferential movements. . . . They give us premonitions of approach to acceptable meanings" (EN:300; also AE:50, 59; HWT:124, 280–283; RPh:88–89).

Dewey uses the terms "practical wisdom," "skill," "general insight," "judgment," "discrimination," and "organized ability in action," in various passages on practical arts quoted above. These usages amount to claiming legitimacy for practical understanding as knowledge. This practical knowledge, Dewey adds, has a crucial social dimension. "Experience," for Dewey, denotes "the accumulated information of the past and not merely the individual's own past but the social past, transmitted through language and even more through apprenticeship in the various crafts" (LW11:70). Furthermore, in Dewey's view, intuitive judgments have the same standing as formal inferential judgments insofar as both are hypotheses, rooted in past experience and reflection, to be justified prospectively (HWT:124). The greatest significance of tacit knowing, however, lies not in its role in natural science, but in its implications for social science. Given the complexity of social phenomena, explicit formal theories will fail to capture crucial relationships; these can, nonetheless, be understood tacitly by skilled practitioners and researchers— one of the subjects of Chapter 3.

Justification and Quantification

Dewey's emphasis on discovery and recognition of tacit knowing might encourage the mistaken, but not uncommon, view that Pragmatism is indifferent to justification. The neo-pragmatism of Rorty which inappropriately links Dewey's thought to today's skeptical, relativist, and even nihilist mood, fosters this error. The conflation of Dewey with James, and the selective reading of James's pragmatism also contributes to such misinterpretations of Dewey (Tiles 1988:110–111). Dewey replies, "I have never identified any satisfaction with the truth of an idea save that satisfaction which arises when the idea as working hypothesis . . . is applied in such a way as to fulfill what it intends" (MW4:109). Dewey is indeed concerned about warranted assertability and about testing our beliefs against experience (Tiles 1988:105). Preoccupation with epistemological questions, however, has distorted the discussion. Justification is better treated as a question of how we warrant our knowledge of particular things, not how knowledge is possible per se. For this purpose, one does best to study actual scientific practices, as the postempiricists later did.

Dewey's account of justification was anticipated earlier in this chapter. Given the idea of a discovery-justification continuum, the same considerations that bear upon the plausibility of initial and partially explored hypotheses are relevant to justification of more fully investigated ones. These considerations include: (a) the contribution of a hypothesis, acted on experimentally, toward resolving the conflicted situation for which it was first proposed; (b) the refinement and development of an experimental intervention in order to produce an intended effect with greater magnitude and precision; (c) the fruitfulness of a hypothesis as an instrument for exploration in search of further discovery, (d) the capacity of a hypothesis, or system of hypotheses to unify phenomena in a domain and across domains; and (e) the culmination of the above considerations in reflectively settled practices.

(a) The first test of a hypothesis is in bringing order to a specific problematic situation. "If ideas, meanings, conceptions, notions, theories, systems are instrumental to an active reorganization of the given environment, to a removal of some specific trouble and perplexity, then the test of their validity and value lies in accomplishing this work" (RPh:156). In the developing study of electricity, for example, Benjamin Franklin's hypothesis was that a single "fluid" subject to a conservation principle accounted for the manifestations of both positive and negative electricity. This immediately resolved puzzling questions about how one electrified body influenced another, and how and when sparks were passed from one body to another upon contact (Roller and Roller 1954).

(b) A key element of justification in Dewey's Pragmatist view is that once a discovery is made, it is refined until it can be produced with regularity and with a minimum of contaminating side effects. Experimenters strive to increase the magnitude of the effect to make it both more demonstrable and more useful for further experiments. This purifying and amplifying is exemplified in the development of the static electricity generator by Hauksbee, and the later development of the Leyden jar, both of which consistently produced ever larger and more dramatic sparks—providing powerful and reliable energy sources for further research. Gray and his successors refined his discovery of electrical conduction, reaching greater distances with decreasing loss due to resistance, and providing a standard part of experimental apparatus. Volta tried different metals and surrounding solutions to make a more effective electric pile (battery). He added more and more layers of alternating metal plates, finding that the electric force increased additively. Thus a reliable electric battery, producing substantial current, became available for research into electrochemistry and electromagnetism. The discovery of electromagnetic induction by Faraday was refined and enhanced into the technology of the electrical generator. Successive refinements provided massive current and voltage for further experiment and for industrial technology and domestic lighting. In all of these cases, the refinement, stabilization, and enhancement of the phenomenon originally discovered—what would later be called "research and development" in industry—has a strong justifying effect. Where highly refined measuring devices are unavailable or where the work is altogether qualitative—in social science, for example—justification of this sort becomes crucial.

(c) Fruitfulness in finding further knowledge is a key element in Dewey's account of justification. "The verifiability (as positivism understands it) of hypotheses is not nearly as important as their directive power. . . . The justification of such hypotheses has lain in their power to direct new orders of experimental observation, and to open up new problems and new fields of subject-matter" (LTI:519). It is not "as if a theory could be tested by directly comparing it with facts—an obvious impossibility—but through use in facilitating commerce with facts. It is tested as glasses are tested; things are looked at through the medium of specific meanings to see if thereby they assume a more orderly and clearer aspect" (EEL:198). "What is known . . . is . . . that which we think with rather than that which we think about" (DE:188). The success of these operations, more than direct experimental tests, is what lends credibility to a theory. Benjamin Franklin's one-fluid theory of electricity was taken as justified, not only because of its initial success in explaining Franklin's own experiments, but also because it turned out to explain other puzzling phenomena, and to open up still further questions (Kuhn 1970:18). Franklin's theory provides a convincing account of the "Leyden jar," not as a literal container holding electricity in its interior, but as an electric capacitor quite independent of its shape.[5] Hacking expresses Dewey's view in an illustration from particle physics. He mentions a physics experiment concerning quarks, which involved "spraying" a target with electrons. Hacking concludes, "so far as I am concerned, if you can spray them they are real . . . Nor perhaps would I have been convinced of electrons in 1908. It was the fact that we can spray . . . electrons . . . to find out something else [that convinced me]" (1983:23–24).

(d) Validating an idea in the three ways described above excludes grand but unfounded conjectures. That idea can then gain further validity in the eyes of scientists if it unifies phenomena within a domain, or unifies several distinct domains (Shapere 1971). In Dewey's words, "scientists bind facts together in systems of increasing temporal-spatial extent . . . [and] range of applicability" (RPh:xv). Modern natural science presents a long history of such unifications across domains. Newton brought together planetary and terrestrial motion under his law of gravitation. The law of conservation of energy brought under one principle heat, mechanical energy, and electricity. Faraday, through his discovery of induction, showed the unity of electrical and magnetic energy, and James Clerk Maxwell gave a unified theoretical account of electricity, magnetism, and light. Darwin drew together geology and natural history in his evolutionary theory, and the theory of evolution is still in the process of being integrated with genetics. Einstein astonished the world by showing the unity of matter and energy in his theory of relativity. Bohr's atomic theory gave an account of the long-investigated relationship between matter and electricity. Quantum mechanics, developed for atoms and particles, was applied to analysis of molecules, which led to the synthesis of quantum physics and chemistry. This, in turn, was applied to biology, leading to discovery of the function of DNA, and the cracking of the genetic code. Finally, there has been, in recent years, a dramatic integration of the very large and the very small—cosmology with subatomic particle physics—in accounts of the origin of the universe. This is unification from below, drawing upon knowledge already well-established and leading to further confirmation through its fruitfulness in opening up a wide range of fresh investigations. These unifications proceeded despite the paradigm shifts that mark off twentieth-century physics from classical physics.

(e) Reflectively settled practices. All of the above considerations contribute to experimental and theoretical practices, which become settled achievements, constantly in use, performing reliably, taken for granted by practitioners and theorists. "The criterion of what is taken to be settled, or to be knowledge, is being so settled that it is available as a resource in further inquiry; not being settled in such a way as not to be subject to revision in further inquiry" (LTI: 8–9). Such practices include the use of particle accelerators to study exotic fundamental particles, and the routine use of quantum mechanical equations to interpret data on molecules and subatomic particles. These practices are *reflectively* settled in that agreement is not based on custom and acquiescence, but on use, publication, criticism, and discussion within a scientific community. Agreement alone, without reflection, "seems to testify to custom rather than to truth" (EEL: 203). In the field of electricity, there is an abundance of such reflectively settled practices. Scientists as well as lay people take for granted the battery, the electromagnet, the vacuum tube and transistor, the cathode ray tube, the X-ray machine, the laser, and the practices of generation, transmission, and use of electricity associated with them. These cannot be dismissed as "mere" commercial technology, since they are fundamental to laboratory apparatus as well. Furthermore, the theoretical practices explaining these devices—Maxwell's laws, relativity, and quantum mechanics—are also reflectively settled.[6]

One field in which justification by formal, controlled experiment— summative evaluation—is the essence of what we call "science" is that part of medical research devoted not to basic science but to the evaluation of therapies. "It is not scientifically proven," we are wont to say, if a particular drug or treatment method has not undergone controlled clinical trials that show a better cure rate than a placebo or spontaneous remission. For Dewey, such evaluation of a fixed treatment approach is not science at all—not an open-ended inquiry into a conflicted situation (LSS:266). Science proceeds by identifying what the problem is, not by solving a preestablished problem, or testing a preestablished entity or hypothesis. "In the laboratory there is no question of proving that things are just thus and so, or that we must accept or reject a given statement; there is simply an interest in finding out what sort of things we are dealing with. Any quality or change that presents itself may be an object of investigation, or may suggest a conclusion; for it is judged, not by reference to pre-existent truths, but by its suggestiveness, by what it may lead to" (EEL:208). Scientists discover their goals in the course of inquiry, Dewey asserts; they do not pursue fixed ends. Scientific inquiry moves toward discovery by the creation of new phenomena, not the repetition of established ones. Narrowly focused summative evaluation uses "techniques that have proved efficacious in inquiries that are conducted scientifically," but this does not qualify it as science (LSS:226). Without arguing over terms, one could concede that this is science in one sense of the word, but not in the sense that refers to the march of physics and other natural sciences from Galileo and Newton to Einstein and Heisenberg. "Science" as primarily meaning summative evaluation is a usage that, when adopted by social scientists, is profoundly misleading. Its focus on justifying existing knowledge stifles the creation of new knowledge. Indeed, it undermines justification as well, if, as Dewey asserts, the justification of old knowledge proceeds through its application in making new discoveries.

Even for well-established claims, "verifications and truths could not be absolute" (1925:12). This is not to say, a scientific claim is arbitrary; it is still a matter of good reasons (Kuhn 1977:328). Polya's statement of the case could have been Dewey's: "Strictly speaking, all our knowledge outside of mathematics consists of conjectures. . . . There are of course . . . highly respectable and reliable [i.e., reflectively settled] conjectures as those expressed in certain general laws of physical science . . . [Nonetheless] anything we learn about the world involves plausible reasoning" (1954:2). A scientific theory becomes accepted not because it is conclusively proven beyond the possibility of argument. Scientific evidence gives security, not certainty. "We can afford to exchange a loss of theoretical certitude for a gain of practical judgment" (QC:213). Because scientific findings are not certain, they cannot compel belief. As Planck put it, in what has become a classic dictum: "a new scientific truth does not triumph by convincing its opponents and making them see the light, but rather because its opponents eventually die, and a new generation grows up that is familiar with it" (quoted in Kuhn 1970:151). Dewey uses similar language, though with respect to social changes, "important reforms can not take effect until after a number of influential persons have died" (HNC:109). Since scientific evidence is not clinching, there is in the scientific community an inevitable amount of conflict, resultant public discourse, and social learning. These processes loom even larger in the social sciences, as examined in Chapter 3.

To sum up, Dewey by no means neglects justification, but he offers a critique—what we now recognize as a postempiricist critique—of the prevailing positivist notions of justification. Furthermore, he provides an alternative account—justification of claims through refinement, stabilization, and enhancement, and through their use as tools for further investigation. This breaks down the split between justification and discovery. It eliminates the braking effect on discovery that comes from diverting attention and resources into premature formal tests—the only purpose of which is justification, and the claims of which are nonetheless, suspect. Having clarified Dewey's position on justification, it is now possible to state fully his view on the related issue of the role of quantitative measurement in science.

Quantification

"The work of Galileo was not a development, but a revolution. It marked a change from the qualitative to the quantitative or metric . . . from intrinsic forms to relations" (QC:94–95). In this passage, Dewey shows his respect for the role of quantification in the emergence of modern science. In context, however, it appears that the key term is, "relations." Measurement and mathematics are seen as instrumental to the discovery and use of such relations in the physical world. Where such relations can be formulated and apprehended in qualitative terms, quantification may not be necessary, and may sometimes be inappropriate. "It is ultimately the nature of the problem in hand which decides what sort of comparison-measurement is required in order to obtain a determinate solution" (LTI:205). Both those who insist on quantification and those who reject it utterly "miss the point. Both take propositions as ultimate and complete when, in fact, they are intermediate and instrumental" (205–206).

One reason for the intense concern with numbers among philosophers of science is the emphasis on rigorous justification, understood in logical-empiricist terms. Shifting one's concern away from such justification immediately relaxes the short-sighted pressure toward quantification. Instead, it invites exploratory experimentation of a qualitative nature. But in physics, discovery also appears to be closely linked to mathematically organized measurements. There is a notion attributed to Galileo that the language of nature is mathematics, and we must learn her language if we would uncover her secrets. Galileo's own discoveries concerning motion required quantification, and Kepler's discovery of elliptical orbits depended on Tycho Brahe's precise measurements. Dewey is both aware and appreciative of achievements dependent upon quantification. On the other hand, the discoveries made possible by Galileo's telescope—moon craters, phases of Venus, and satellites of Jupiter—were qualitative.

The history of research on electricity, again, is a case in point (Roller and Roller 1954). For two centuries after Gilbert, and on into the nineteenth-century, the great scientific advances were made almost entirely on a qualitative basis. As already stated, qualitative discoveries—such as the Leyden jar, electrical conduction, the voltaic pile, and the electromagnetic generator—were refined and enhanced until the observer could judge clearly that the results were of substantial magnitude, and the scientist could put them to good use in further inquiry. Measurement, in this case, was not an essential instrument, but an added refinement, and perhaps, an obstacle. Mathematical formulations of the extant knowledge of electricity were established by Charles-Augustin Coulomb and Andre Ampere at the turn of the nineteenth-century. Joseph Agassi (1971) argues that this formalization was premature and restrictive of further discovery. It was Michael Faraday's bold qualitative theorizing about electrical and magnetic fields that facilitated his great discoveries and paved the way for James Clerk Maxwell and Albert Einstein. When Maxwell was formulating his laws, measurement of electrical current and voltage was well-advanced and theoretically useful, but the basic discoveries he accounted for had been reached on a qualitative basis.

The turning points that made the study of electricity and magnetism a modern science preceded quantification. The modern revolution in chemistry, however, depended on measurements of great precision by Antoine Lavoisier—though considerable qualitative knowledge of chemical properties through qualitative investigation was a necessary prelude (Kuhn 1970:70–72). In biology, qualitative inquiry was more important than in chemistry, and continued to be of value for some purposes into the twentieth-century. Dewey asserts that each field, perhaps each topic, has its own unique problems and needs particular methods adapted to these tasks. "Every phase of experience must be investigated, and each characteristic aspect presents its own peculiar problems which demand, therefore, their own technique of investigation" (EEL:212). This observation bears strongly upon Dewey's recommendations for the pursuit of social science.

For purposes of simplification, the discussion in this chapter has proceeded as if scientific inquiry could be identified with the individual investigator. For Dewey, however, each investigator is part of a scientific community.

Scientific Community

Science, in Dewey's view, is essentially a community activity, and the scientific community is a uniquely democratic one, providing a model of what political democracy might be. Dewey portrays an ideal community, a reconstruction with a normative element, not a literal description. First let us examine that ideal, and later consider the actuality. Scientific practitioners are interdependent. The work of any one investigator "depends on methods and conclusions that are a common possession and not of private ownership" (1936:142). The findings of a single person are only accredited as knowledge through consideration by other scientists. "The authority of science issues from and is based upon collective activity. In the measure that it is cooperatively confirmed, it becomes a part of the common fund of the intellectual commonwealth . . . [The] contribution the scientific inquirer makes is collectively tested and developed" (1936:142). The goal of individual scientists is to publish their work and make it available to the whole community, not cling to it as a private possession. Any new "fact or truth is put at once, freely and voluntarily, at the disposal of the whole scientific public" (LW11:277). Community, for Dewey, involves coordinated activity that is conscious and deliberate—not merely customary, and is valued by the participants. Scientists are aware of their membership in a community, and take great pride in it; they are aware of its norms and abide by them.

Democratic community for Dewey involves the working out of common purposes through discourse about practice. This is especially true in science. "Even when, temporarily, the ideas put forth by individuals have sharply diverged from received beliefs, the method used in science has been a public and open method which succeeded and could succeed only as it tended to produce agreement, unity of belief among all who labored in the same field" (1936:142). There are, in principle, no authorities and no coercive powers that could compel belief. Opportunity to present findings and to critique the findings of others are, in principle, strictly equal. Scientific papers are presented anonymously for peer review. No name, title, or rank should give any single author preferential access to publication. These features approximate Habermas's construct—the ideal speech situation.[7]

This is, of course, an idealized view of science. Real scientific communities—even the smaller-scale, more autonomous, and less frenetic ones of Dewey's time—have their share of hierarchy and privilege, uncivil conflict, ideology, rigidity, and even occasional outright fraud. Dewey, however, argues in terms of the norms that constitute the practice of science rather than the motivation and behavior of individual scientists (EN:151). In terms of these norms, such behavior is simply unscientific. Furthermore, actual scientific communities, Dewey would claim, achieve a good approximation of the ideal. They are largely successful in socializing their members into their norms and enforcing compliance. When, on occasion, serious violations occur, the community mobilizes to investigate them and prevent their recurrence.[8]

Dewey's view of the scientific community appears paradoxical in light of obvious individual effort and contribution by particular scientists, and their disagreement with and competition with one another. Indeed, a common metaphor for science is the "market-place of ideas," thriving on the self-interested activities of isolated individuals. This view, in Dewey's eyes, is based on a fundamental misunderstanding, not only of science, but also of economic life. There is a failure to see how much each individual entrepreneur's or scientist's successes are dependent upon the efforts of others, upon organized systems of communication and distribution, and upon the fruits of technology which the individual had no part in creating. "The notion that intelligence is a personal endowment or personal attainment is the great conceit of the intellectual class, as that of the commercial class is that wealth is something which they personally have wrought" (PP:211).

The ideal scientific community goes a step beyond the ideal speech situation. It not only accepts worthy contributions regardless of the identity of the author, it positively encourages diverse, daring, and dissenting views. "It is of the nature of science not so much to tolerate as to welcome diversity of opinion" (FC:102). Science not only permits free deliberation over a given claim, it promotes discovery—leading to the obsolescence or transcendence of old conflicts, and the building of new unities. The scientific community is thus an institution for conflict-resolution, and not simply for adjudication. Democratic communities are not characterized by the absence of conflict, but they could not survive or remain democratic if they were not effective in resolving conflict—without resort to hierarchy and coercion. The scientific community has had, in Dewey's view, a remarkably successful record of conflict-resolution and consensus-building. This is achieved in a dynamic, growing, changing field without evasion of conflict through custom, tradition, and authority. Dewey attributes this success to the methods of science—the norms of the scientific community.

Under conditions of normal science, Dewey's claims seem accurate but unsurprising. When there is a reigning paradigm, a high degree of consensus prevails on the interpretation of observations, and on standards of acceptance of findings. Conflicts of interpretation can be adjudicated against such consensual concepts and standards. But what of conditions of paradigm crisis and scientific revolution, when previously accepted concepts and standards are now challenged and alternative world views are in contention? Even revolutions within science are remarkable for their nonviolence, if not always for their civility. The violence and coercion which occurred during the Copernican revolution, for example, came from theological and political institutions outside of the scientific community. The modern scientific revolution of quantum mechanics and relativity was embraced rapidly by large segments of the scientific community, and the conflict was over, for all intents and purposes, a generation later. For Dewey, what is crucial in such resolutions is the willingness to submit claims to experimental test and abide by the results. But when competing paradigms are at stake, can the two sides agree on what constitutes a fair test? This question, however, depends on the traditional view of experiment solely as a means of justification. Dewey's conception of experiment, not the conventional positivist one, accounts for the success of science in resolving even disputes across paradigms. In Dewey's view, theories are tested through use as instruments for the pursuit of further knowledge, and through refinement of scientific practices based upon them. For example, the fruitfulness that the new quantum mechanics exhibited from the start, and throughout the process of application largely accounted for its enthusiastic acceptance.

If one accepts the claim that the natural science community has been uniquely successful in resolving conflict, the question remains whether that success is attributable to its general method of inquiry. If so, this model might be applicable in the social domain. Alternatively, the success in conflict-resolution could be due to uniquely tractable features of natural phenomena. Dewey, himself, argues that the physical domain is far less complex than the social. The approximation of treating certain phenomena as closed systems is much more applicable.[9] Hence, the results of physical science inquiries are more determinate and more decisive in resolving conflicts. On the other hand, Dewey believes that the broad scientific method of inquiry and discovery could vastly improve our attempts at handling social conflict. Taking these two views together, Dewey can be seen as suggesting that, with regard to tractability, there is a difference in degree, but not in kind, between the physical domain and the social.

If the scientific community is to be a model of democratic community generally, however, it must also include processes for resolving value conflicts. For Dewey, science should indeed confront such conflicts and resolve them through ethical inquiry. But scientific communities, as presently constituted, largely evade such questions, and indeed, justify excluding them. To the extent that issues of the consequences of science for human welfare are taken up, scientists appear no more adept at discussing and resolving them than other citizens.[10] Dewey believes that ethical deliberation, like scientific work, requires inquiry and discovery. Thus he believes that scientific method has much to teach us about ethics. But Dewey is also clear that in ethical deliberation, inquiry into one's own desires and purposes, and the desires and purposes of others, is central to the investigation (E:176, 270). Ethical deliberation also requires the ability to interpret language, exercise moral imagination, and critique conventional wisdom. It requires acquaintance with historical antecedents of current problems, and knowledge of the social and economic issues at stake. Natural science does not call for knowledge of or skill in investigating these aspects of experience. Indeed, intensive professional natural science education preempts time and instructional resources that might have been devoted to acquiring such knowledge and skill (LW11:187, 189).

To sum up, Dewey's thesis about scientific community and democracy holds, but to a limited extent. The lessons of welcoming diversity, insisting on publicity, and pursuing conflict-resolution through inquiry remain. But democratic communities must develop skills and methods of ethical deliberation not required in the scientific community as presently constituted. Were this to be accomplished, democratic political communities would have something to teach scientists, as well as something to learn from them. In Dewey's view, scientists do, indeed, need to learn such lessons. They are faced with ethical questions about the applications of science for which, Dewey argues, they are responsible. Despite the culture of specialization which encourages scientists to avoid such questions, that responsibility is inherent in the role of human beings and citizens who take a moral point of view.

Applied Science: Science and Human Values

Dewey makes three arguments in favor of applied science and the social responsibility of science. Two of these arguments are flawed, but are not necessary to make Dewey's case; the third argument, it is claimed here, is sound and is sufficient. First, Dewey argues that science arose from the practical arts and had as its goal, the improvement of human well-being. This origin, however, does not preclude science from becoming functionally autonomous and pursuing purposes of its own. Such purposes would be to satisfy esthetic needs, needs for power, and curiosity, pose mental challenges, overcome superstition, answer cosmological and perhaps spiritual questions, and actualize grandiose visions. Second, Dewey argues that science cut off from application becomes precious and sterile: "Inquiry loses stimulus and purpose. It degenerates into sterile specialization, a kind of intellectual busy work carried on by socially absent minded men" (RPh:148–149). This may be true of social science, since applied questions of human well-being are near the core of theoretical questions about social structure and process. But natural

sciences, as mature autonomous disciplines, have proven very successful in generating from within, bold new questions and powerful motivations for fresh discovery. Third, Dewey observes that as human beings
and citizens, scientists have moral obligations concerning the consequences of their work.

It is customary within our complex society to make ethical choices
from the perspective of one's roles, especially one's professional or voca-
tional role. One is inclined to say, "my responsibility as a scientist is to
values of truth"; "my responsibility as a corporation executive is to generate returns for the stockholders;" "my responsibility as an engineer is
to design and build well on the project to which I've been assigned."
Moreover, in these assertions there is usually an additional clause, provided by the culture, which rationalizes the evasion of responsibility altogether. For example, "my responsibility as a businessman is to make
a profit, while the market assures—as if by an invisible hand—that this
results in social well-being." Scientists might reason, "my responsibility is to advance our understanding of the physical world, while it is up
to ethicists, political leaders, and voters, to decide about the uses to
which such discoveries will be put." Dewey points out that such role-
based choices assume a prior ethical decision—the decision to choose
from within a professional role and not from one's larger roles as citizen
and human being. "The man who decides to put business activity before
all other claims . . . does make a choice about . . . good. But he makes it
as a man, not as a businessman" (HNC:218). We must make such decisions, as Dewey says in another context, "as a human not . . . in any special professional capacity" (RPh:xli). Our culture of specialization—
both generally and academically—pays little attention, however, to that
more basic decision and the standards that should guide it (LW11:128).
It may, therefore, take a crisis—an economic depression, war, or episode
of rapid social change—to remind us of the larger decision that we make
unreflectively, under the influence of the prevailing culture. Dewey tells
the story of an engineer acquaintance, who said, "'do you know I have
only begun to think since 1932.' . . . He meant he had not had to consider the relation of his work, that of the engineering profession, to the
whole social and economic construction before that collapse of 1929 in
the way he has to do now" (LW6:224).

To be sure, the physical universe exists apart from human beings, and
our conclusions about it should not be dependent on our wishes. "Humanity is not, as was once thought, the end for which all things were
formed; it is but a slight and feeble thing, perhaps an episodic one, in the

vast stretch of the universe" (PP: 175). Nonetheless, humans have to decide, on their own grounds, whether and why they will study nature.
"But for man, man is the center of interest and the measure of importance" (PP: 175). To study science for its own sake, which is to say for
the esthetic enjoyment and intellectual challenge, is not without consequences. "The magnifying of the physical realm at the cost of man is
but an abdication and a flight. To make physical science a rival of human
interests . . . forms a diversion of energy which can ill be afforded"
(PP: 175–176). This is not, however, the full cost. Science will inevitably
have social consequences, and these will often be malign unless scientists and laypeople both take responsibility. "The instrumentality becomes a master and works fatally as if it possessed a will of its own—
not because it has a will, but because man has not. The glorification of
'pure' science under such conditions is . . . a shirking of responsibility" (175).

There are several standard defenses of pure science which must be answered to support Dewey's view. First, it is argued that motivations internal to autonomous science will ultimately be more fruitful in applications than research that pursues such applications directly. Whether
or not the empirical claim is true, what is at stake here is only whether
application is immediate or delayed. This argument concedes from the
outset the social responsibility of science, and thus is no challenge to
Dewey's position. Second, there are those who see no need for justification of science except, say, that it enriches our lives with knowledge,
or that it demystifies the wonders of nature. But this approach also concedes that there is a human purpose for science—the purposes of en-
richment and of demystification—"the need is practical and human,
rather than intrinsic to science itself" (QC: 312, also 138, 221–222). This
contemplative purpose can, then, be challenged as to whether it is more
worthy than applying science to fill human material needs and to advance democracy. Third, applied science in the form of industrial production has befouled the environment and subverted the democratic
public by offering an orgy of consumption. Dewey sees this not as intrinsic to application, but the result of leaving application to the market
system and not to democratic discussion and planning for human welfare (LW6: 44–45; ION: 138; PP: 174). "The adulteration of knowledge is
not due to its use, but to vested bias and prejudice . . . to contempt or
disregard of human concern in its use" (PP: 175–176). A fourth argument
is that positing a social responsibility of science invites government regulation, portending a loss of freedom of thought and speech. Government

choices in this sphere would be, at best, fallible, and, at worst, corrupt and tyrannical. Dewey can be read as responding in two ways. (a) He is engaged in persuasion, not coercion. He is appealing to each individual scientist voluntarily to recognize her or his own responsibility. "It is a question of acknowledgment on the part of scientific inquirers of intellectual responsibility; of admitting into their consciousness a perception of what science has actually done through its counterpart technologies, in making the world and life what they are. This perception would bear fruit by raising the question of what science can do in making a different sort of world and society" (ION: 137).[11] (b) To the extent that there is to be government intervention—as there already is through funding decisions—it should be based on a thoroughgoing participatory and discursive democratic process, not left to nonresponsible officials operating on ideology or yielding to lobbyists' pressure.

Conclusion: Social Intelligence

Dewey is not at all interested in developing philosophy of science for its own sake, or even for the sake of improving natural science research—which he sees as having no need of external assistance. His purpose is learning from the success of natural science in order to identify a general "method of intelligence," which can be applied in social science, in ethics, and in public discourse. Dewey devotes the book *How We Think* to explicating this method for general use, and to indicating how schools might seek to guide students in their acquisition and mastery of it. There is much in this method that is shared with the broad array of empiricist approaches. That is, there is a commitment to put ideas to the test of experience, and this commitment works against superstition, fantasy, prejudice, and vested interest. It has a thrust toward healthy skepticism about particular views, but not about the possibility of knowledge altogether. But what is more particular to Dewey's Pragmatism is the constant emphasis on experimental intervention to gain new knowledge through which to resolve conflicts. The concern of the method of intelligence is prospective: the production of new discoveries—indeed, the rapid production and testing of findings and discarding of failed ones—issuing in a vast expansion of the overall stock of usable knowledge.

3 Social Science

Introduction

Dewey sees a broad unity of method for both natural and social sciences. His stance as commentator on these two fields is quite different, however. Dewey reconstructs the methods of natural sciences in order to come to an understanding of a going concern. He seeks to build a project of social science inquiry from the ground up. After witnessing substantial expansion and paradigm formation in the positivist-oriented social sciences, in 1926 Dewey writes, "he would be a shameless braggart who . . . claimed that the result is yet adequate" (1926:9–10); and again, in 1948, "[social science] is not as yet . . . worthy of being designated scientific" (RPh:xxv). Despite vast development in social science since mid-century, its mainstream follows the same positivist lines as when Dewey made his critique (Ross 1991). The principal countertradition, the newer interpretive approaches inspired by anthropological field work and literary interpretation, lacks the experimental thrust that is central to Dewey's conception of science. Were Dewey alive today, his assessment would likely be changed only at the margins. It is in the less prestigious and more practice-oriented fields such as community mental health, progressive education, organizational development, clinical studies in child development—and in methodological approaches such as reflective practice, action research, and participatory research[1]—that Dewey might see some realization of his conception. Dewey's alternative still has the power to challenge, shock, and inspire. It stresses ex-

72

ploratory experimentation in natural settings—in a spirit of audacity, invention, and discovery, strongly motivated by critique of existing institutions, and by ethical concerns.

Through experimentation/invention, new possibilities are opened up for win-win solutions to social conflicts, and the transformation of social institutions and policies. This would greatly advance social science as science, as well as contribute to the betterment of human life. "The assumption is generally made that we must be able to predict before we can plan and control [i.e., have pure social science first, then application]. . . . The reverse is the case . . . We should take measures to bring the event to pass . . . only then can we genuinely forecast the future in . . . social matters" (SSSC:67). Practical knowledge precedes scientific knowledge and is the basis for building the latter. Discovery precedes and makes possible justification. In stressing discovery, Dewey frees us from the tight constraints of formal experimentation on behalf of justification, making bold intervention scientifically legitimate. Justification follows social invention, when promising experimental effects are refined and enhanced until the main causal influences become prominent, and reflectively settled practices ensue.

By invention, Dewey means devising new organizational forms and processes, and new social and economic policies—in particular, those which enhance both democracy and task-effectiveness. Dewey warns that social inventions are works-in-progress, steps in a continuum of inquiry, not finished achievements (LTI:9, 11, 246). They must be continually improved and refashioned. Inquiry has as much to learn from errors as from successes (1928a:105; RPh:208; HWT:115; EEL:101; ACF:31–32). It is easy to dismiss new and still-evolving organizational forms. Dewey welcomes criticism for the sake of ongoing improvement, but not as a sufficient basis for terminating an experiment. To judge anything short of perfection, as proof that change is impossible, is faint-heartedness, if not self-serving apologetics for the status quo. In Sarason's words, "Why should any effort at innovation be expected to be other than a first approximation . . . ? The first computer is truly a museum piece compared to the computer of today. The changes took place in a developmental process characterized by feedbacks . . . a self-correcting process" (1996:355).

Let us proceed directly to an example of social invention, noting features of exploratory experimentation, before turning to a more abstract account of Dewey's philosophy of social science.

Social Inventions

WORKPLACE DEMOCRACY: THE MONDRAGON COOPERATIVES

A major social invention in the economic sphere is the Mondragon Cooperative system in the Basque region in Spain (Whyte and Whyte 1991). Over a thirty-year period, and continuing today, this complex of industrial producers' cooperatives came to employ more than twenty-thousand worker-owners, provide educational and social services for more than five times that number, and grow steadily, despite European recession and global competition. This record was achieved through constant experimentation—establishing a new model of cooperative organization at the outset, and developing this model to respond to a dynamic environment. The Mondragon Cooperatives are a new phenomenon that reveals possibilities of individual and collective human functioning not previously experienced.

As in Dewey's Pragmatist approach (see Chapter 1), Mondragon's founding was conflict-driven—a response to severe unemployment in the countryside of Spain's Basque region under Franco's rule. Mondragon's development was also strongly value-driven, in keeping with Dewey's approach (RPh:xxvi–xxvii). Whyte and Whyte (1991) sum up the value positions of the priest Arizmendiarrieta—founder, theorist, and inspirational force behind the cooperatives—views which sound very close to Dewey's. Arizmendiarrieta's program shares with Dewey's the commitment to full employment, dignified work with a decent wage, and worker ownership and management (see EBNS). "Work should not be seen as a punishment but as a means of self-realization. There should be dignity in any work. He [speaks] of the need for cooperation and collective solidarity. He combines a social vision with an emphasis on education for technical knowledge and skills" (Whyte and Whyte 1991: 29; also 256–263). Like Dewey, Arizmendiarrieta emphasizes education in skills and attitudes for cooperation (LW11:192; Whyte and Whyte 1991:256). The goal of economic organization is to serve the workers. Profit is important as a measure of success in the market, but is not the primary aim. "Leaders of Mondragon recognize profits as the essential means for achieving their ends of social and economic development" (214). Arizmendiarrieta writes, "'The cooperativist . . . utilizes capital . . . to make more gratifying the working life of the people'" (254).

Arizmendiarrieta's approach, like Dewey's, is also theory-driven—not formal theory, but political, social, and economic thought; speculative philosophy and liberal theology (LTI:499; PESE:257; PP:32–34). He draws upon the tradition of cooperatives among the Basques, Catholic social philosophy, wide reading in sociology, Marxism, Paolo Freire, and other sources (Whyte and Whyte 1991:247). Recognizing that decentralization is favorable to democratic management, but that the market favors large-scale production and marketing, he theorizes that a federation of cooperatives could meet both decentralist values and centralizing pressures, thereby resolving a fundamental conflict (264). A bold theoretical innovation by Arizmendiarrieta is a pattern of ownership which gives workers a financial stake in the cooperatives but does not permit them to sell their interest, as ordinary ownership of shares would have done. This proceeds from a communitarian understanding of property relations. This arrangement has proven successful in providing financial strength and intergenerational continuity to the cooperatives.

Like Dewey's approach, the Mondragon Cooperatives are both democratic experiments and experiments in democracy. All major policy changes require a two-thirds vote of the entire membership, assembled in a general meeting. A vivid example is provided by the decision in one large cooperative to reduce wages in response to the European economic recession of the late 1970s and early 1980s. There was a fifteen-week process of drafting statements, disseminating educational material, and holding discussion meetings. Moderators were trained to lead group discussions, and all members were polled in an advisory opinion gathering effort. Interest groups were formed to draft alternative policy proposals and generate support for them. Although there was heated disagreement, a compromise policy, which still exacted stringent sacrifices, was worked out. In the end, the compromise was passed by the required two-thirds majority (Whyte and Whyte 1991:134–141). Democracy in Mondragon is a matter of facing conflict, not minimizing or avoiding it. "Mondragon people take pride in their ability to resolve conflicts of interest and ideas" (311; also 273). "The basic idea is that life in a cooperative should not be carried on as if it were a zero-sum game in which some win and some lose" (275). Since the Mondragon Cooperatives comprise a large and complex community, representative democracy is the principal governance mechanism. Through "social councils," experts in technology, management, and marketing are kept in touch with the viewpoints, ideas, and needs of the workers. Problems of worker engagement, education, and active participation have not yet been fully solved, however, and the social council activities have frequently come up for review (230–233). This indicates a need for ongoing innovation and experimentation, and should not be taken as a verdict of failure of democracy in large-scale cooperative enterprise.

This type of democracy requires that individuals change, and this, in turn, requires enough support to deal with the inevitable anxieties that accompany change. The leadership style of Arizmendiarrieta, the founder of the cooperatives, is characterized as a "combination of challenge and support" (Whyte and Whyte 1991:267). Arizmendiarrieta is notable for not assuming formal leadership positions himself but, instead, enabling others to develop leadership skills. Subsequent generations of leaders model their leadership style upon that of the founder. A manager "in explaining his decision [to trust workers and supervisors to take up management tasks] told us that he too had been a student of Don José Maria and the founder had led him to believe that such people, if given the chance, could measure up to the challenge" (191; also 268).

Arizmendiarrieta, like Dewey, is concerned with "continuous critical examination" and ongoing revision as essential to experimentation and social invention (LTI:161; Whyte and Whyte 1991:234). He "stresse[s] the need for constant reevaluation of the cooperative experience . . . stresses the need for people with open and flexible minds, capable of adapting to constantly changing conditions" (261). "'By making mistakes we end up learning'" (257). Arizmendiarrieta's often quoted expression on this subject is, "'We build the road as we travel,'" echoing Dewey's, "unceasing creation of an . . . new road upon which we can walk together" (Whyte and Whyte 1991:257; FC:176). The Mondragon Cooperatives undergo frequent revision for three reasons:

First, insofar as the environment remains constant, they wish to learn from experience in order to achieve more of their goals. "Different systems of leadership have evolved, and with them, a growing sense of teamwork. For example, a furniture factory now operates completely through work teams. Thus the formal system has led to the ongoing evolution of a democratic process" (Benello 1992:96).

Second, the cooperatives must deal with the internal effects of their responses to external changes. In particular, increasing size and increasingly sophisticated technology threaten democratic governance and call for organizational innovations to maintain meaningful worker participation. In response, there have been ongoing efforts to strengthen the capacity of the "social councils"—which represent workers' interests in the periods between general membership meetings—to interpret for workers the "complex and technical" data "on which management decisions are made" (Whyte and Whyte 1991:233).

Third, the cooperatives have to reckon with frequent changes in the economic environment—rapid changes in technology, severe fluctuations in the European economy, and the intensified competition that accompanies economic globalization. One of Mondragon's general responses to the changing external environment is to invest heavily in education and research on new technology, product development, and marketing (Whyte and Whyte 1991:215–221). Another major response is spinning off new cooperatives to serve new markets, thus maintaining decentralization and flexibility. At the same time, institutions coordinating the work of individual cooperatives are developed. An additional cushion against external changes involves investing heavily in reorganization in order to save faltering production units. This is accomplished not by tolerating persistent financial losses—turning the enterprise into a welfare delivery system, as in some socialist economies—but through rigorous restructuring of management, technology, and marketing. Such reorganizations resemble those of capitalist firms, with the notable exception that wholesale slashing of the workforce does not occur. If job cuts are deemed necessary, jobs are found in other cooperatives for every displaced worker. In one case, the cooperative "struggled through a reorganization in 1983, and then, when that failed, underwent a much more drastic reorganization in 1985. The case illustrates the lengths to which the members and leaders of the complex will go, to rescue failing cooperatives and save jobs" (Whyte and Whyte 1991:181). This is another extraordinary feature of Mondragon, compared with other economic arrangements.

The Mondragon experiment involves the creation of a system, not unconnected, independent components. "To obtain the benefits of large scale, along with the benefits of small individual units, Mondragon has evolved a system of cooperative development . . . coordinated by a management group elected from the member enterprises. These units are either vertically or horizontally integrated and can send members from one enterprise to the other" (Benello 1992:94). Mondragon "has created a total system where one can learn, work, shop, and live within a cooperative environment. . . . In such an environment, motivation is high because members have an overall cooperative culture which integrates material and moral incentives, and which extends into every aspect of life" (96). The system's complexity is addressed in a number of ways. There exists an elaborate formal organization with constitutional provisions for democratic control. Additionally, improvised and tacit procedures are used in areas where formal methods would be ineffective.

Through specialized postgraduate education, research and development, and individual study, explicit, codified information is absorbed from without and generated from within. For example, "A physicist by training, Mongelos had no formal education in personnel administration, but after taking the position of director, he immersed himself in the literature of personnel and human relations" (113). Tacit knowledge and practical skill are acquired concomitantly through apprenticeship and through lateral movement among various positions. Mondragon has a remarkable record of developing successive generations of leadership and technical expertise from within the cooperatives and through its associated schools and laboratories. In discussing the systemic and tacit nature of Mondragon's organizational culture, Whyte and Whyte report that, "the elements of culture need to be compatible with one another and mutually reinforcing . . . Furthermore, one cannot assume that the culture consists of what is written down and disseminated in company policy statements: the 'espoused theory.' One infers the nature of a culture from the study of behavior, which leads to the 'theory in use.' At the same time, it is important . . . to write down and disseminate the basic elements of [this] culture . . . [as] reference points for study and debate" (295).

Economic and democratic performance are constantly monitored in the Mondragon Cooperatives as indicators of a need for ongoing revision. Economic production is evaluated rather easily through quantitative measures such as profit, gross revenue, capitalization, and workforce—all of which grew rapidly, on average, and did not decline even in difficult years. "Spain's industrial output grew at an annual rate of 1.5 percent in the period 1976–1983 while Mondragon averaged 6 percent for those years" (Whyte and Whyte 1991:204). Guided by their community-oriented values, the Mondragon Cooperatives sought and achieved extraordinarily low percentages of business failures and worker layoffs (132, 206). These figures are readily available unambiguous, quantitative indicators. Evaluation of success in achieving democratic ideals, however, is not so straightforward. This is assessed through qualitative reports of observers and through observations and interviews of social scientists from outside the community.

For Dewey, the question of evaluation ultimately turns to the achievement of reflectively settled practices. Although Mondragon is noted for its flexibility—its constant adaptation to a changing environment—there is at least one feature that has remained quite stable—the system of property relations established at the outset. "The system of individual accounts with automatic loan-back, along with the partitioning of the surplus into an individual component and a collective component, represents a method of giving the worker a sense of individual owner-ship along with a sense of collective participation in an organization" (Benello 1992:97). This arrangement can be considered a well-tested, successful, and consensually approved practice, and the theory underly-ing it, therefore, can be regarded as knowledge in Dewey's view.

The flourishing of the Mondragon Cooperatives over their more than thirty-year life span qualifies them, viewed as a single system, as a reflec-tively settled practice. Not only does this support knowledge claims, it disconfirms theories of human organization and motivation which pre-dict that such well-functioning cooperatives are an impossibility. "Mon-dragon . . . speaks to the claim of the weakness and fallibility of human nature in specific and concrete ways" (Benello 1992:99). "Until it [Mon-dragon] happened, it was easy to write off experiments in economic de-mocracy as marginal and unrealistic utopian ventures, totally irrelevant to . . . any sizable portion of an existing economy. This can no longer be said" (97). The experience of Mondragon underlines the importance of skilled and resourceful leadership equipped with knowledge of organi-zations as systems. "Mondragon . . . demonstrates that . . . when [orga-nizational] skills [on a high level] are present, the traditional opposition of democracy and efficiency vanish, and the two reinforce rather than oppose each other" (97). Thus a bold, creative social invention resolves what seems to be a fundamental conflict, finding a way to achieve both of the goals in question. Furthermore, what might have been an inter-minable debate is instead worked out in experience, within the Mon-dragon community—through experiment and not by discussion only. Benello echoes Dewey's Pragmatism with its insistence on settling con-troversies in practice: "here, the ideological debate gives way to concrete know-how" (97, also 99).

Dewey would view the understandings embodied in the practices of Mondragon as knowledge in a limited sense, because they have been tried and accepted in one particular community. With respect to other sites, however, they can only be seen as working hypotheses, albeit per-suasive ones. The ideas suggested by the Mondragon experiment con-tribute to the discourse on economic organization in the wider world. "Mondragon is important because it serves as a model" (Benello 1992: 97). Among those interested in workplace democracy, decentralization, and other transformational approaches, Mondragon is the touchstone. Every author mentions it, and some build much of their analysis around it.[2] Its successes and failures are charted and evaluated. Questions are raised as to how democratic and progressive the cooperatives really are (Kasmir 1996). Its methods are carefully studied with a view to possible replication. "Mondragon has awakened worldwide interest. The Mitterand government in France [had] a special cabinet post for the development of cooperatives, the result of its contact with Mondragon. In Wales, the Welsh Trade Union Council is engaged in developing a system of cooperatives patterned after Mondragon . . ." (Benello 1992:95). The International Cooperative Association helps cooperatives form and develop, based on Mondragon's principles. Evidence will be forthcoming as to whether and how the Mondragon model can be adapted to different environments. That evidence will contribute to ongoing experimentation and discourse. It will be crucial to see whether Mondragon remains an isolated case or inspires and gives guidance to many other successful cooperatives. This is what Dewey means by the statement: "Knowledge of social phenomena is peculiarly dependent upon dissemination, for only by distribution can such knowledge be . . . tested" (PP:170–171; also LTI:490). Within the limited circle of workplace democrats, discussion about Mondragon dominates. Outside this circle, however, Mondragon is scarcely known. It is not the stuff of economics textbooks and business magazines, much less the daily news media. If Dewey's ideal of public communication about social experiments were to be realized, Modragon would move to the center of public discourse.

Having reviewed in some detail this particular example of social invention, let us survey a wide range of such inventions, to establish the scope of activity in this sphere.

SOCIAL INVENTION: ADDITIONAL EXAMPLES

To the case of Mondragon can be added three other examples of large-scale networks of cooperative enterprises—to say nothing of countless smaller coops. "In Italy's Emiglia Romagna region, three small, linked networks represent some 2,700 coops of all kinds, led by sophisticated 'flexible production' industrial coops. Together they employ over 150,000 people, and have significant political constituencies. . . . Growing since 1927 in Canada's Maritime provinces, the Co-op Atlantic federation of 166 purchasing, retailing, producer, housing, and fishing cooperatives employs 5,850 workers and counts over 170,000 families as members in a network that permeates the region. Japan's Seikatsu network, started in Tokyo in 1965 as a buying club, now includes 225,000 member households organized at the neighborhood level, and has established over 160 worker-owned producer cooperatives to meet its members' needs" (Bowman and Stone 1996:12–13; also Morrison 1995). While sharing common properties as worker-owned and managed businesses, each of these examples illustrate unique features in responding to their environments and expressing the creativity of their members and leaders.

Dewey's foremost example of social invention is progressive schooling—in the rigorous sense that he intended, not the watered down versions that later claimed the name. Dewey engages in an ongoing effort to critique and advance progressive pedagogy and curriculum, but he judges the movement to have achieved, already, substantial improvements over traditional schooling (see *Schools of Tomorrow* [ST], PESE, EE). The minority of schools that are fully progressive in their practices, not just in name, can be a model for all of schooling. Were progressive schooling to become widespread, it would amount to a transformation of the educational system, one major section of society. What is more, the graduates of such schools, much better-equipped as citizens, would have a profound effect on democratic political life. Four notable experiments which continue Dewey's legacy today are the School Development Project (Comer 1993), the Central Park East schools (Meier 1995), the Coalition for Essential Schools (Sizer 1992), and the school system of Reggio Emilia in Emilia Romagna province in Italy (Edwards, Gandini and Forman 1993; Katz and Cesarone 1994). These are just a few among many schools or groups of schools that continue the progressive movement (Wood 1992; Rose 1995). The School Development Project is discussed at length in Chapter 6. By introducing new forms of school community, governance, curriculum, and pedagogy, the best progressive schools reveal unsuspected potential in their students, and highlight the tensions between educational aims and social contexts. They give us new knowledge as they give us new effective practices.

In the economic sphere, in addition to the Mondragon Cooperatives, a widely discussed example of social invention today is the Grameen Bank in Bangladesh (Yunus 1997). The Grameen Bank has provided credit to make possible entrepreneurial enterprises for thousands of poor women, yet experiences a very low default rate on loans. This example demonstrates how placing repayment responsibility upon groups rather than individuals can enhance small business success and reduce loan

defaults. The micro-credit approach pioneered by Grameen has been celebrated by political figures and experts, and attempts are underway to
replicate it in many nations.

At the level of provinces within nations, Emilia Romagna in Italy
(R. Putnam 1993; Fitch 1996), and Kerala in India (Franke and Chasin
1989), have achieved broad-based bottom-up development and social welfare, through innovative government-private partnership, cooperative
enterprises, and responsive government programs. These approaches follow neither the socialist nor laissez-faire capitalist models, and have
demonstrated the possibility of alternatives. At the level of national systems, given the collapse of Communist regimes, and today's economic
crisis and backsliding in western European social democracies, there is
distressingly little to report. Specific policies at the national level offer
interesting examples, though many of these efforts have been buffeted
by recent shifts in the global economy. Worthy of mention, nonetheless,
are the incomes policies of small European states and the, once sturdy
but now disintegrating, solidary wage policy and system of job retraining in Sweden (Katzenstein 1984; Alperovitz and Faux 1984:225–235).
The undermining of these nation-level alternatives by global exploitation of low wage production in developing countries has convinced
the faint-hearted that no alternative to laissez-faire market systems exists. Thus it is important to stress the contextual effects, to highlight social inventions operating below the nation-state level, and to note that
rapid socioeconomic change in western societies suggests an open-ended
future.

The systematic professional practice of mediation and conflict-
resolution is another well-established social invention, which has received recent public attention when called upon to relieve crowded court
dockets, undertake violence-prevention in schools, resolve environmental conflicts, settle international disputes, heal bitterness in the wake
of civil wars, and so on (Burton 1987, Fisher and Ury 1981; Lantieri and
Patti 1996; Moore 1996; Susskind and Cruikshank 1987; Ury, Brett and
Goldberg 1988). The practice of mediation actualizes the abstract ideas
of conflict-resolution so central to Dewey's thought. It is therefore of
special theoretical significance here. In addition, it has the potential to
be an essential social institution. A major portion of public issue disputes might be referred for mediation, independent of or in conjunction with legislative, executive, and judicial efforts at settlement. In the
process, substantial numbers of citizens would be educated in skills
of deliberation, dialogue, inquiry, and implementation. Thus conflict-

resolution could become a central aspect of a Deweyan progressive politics. Conflict-resolution has the double status of being a social invention, as well as an institution that fosters further social invention in the search for integrative solutions to conflicts.

Several additional notable examples of social invention will be mentioned briefly here. Grassroots community organizing is now a systematic practice with trained professionals, thousands of citizen participants, and notable influence on particular communities around the United States (Boyte 1989; Delgado 1986; Wypljewski 1997). Support groups, variations on the model of Alcoholics Anonymous—though an easy target for criticism and satire—are a remarkably democratic form for providing information, social support, and healing for people in distress due to addiction, illness, loss, trauma and other vicissitudes (Wuthnow 1994). Though largely nonpolitical or even antipolitical, their potential for political mobilization should not be underestimated, as Frank Riessman (1992) has pointed out (cf. Cuoto 1992). Group dynamics and organizational development are so well-established in the profession of management consulting that it is hard to believe these were social inventions by Kurt Lewin and his students following World War II (Marrow 1969). The work of Lewin and colleagues at the National Training Laboratories also exemplifies research subjects becoming participants in ongoing evaluation and redesign of experiments (Marrow 1969). Another recent approach is deliberative polling. Having taken a public opinion survey of a random sample of citizens, the researchers take the unprecedented step of gathering these people together to discuss issues, obtain information from experts, and question politicians. Early findings suggest that participants gain knowledge, change opinions, and become more committed to participation, and also maintain these gains nine months later (Fishkin 1991; 1996; Luskin et al. 1996).

These are among the best known and most successful examples, but far from the only ones. Experiments are being conducted with community development banks (Krimcrman and Lindenfeld 1992), community policing, worker-owned businesses (Krimerman and Lindenfeld 1992; Bowman and Stone 1996; *GEO*), small business incubators (Osborne 1990), civic journalism (Charity 1995; Rosen 1996), consumer cooperatives, "Pigovian" taxes (Hawken 1993), community land trusts (Meeker-Lowry 1988), labor and mental health groups (Lerner 1986), deliberative forums (Yankelovitch 1991), participatory research (Fischer 1990; Merrifield 1989), consensus building procedures (Avery et al. 1981; Saint and Lawson 1994), electronic town meetings and other forms of teledemocracy (Becker and Scarce 1986), dialogue groups (Pogrebin 1991:Ch. 14, 16), ecological villages (Weisman 1998), local currency systems (Meeker-Lowry 1988), community mediation boards (Schwerin 1995), consensus councils in American states (*New York Times,* June 14, 1998), sustainable lifestyles (*In Context, Yes*), co-housing (McCamant and Durrett 1994), watershed councils (*New York Times,* June 14, 1998), and many more (Alperovitz 1996; Coop-America *Quarterly; Doing Democracy; In Context;* Lappé and Dubois 1994; Meeker-Lowry 1988; *New Options, Yes*).

None of these examples is more than a blip on the radar screen of public attention today. Even the most celebrated (e.g., Mondragon), are rare exceptions to customary practices, rather than the rule. The issue for Dewey, however, is prospective, not retrospective. Do these models have the potential for ongoing development, refinement, and implementation on a larger scale—and thus for making major improvements in social functioning and social scientific knowledge? Can they mobilize the political strength to survive and grow in the face of hostility from large corporations and local elites, discrimination by lending institutions, and unfavorable state and federal legislation? Can the ideas and ideals they represent attain public visibility, and capture the imagination of citizens, workers, students, designers, scholars, and teachers (Weisman 1998). Dewey asks us only to have faith enough to experiment further, and determination enough to organize politically: "faith in the ability of human nature to achieve freedom for individuals accompanied with respect and regard for other persons and with social stability built on cohesion instead of coercion" (FC:162; also 126–127; CD:228; DEA:219). This is an open faith which energizes exploration, not a dogmatic faith which insists that these are precisely the solutions we need, and feels licensed to impose its views by force on others.

Most social inventions, such as the ones just discussed, are of modest size. In a world where large institutions lack an experimentalist vision, these are easiest to initiate and sustain. Even the very substantial Mondragon complex is a local, not a national, social invention. It could become the prototype, however, of a society-wide worker self-managed economy—just as the individual progressive school could be a prototype of a general progressive education system. Vanek (1970) and Schweikart (1980) have posited general theories of an economy where the principle units are worker-owned and managed. Bowman and Stone offer an economic and political strategy for expanding the cooperative sector until it becomes the dominant economic form (1996:9–23). Federations of coops would support one another. They would retain profits from their high productivity, and invest these in new coop startups. They would encourage workers who have ownership, through employee stock ownership plans, but not control, to fight for democracy in their firms. And, in the face of corporate opposition, they would mobilize constituencies to seek favorable, or at least neutral, state policies. Elements of such a strategy are already in place. There exist agencies which conduct research and disseminate information, provide training and venture capital for new firms, and lobby for supportive legislation (Krimerman and Lindenfeld 1992). In addition to such a bottom-up strategy, let us consider social experiments that are pursued on a national scale from the outset.

Macroscopic Social Inventions and Experiments

Several extant efforts are illustrative of both the possibilities and limits of macro-level programs for social intervention and experimentation. Consider the efforts at stabilizing the U.S. economy using Keynesian fiscal and monetary policy, about which a substantial historical record has accumulated. Dewey was greatly concerned with recurring economic depression, but was not conversant with Keynes's theoretical basis for solving that problem (Ratner 1989:xix). Dewey would have preferred a more comprehensive socioeconomic theory oriented to an entire "cooperative industrial order" (LSA:61; LSS:229), but was not averse to partial interventions. The imperfect implementation of Keynesian ideas, however, has created an ambiguous quasi-experiment, not the clear-cut test Dewey would have wished.

Among economists, the experience of World War II, the empirical achievements of Simon Kuznets, and the formalization by John Hicks, led to acceptance of a version of Keynesian economics, which became the new conventional wisdom in the field. In the larger public arena, however, Keynesianism became an ideological and political battleground between conservatives and liberals. Although opposition gradually eroded over the decades, Keynesian policies often could only be implemented covertly through "military Keynesianism"—pursuing deficit spending by greatly increasing the military budget under the rationalization of security needs (Galbraith 1958). Given rigidities of ideology, and of budget-making processes, fiscal policy responses to changes in the economy were neither timely, nor finely graduated in proportion to need. Thus the outcomes of these policies were quite ambiguous as evidence on the validity of Keynesian theory. Nonetheless, by the 1970s a Keynesian consensus seemed to have emerged—including pragmatic individuals in the business community and the Republican party, both of which had been centers of opposition. Such a consensus existed despite continued polemics from the far right and from monetarist economists. A stripped-down and distorted version of Keynes's theory—"neo-Keynesian conventional wisdom," is what became adopted (Dean 1981:20).

In any case, the "stagflation" of the late 1970s, when high interest rates coexisted with high unemployment, was taken as evidence against Keynesian theory. Whether this problem was intrinsic to the policy and its theory, or a result of exogenous factors—the oil price shocks, paying off the Vietnam War debt—is ambiguous. In any event, the fragile consensus broke down, permitting renewed flourishing of monetarist theory and other schools (Bell and Kristol 1981). This period produced critiques of Keynesian conventional wisdom, and, more fundamentally, reexamination of fundamental Keynesian and neoclassical assumptions. It also produced ideologically driven polemics in the guise of scholarship. Public and scholarly discourse fell far short of the Deweyan ideal, but was not devoid of constructive efforts which can be called scientific in Dewey's sense. In the 1990s, a plurality of theories continues to flourish, and hybrid policies are pursued by the federal government (Prychitko 1998:4).

This experience confirms Dewey's contention that when variations in policy are chaotic, evidence on the causal effect of those variations brings only further confusion (SSSC:68). Dewey's proposal would have been for the parties to the debate to suspend their battles and agree to clear-cut policies that would provide a meaningful experimental test. That is, policies would be designed to give full expression of Keynesian assumptions in government policy, and criteria would be agreed upon in advance as to what constitutes success and failure. Such an approach, even were it politically feasible, seems unrealistic as social science, given the immense complexity and nonlinearity of the economic system. (I return later to the issue of complexity, with this example in mind.) Measures and predictions of economic performance—e.g., unemployment, inflation, and overall output—are limited in both reliability and validity. Figures are constantly being revised and reevaluated. Elaborate computer simulation models predicting short-term economic performance have a modest rate of success, and may be useful only until some basic system shift occurs. This is not to say that we cannot learn from experience. Over long enough periods of time, unanticipated effects emerge, exogenous effects can be recognized and accounted for, and policies reach stability after many adjustments—in short, reflectively settled practices can be achieved. Such learning is very slow, and cannot settle decisively the deep differences of belief and ideology that mark the debate on economic theory and policy. In the absence of decisive adjudication through experimental results, we can return to the broader Deweyan prescription for public discourse and conflict-resolution, issuing in public judgment; this involves deepened communication aimed at mutual understanding, movement from positions to interests, innovative fashioning of mutually satisfactory solutions, and extensive public discourse for the interpretation and critique of the imprecise experimental results. A more detailed example of such discourse is offered in Chapter 6.

Incomes Policy

The second major macroeconomic problem in Dewey's program— maintaining full employment—has been addressed by the incomes policies of small European countries, notably Austria (EBNS:309–311; Katzenstein 1984). Through a corporatist mechanism of negotiations between the government and labor and business federations, wage and price increases in each economic sector are limited to the rate of productivity increase in that sector. This approach appears to have provided for several decades of steady growth without inflation. But it has not been equal to the challenge of globalization, with intensified competition from low wage production in developing countries. That an incomes policy in Austria was possible at all may be traced to a much higher degree of consensus than has been experienced, or even appears possible, in the United States—"'a remarkable social consensus . . . between Socialists and conservatives, bosses and workers, rich and poor, which spares this tiny country the bruising confrontations that thwart policy-making in most other Western nations'" (Lewis, quoted by Katzenstein 1984:26). In Austria and Sweden, this is rooted in the rise of powerful labor unions and associated social democratic political parties. Paradoxically, the deeper class divisions in these societies led to strong labor unions and workers' parties which had a solid enough position not only to struggle against capital but also to engage confidently in conflict-resolution. Furthermore, the wrenching historical vicissitudes of the

Great Depression and World War II generated powerful motivations to seek social peace through constructive, mutually enhancing accommodation between classes (29). On the other hand, there is an undemocratic side to this consensus formation. Agreement among the leaders of peak associations who "enjoy very strong powers over a compliant membership" is hardly Deweyan participatory democracy (27). Given the degree of consensus in post-war Austria, however, and the rather systematic policy formation and implementation based on it, something close to a macroscopic social experiment, such as Dewey proposed, can be seen here.

This experiment was, as Dewey would recommend, characterized by ongoing monitoring and revision. "Using overly optimistic forecasts for 1975, business and labor concurred on wage increases that in hindsight were far too high; but both adopted remarkable restraint from 1976 onward" (Katzenstein 1984:49). The results during the 1960s and 1970s initially appear to pronounce the experiment highly successful (49). Nonetheless, "the unambiguous determination of the economic effects of policy is not an easy task" (48). Many other variables affected the success of these economies: the wider vicissitudes of the European economy with its overall sustained growth in the 1960s and 1970s, the historical capacities and traditions of this particular country, low levels of military spending, and so on. And finally, we need to consider the performance of the Austrian economy during the European economic recession of the 1980s. Again, there is much to be learned from the experience of Austria's incomes policy, but there is by no means enough evidence to settle decisively the issues it raises. For other nations seeking to adapt the Austrian model to their own circumstances, public discourse, further experimentation, and public judgment remain necessary.

National Programs, Quasi-Experiments, and Deliberate Social Policy Experiments

Although the New Deal was not the systematic social experiment and social transformation that Dewey sought, it did provide some rough experiments in national planning; these appeared in the form of the Tennessee Valley Authority, the Rural Electrification Administration, and other significant government economic interventions. In addition, two World Wars brought about national intervention on behalf of war production (EBNS: 311–315). The absence of young men from the labor market during World War II resulted in a brief but influential period of full

Social Science   89

employment, which may be viewed as a quasi-experiment. Women and
African-Americans gained unprecedented access to industrial jobs, while
inflation was checked by wage and price controls. Because these programs were the result of political compromises, both initially, and in
their continuation and revision, they do not qualify as deliberate and explicit social experiments. Nonetheless, there is a wealth of experience
left by these programs, from which working hypotheses for future efforts
may be formulated. My purpose here is not to offer a plan for such investigations, much less anticipate the conclusions, but simply to point
out historical quasi-experiments that approximate, but do not fully realize, Dewey's conception of social science.

   There have been sustained efforts in applied social science to persuade
the government to commission policies framed as experiments (Rivlin
1971; Riecken and Boruch 1974; Gueron 1986). Such experiments, as
authorized and implemented, meet Dewey's criteria only imperfectly.
They lack the open-ended exploratory quality that Dewey stressed—
the willingness to discover the goals of the inquiry, as well as its means,
in the course of experimentation. Favoring the "single treatment" approach, they ignore systemic factors that must be treated in order for
real change to take place. Nonetheless, these attempts were made in
the Deweyan spirit, and the experience gained from them should not be
disregarded.

Political and Ethical Constraints on Macro-Experiments

   Although the creation and development of producer cooperatives are
realizations of Dewey's ideal of social experimentation, Keynesian fiscal
policies, and New Deal and wartime government interventions fall far
short of it. Could Dewey's policy experimentation program ever be implemented at the national level in the U.S., given the practical, political,
and ethical constraints? If so, could it be done without the ethically
unacceptable manipulation of its citizens? Would it be possible to implement a limited approximation of Dewey's program without vitiating
its unique features and prospects? In other words, could a democratic
government—subjected to myriad pressures in a corporate-capitalist society and whose policies are created by horse trading and compromise—
conduct anything approximating a theoretically guided and impartially
evaluated social experiment? Frankel raises these issues forcefully (1977:
11–13). Dewey, himself, acknowledges "the practical difficulties in the
way of experimental method in the case of social phenomena" (LTI:

508). "Consequences [are] . . . not as capable of definite or exclusive differentiation as in the case of physical experimentation . . . Social phenomena do not permit the controlled variation of sets of conditions in a one-by-one series of operations" (LTI:509). Given the vacillating and deeply compromised policies reached by political log-rolling, "the only alternative seems to be a concentration of power . . . in administrative bodies possessed of large powers;" itself, a threat to democracy (FC:65). In addition, "planned policies initiated by public authority are sure to have consequences totally unforeseeable—often the contrary of what was intended—as has happened in this country rather notably in connection with some of the measures undertaken for the control of agricultural production" (FC:62).

Dewey's response to ethical difficulties is further discussed in the section entitled "democratic experimentation." With respect to practical difficulties, Dewey calls for maintaining the spirit, if not the letter, of science. But if the rigorous strictures of scientific inquiry are relaxed too much, what is there to constrain legislators from returning to sloganeering and log-rolling? Dewey's second solution is a highly trained, civil service (FC:65). Even if we view Dewey's proposal in its historical context, when civil service reform in the U.S. was urgently needed, it remains an attempt to bypass the political process and is hardly compatible with his commitment to democracy. Furthermore, it appears doomed to fail, as target groups capture the agencies meant to regulate them.

The possibility of government experimentation depends on a working consensus. "Even as they now exist, the forms of representative government are potentially capable of expressing the public will when that assumes anything like unification" (LSA:85–86). Such consensus was achieved around war aims during World War I (EBNS:311, 315). And the urgencies created by the Great Depression seemed to Dewey to be capable of evoking such unity. In 1935, Dewey expects liberals, first, to recognize and unite around the need for social control of economic forces (LSA:90–91). For wider agreement, Dewey counts on the "American method of back-and-forth give-and-take discussion until final decision represented a workable consensus of the ideas of all who took part" (MW8:443). In more sober moments, Dewey, though still a visionary, acknowledges that the development of public discourse and the emergence of consensus may take years, decades, or generations (FC:176; HNC:109; 1936:145).

So, it would be wise to concede the limitations of national macropolicy experiments, at least until such time as public consciousness, perhaps changed by participatory experiences, provides a more propitious environment for such undertakings. Meanwhile, continued experimentation in pilot projects and micro-level settings can provide opportunities for citizen participation. Moreover, local projects are not irrelevant to macro-level outcomes—as the Grameen Bank and Mondragon Cooperatives suggest. Dewey rejects a strict dichotomy between the macro- and the micro-level, just as he criticizes other dualisms (HNC:9–10; ION:126–186; LSA:61; E:323). He would have been sympathetic to recent theorizing about macro-micro linkages (J. Alexander et al. 1987; Bohman 1991; Knorr-Cetina and Cicourel 1981). He would have recognized the macro-political relevance of today's experiments-in-progress, often revolving around citizen or worker participation in education, micro-credit, organizational development, democratic management, job training, conflict resolution, local economic revitalization, community organizing, and so on (e.g., Schon 1983; Whyte 1991). Successful experiments in these fields could have substantial impact on solving national policy problems, on improving experimental methods, and on creating a climate for national policy experiments.

Issues of national policy are too urgent to be left to politics-as-usual, even as lower level social experimentation continues to mature. Keynesian economic and incomes policy experience suggest how theory formation and practical application, if not deliberate experimentation, occur in imperfect democracies. Although they may not be scientific findings per se, historical learning and public judgment emerge from such applications. Absent experimentation, Deweyan programs could concede a place for more conventional social science methods, including controlled observation and policy evaluation, while still recognizing their limitations. That Keynes developed his theory on historical experience and not on experimentation, is instructive.

With these examples in mind, I will formulate Dewey's approach to three topics in philosophy of social science: experimentation; differences between natural and social science; and interpretation and explanation.

Dewey's Philosophy of Social Science

EXPERIMENT

Views on experiment in mainstream philosophy of social science are shaped by a strict focus on the "context of justification." To experiment is to validate or falsify a given hypothesis, not to create new phenomena and discover new relations. This requires controlling extraneous variation. Experiments in social science can rarely meet these standards, however. Ernest Nagel, for example, views them as desirable in principle but largely unrealizable in practice. "Field experiments" do not permit sufficient control of variables nor enough possibility of replication (Nagel 1961:450–451, 457). Laboratory experiments, while offering greater control of variables, restrict severely the range of social processes that can be studied, the range of variation that can be introduced, and the validity of extrapolation to natural settings (456).

Nagel makes no attempt to argue for social experimentation while allowing for these difficulties because he believes there is a viable alternative form of "controlled empirical inquiry" (Nagel 1961:457). This alternative is observation in natural settings where variables can be measured and their effects statistically controlled (Nagel 1961:457–458). In this approach, investigators view naturally occurring variation as if it were an experimental treatment, and apply statistical modeling to the findings. Thus, they test theories and suggest causal connections (Rosenberg 1988:175–176). Campbell and Stanley (1963), for example, elaborate creative possibilities for "quasi-experiment," showing that well-chosen observations can exploit existing variation to test empirical claims.

Nagel affirms this approach even as he acknowledges the limitation "that the variables assumed to be relevant . . . can't be manipulated at will . . . or may not even have been planned by anyone" (Nagel 1961:457). This limitation is precisely what concerns Dewey: "The social situation out of which these facts emerge is itself confused and chaotic because it expresses socially unregulated purpose and haphazard private intent" (SSSC:68). Haphazard or tightly constrained variation leads to indeterminate or inconsequential outcomes: "we shall add intellectual confusion to practical disorder" (68). Dewey's answer is exploratory experimentation in which the premium is upon bold innovation—"large and far-reaching ideas," audacity of imagination, and dramatic interventions based upon them (QC:138; 310). This increases the range of variation, if not its specificity, producing novel effects, if not yet isolating the variables responsible (QC:87). As in natural science, this approach enables discovery of significant relationships by means of creation of phenomena.

The experiment is repeated, varied, strengthened, and refined until the novel effect can be reliably reproduced. Reflectively settled practices, which solve significant social problems, are a mature result of a long course of successful social experiment. The results may be so palpable and the procedures for producing them so explicit, that formal experimentation finally becomes relevant. The function of formal, controlled experiment is to tidy up the project, provide even more credible confirmation, or eliminate misleading explanations of the effects. In Jerome Bruner's words (with regard to schooling, but generalizable to other fields): "Develop the best pedagogy you can. With a mixture of psychology, common sense, and luck you may *produce an effect* on learning that is worth studying. Then *purify* . . . and [finally] experiment [in the formal controlled sense]. But first, *invent*" (1966:113, italics added).

Consider an illustration of the difference between haphazard, limited existing variation and the variation introduced by exploratory experimentation. Instead of searching out traces of rationality in ill-informed and apathetic voters (Key 1966; Popkin 1991; Page and Shapiro 1993), one can intervene in an attempt to develop the as yet unrealized potential for rationality. One can create forums which engage voters in discourse and expose them to information, and then see how they respond (Becker and Scarce 1986; Fishkin 1991, 1996; Luskin et al. 1996; Yankelovitch 1991). In such experiments, rather than rush to measure change and claim success, one can repeat the experiment numerous times, polishing the techniques of discussion leadership, information delivery, and ongoing support and information services. One can thus amplify the variation induced by intervention, and produce more palpable results.

This approach to experiment and justification is taken directly from Dewey's analysis of natural science, but not necessarily from the extraordinarily developed and refined sciences of today. As the social sciences are less mature than the natural sciences, the experience of early natural science is especially relevant, while that of twentieth-century science may actually be misleading (LTI:77, 487, 492; RPh:xxv; HNC:322; PP:169). Social inquiry, as an immature discipline, has the opportunity to grow based on the reconstruction of everyday practices—much as the young natural sciences did from agriculture, construction, mining, navigation, and war-making (EN:128; LTI:72). "Scientific inquiry always starts from things of the environment experienced in our everyday life, with things we see handle, use, enjoy and suffer from" (QC:103). This link between social inquiry and general practices is unlike hypothesis formation and problem generation in the mature sciences, which are "mainly set by subject-matter already prepared by the results of prior inquiries" (LTI:493). Likewise, social inquiry can test its conclusions against everyday qualitative observations, much as the natural sciences once accepted as confirmation the sight of a spark, the deflection of a needle, the appearance of a flame, the change in state of a solid, liquid, or gas, and the sensations of heat and cold. Furthermore, in generating new hypotheses, philosophical theorizing looms large for social inquiry as it did for the early natural sciences (see 1926; Heilbron 1982).

COMPLEXITY

Dewey notes a qualitative difference between social science and natural science experiments. He sees social phenomena, unlike physical ones, as irreducibly complex. To escape triviality, any social inquiry must account for a host of intricately, nonlinearly, interrelated aspects. "The relations that determine . . . what human beings experience . . . are indefinitely wider and more complex than those that determine . . . physical [events]" (QC:270; also 1929c:11). Many "social phenomena do not permit the controlled variation of sets of conditions in a one-by-one series of operations" (LTI:509). Even when this is possible—as, for example, in controlled trials of particular teaching methods in schools— the result is likely to be indeterminate or unimportant. "Simplifications which end in leaving out of account some of the conditions which are active anyway defeat themselves" (LW14:261). Dewey warns that "the 'essence' of [knowledge of human affairs] is that we cannot indulge in the selective abstractions that are the secret of the success of physical knowing. When we introduce a like simplification into social and moral subjects, we eliminate the distinctively human factors" (QC:216). Mainstream social scientists seeking to isolate the contribution of individual variables, whether through multivariate statistics or controlled experiments, reduce complexity by simplifying assumptions and models. Such simplification is the only condition under which knowledge, as these approaches understand it, is possible. If we insist, nonetheless, on the sort of complexity that Dewey delineates, an altogether different account of knowledge is required. Knowledge, for Dewey, is embodied in reflectively settled practices—in the skills and intuitive discriminations and judgments of practitioners. Thus, tacit knowing, which accommodates more complexity than explicit formalized knowledge, is an essential part of a Deweyan account of social science.

Though the corrigibility of scientific knowledge applies generally, in Dewey's view, it is especially true of social science inquiry, given its complexity. Social scientific results are underdetermined; they are provisional way stations in an ongoing course of research, not terminal points. There are four appropriate responses to such underdetermination, in Dewey's view. First, continue refining and developing existing achievements—move toward reflectively settled practices, toward security if not certainty. Second, search for fresh social inventions and discoveries. Dewey believes, following Bacon, that there is a vast amount yet to learn, and much present knowledge is destined soon to be obsolete, so emphasis should be placed more on discovering new practices and knowledge than on shoring up existing ones (RPh:31). Third, through discourse, arrive at the best judgments possible for reasonable policy choices on urgent issues, based on present information (PP: 177). Fourth, clarify the meaning, significance, and justification of tacit knowing.

Tacit Knowledge and Its Justification

Given the complexity of social phenomena, it may not be possible to disentangle the variables responsible for a reliably produced result. If one can produce it consistently, however, one can be said to have tacit or practical knowledge. And the articulation of that practical knowledge, as principle, maxim, metaphor, ideal type, or conceptual scheme is another form of knowledge. As Polanyi observed, principles facilitate the conduct of an art, but do not replace the art (1962:30–31). Dewey saw them as tools for exploring emergent situations. Consider that two different, even incompatible, principles can nonetheless each evoke successful practice. Thus they are not true or false in the strict logical sense. When we, loosely, say they are true, we mean that they are fruitful. They either elicit the tacit practical knowledge already inherent or stimulate us to improvise and discover new practices.

This sort of knowledge appears distinct from knowledge achieved in the physical sciences, as law is distinct from metaphor, the determinate from the suggestive. For example, Dewey's principles of progressive pedagogy may work wonders when employed by a skilled and sensitive teacher, but they are far removed from the precision and impersonality of Newton's laws or Maxwell's equations. Perhaps, as the postempiricists suggest, the determinateness of physical laws has been oversold (N. Hanson 1958; Polanyi 1962: Cartwright, in Bohman 1991). Even so, in this regard there is a profound difference between natural and social sciences in degree if not in kind.

Dewey emphasizes that the laws of physics are susceptible to mathematical formulation that permits flexible elaboration, manipulation, and transformation—hence far-reaching inference (HWT:113). Metaphors, models, and the like are also susceptible to transformations and implications, but by association, not deduction. They may have great emancipatory power, however, which is different from inferential power. Dewey seems to suggest at times that social science can repeat the inferential achievements of physics. At other times he appears to emphasize the qualitative, tacit, and suggestive quality of social knowledge corresponding to the complexity of social systems. While not as respectable as the explicit and tested "knowing that," practical, metaphorical, and emancipatory knowledge can reliably produce outcomes of great human significance. In Dewey's view, therefore, these deserve the honorific designation as knowledge.

SELF-DENYING PROPHECY

In experiments with human beings, the subjects have the capacity to be aware of the experiment and its results, reflect on it, and change their behavior accordingly. For a positivist, this compromises the reproducibility of the experiment and the validity of its findings. Nagel points out that, "the conclusions can literally be made invalid if they become matters of public knowledge and if, in the light of this knowledge, men alter the patterns of their behavior upon whose study the conclusions are based" (1961:468). Dewey acknowledges the same phenomenon. "Social inquiry brings the fact of human conduct to consciousness, and this very bringing of our own behavior into reflection changes its career . . . The knowledge and judgment of social inquiry thus becomes an integral factor in the phenomena themselves. Social theory is thus [not] comparable . . . to physics" (MW15:235). But what the positivist regards as contaminating, Dewey sees as enlightening and emancipatory. Once the experiment is underway, the participants are no longer naive, merely passive subjects. Although the positivist's goal of predicting the behavior of passive and unreflective persons is lost, something far more valuable can be gained. Ordinary people can be empowered and can learn far beyond the expectations society has for them. Kurt Lewin and his associates illustrated this principle by discovering serendipitously that when participants in small group experiments attended the experimenter's evaluation conferences, their organizational and task performance improved markedly (Marrow 1969). The participants became "reflective practitioners" or "participatory action researchers" (Schon 1983; Whyte 1991; Elliott 1991). This provides an example of a creative solution to the conflict between expert and lay person. What is a ruined experiment for the positivist is an experiment in participatory democracy for Dewey.

Participatory experimentation creates a new phenomenon: citizen responses to novel ideas and opportunities. It "release[s] new potentialities . . . which . . . then modify social phenomena" (PP:199). This issue of self-denying prophecy sets social science apart from the natural sciences. Another major issue distinguishing social from natural sciences is the role of interpretation.

INTERPRETATION AND CRITIQUE

While affirming a broad unity of method, Dewey insists that each field has its own unique attributes. "Every phase of experience must be investigated, and each characteristic aspect presents its own peculiar problems which demand, therefore, their own technique of investigation" (EEL:212). One ignores these differences at the peril of fruitless investigation and trivial results. "The existing limitations of 'social science' are due mainly to unreasoning devotion to physical science as a model" (SSSC:64). Dewey elaborates further, "'Fact,' physically speaking, is the ultimate residue after human purposes, desires, emotions, ideas and ideals have been systematically excluded. A social 'fact,' on the other hand, is a concretion in external form of precisely these human factors" (SSSC:64). To say that social facts are constituted by human purposes, is to put a heavy burden on interpretation in the conduct of social inquiry. To be intelligible at all, human action must be interpreted in terms of prevailing cultural meanings and rules, or language games and forms of life. To use Taylor's example, one requires an interpretive understanding of the cultural pattern of elections to know that the behavior of marking a particular piece of paper and dropping it in a certain nearby box is the meaningful act of voting (1985:35). Interpretation goes beyond the present intelligibility of cultural patterns, such as elections. These patterns require interpretation in light of their historical development. "Experience is already overlaid with and saturated with the products of the reflection of past generations and bygone ages. It is filled with interpretations" (EN:37). But social inquiry does not stop there. Social scientists are concerned with what makes people choose certain meaningful actions and not others—like voting for one party or another (Fay 1996:119–123). Furthermore, Dewey seeks not simply to understand, but also to change society—to investigate experimentally how to foster political discourse in which voters' preferences are articulated, refined, informed through exposure to other perspectives, and thus changed (see SSSC).

In philosophy of science today, there is a polarized debate which pits the empirical and naturalistic against the interpretive and critical (Rosenberg 1988:4–20; Fay 1996). One side embraces a positivist conception of science; the other rejects it outright, without exploring any other account of science. Dewey does not succumb to this dichotomous thinking. Like Max Weber and Habermas, he seeks to combine interpretive understanding with the search for empirical regularities (Bohman 1991:vii). He is opposed to the extreme "naturalist" view that dismisses the intentions of actors, and seeks only causal relations between behaviors (Rosenberg 1988:19). But Dewey also rejects the "interpretationalist" view that the sole goal of social science is to render human actions intelligible (Rosenberg 1988:14–15, 20; Fay 1996:112–119). For Dewey, successful inquiry brings resolution and unity to a confusing situation— by means of actions which change the world. The interpretationalist criterion of intelligibility calls only for resolution of mental confusion.[3]

Articulation of culturally embedded interpretations passes over into critical reflection. "If we may . . . call these materials prejudices, then philosophy is a critique of prejudices. Emancipation follows when they are cast out" (EN:37). Dewey emphasizes this idea of emancipatory critique: "failure to examine the conceptual structures and frames of reference which are unconsciously implicated in even the seemingly most innocent factual inquiries is the greatest single defect that can be found in any field of inquiry" (LTI:507). Dewey's critique of alienation exemplifies his critical method.

Dewey's analysis of alienation proceeds from his critique of dualisms that shape our thinking on economics—labor versus leisure, production versus consumption, and manual versus mental labor (AE:343; HNC: 272; ION:142). These dichotomies, he suggests, are rooted in dualisms between body and mind, and between theory and practice, both of which are consequences of and reinforcement for the division of socioeconomic classes. These dualisms, in turn, contribute to the sharp separation drawn between economics as an autonomous scholarly field, and all other fields, especially ethics and politics (see LSS). The production-consumption or labor-leisure dualism blinds us to the fact that some basic human satisfactions arise from work—that is, skillful, useful, responsible, creative, and self-directed work (AE:343: HNC:273). When work is reduced to drudgery, people are deprived of these satisfactions (1928a:107–108; ION:129–132). "The philosopher's idea of a complete separation of mind and body is realized in thousands of industrial workers, and the result is a depressed body and an empty and distorted mind" (ION:132). The quality of work life bleeds over into leisure time, shaping the preferences we hold for consumption and recreation. "What [a person] labors at and the reward he gets are things which affect all his capacities, desires, and satisfactions—and not only his own, but those of the members of his family" (E:335). When work has no intrinsic consummations, then "leisure is not the nourishment of mind . . . nor a recreation; it is a feverish hurry for diversion, excitement, display . . . [or else] sodden torpor" (HNC:272; also HNC:144; EN:205). If one is bored, stressed, and powerless at work, one will develop a "feverish love of excitement" and seek immediate sensation (ION:56). Moreover, one will be attracted to symbolic goods that have cultural meanings of power, prestige, and wealth, in a "frenzied use of the results of acquisition for purposes of . . . display" (PP:217).

Furthermore, the competitive ethos of the marketplace creates a general motivation to seek wealth and power at any cost (ION:55–56, 127). The market system tends, in Dewey's judgment, toward the "brutal exploitation of nature and man" (PP:175). "Mankind is in danger of becoming "a race of economic monsters, restlessly driving hard bargains with nature and with one another, bored with leisure or capable of putting it to use only in ostentatious display and extravagant dissipation" (RPh:127). The market in labor, combined with rapid developments in transportation, has created a mobile labor force, which undermines local communities; this, in turn, adds to alienation and provokes frantic consumption (PP:214). Stating these points more generally, Dewey writes that "the ultimate problem of production is the . . . production of human beings" (EBNS:320). It is this critique of capitalist economic life that pushes Dewey toward workplace democracy experiments, such as the Mondragon Cooperatives, and toward an ideal of a cooperative commonwealth. Dewey would today find congenial current alternatives to mainstream economics—in journals such as *Ecological Economics, Review of Social Economy,* and *Review of Radical Political Economics;* in books on sustainable economics (Daly and Cobb 1994), dual labor market theory (Gordon 1972), socialist economic theory (Bowles and Gintis 1986; Roemer 1994; Schweikart 1980), psychology of economics (Wachtel 1989), and so on. Once again, Dewey's value-laden critique and experimentation raise the issue of the place of values in social science.

Values and Science in Social Experiment

Social inquiry, like inquiry in natural science, is not about just any facts, but about significant ones. Furthermore, judgments of significance in social inquiry necessarily involve ethical judgments. "[Social science]

can be nothing less than the work of developing . . . inquiry into the
deeply and inclusively human—that is to say, moral—facts" (RPh:xvii).
"Any inquiry into what is deeply and inclusively [i.e. significantly] human enters perforce into the specific area of morals" (RPh:xxvi). That is,
in the social if not the natural sciences, scientific values overlap strongly
with human values. Ethical deliberation, therefore, becomes endoge-
nous to scientific method in social inquiry. Assessing what is "deeply
and inclusively human" requires interpreting and applying our inherited
stock of ethical principles in new situations. Dewey would also have us
test and critique these principles with regard to their success in illumi-
nating new situations. Interpretation and critique arise both in understanding how facts are constituted, and in understanding what their
moral meanings are—topics discussed further in Chapters 4 and 5.

Experiments in natural settings carry the danger of government or industry manipulation and control of citizens. Dewey both recognizes and
deplores this malign implication: "a more adequate [positivist] 'science'
of human nature might conceivably only multiply the agencies by which
some human beings manipulate other human beings to their own advantage" (FC:171; also PP:197). Dewey believes this problem is not intrinsic to experimentation as such, but stems from treating human situations as if they were no different from physical ones (PP:199). "Any
doctrine [of social science] that eliminates or even obscures the function
of choices of values . . . helps create the attitudes that welcome and support the totalitarian state" (FC:171–172). The democratic experimentation that Dewey advocates is an answer to these ethical problems. Not
only is consent solicited, but active participation is encouraged. Sharing
information on experimental interventions and results is a goal of the experiment and part of its process. Should such experiments fail in their
democratic intent, then the further democratic mechanism of grass roots
organizing and advocacy would provide a second level of protection for
its subjects. James Bohman (1999) offers the example of AIDS activists
gaining a voice in the design of clinical trials of new AIDS drugs. Having
considered Dewey's views on values and science in social experiment,
let us discuss Dewey's democratic experimentalism in detail.

Democratic Social Experiments

For Dewey, democracy in social experiments requires, at minimum,
informed consent. He calls for "obtaining the agreements" of the partic-

ipants in an existing social group that is chosen to become a natural experiment (LTI: 502–503). Taking it a step further, Dewey calls for citizens to actively participate; not simply to be acted upon. He states that the citizens, themselves, are "those who are to . . . execute the operations" (LTI: 502–503). Their willing, even enthusiastic, commitment is a key part of the experimental intervention and is vital for success. This may require that they also have a say in the design and ongoing evaluation and revision of the experiment. Explicit on this point when discussing education, Dewey writes, "every teacher should . . . participate in the formation of the controlling aims, methods and materials of the school of which he is a part" (DEA: 222). Individual participants do not act in isolation from each other or from history; they are already in structured relations with one another. Thus, their conducting experimental operations requires joint culturally patterned activity. "Associated activities are directly involved in the operations to be performed." Furthermore, "these associated activities enter into the idea of any proposed solution" (LTI: 502–503). Thus "any hypothesis as to a social end" has to include an account of existing relations and their intended transformation (LTI: 502–503). Given Dewey's value orientation, these experimental hypotheses are concerned with organizational and cultural structures and processes through which democratic participation can be realized. In summary, democracy in social experiments is: an ethical requirement of informed consent; a means to engaging participants in carrying out the experiment; involvement of participants in planning the experiment; and a goal of the experiment.

Democratic experimentation involves reconfiguring the relationship between experts and nonexperts. Dewey insists that productive interchange is necessary so that expert inquiry is not to be cut off from vital sources of knowledge and become sterile as a result. "In the degree that they become a specialized class, [experts] are shut off from knowledge of the need which they are supposed to serve" (PP: 206). They are liable to the "impotence consequent upon the divorce of theory and practice" (205). Conversely, ordinary citizens, not privy to professional expertise, are handicapped in making wise decisions (207) and may withdraw altogether out of frustration or feelings of incompetence. It is a two-way street—experts must learn from lay people, as well as impart information and skills to them. In Dewey's view, both groups gain in understanding and in task performance, so this constitutes a win-win solution to the conflict between lay people and experts. His advocacy of democratic experimentation can easily be extrapolated to incorporate "participatory research" in which citizens direct and design the inquiry, employing experts as consultants (Fischer 1990; Merrifield 1989; Lindblom 1990:32n). But Dewey, himself, does not take that step.

Collaboration between experts and lay people will not happen simply because we approve of it. There are obstacles to overcome, support and challenge to provide, and concrete steps to take. Social intelligence is needed to make this associated activity work. The collaboration, itself, is a social invention, an experiment—an end as well as a means. As a first step, experts must overcome their stereotypes in order to learn from those less trained and prestigious than themselves. Dewey writes of experts' views of the masses as ". . . intellectually irredeemable . . . [characterized by] bias, frivolity, jealousy, instability, which are alleged to incapacitate them" (PP:206). Respect for the nonexpert, however, should not be construed as the abolition of leadership, expertise, and legitimate, democratically constituted authority. "To decry the very principle of authority [is] to deprive individuals of the direction and support that are universally indispensable . . . for the organic freedom of individuals" (1936:136). Support from peers as well as leaders is essential in helping all participants deal with the insecurity attendant on organizational change. People "require reinforcement and courage that come from a sense of union with others in their position" (LW6:412). When people listen respectfully to others, "what is contributed to each is, first, a support, a reenforcement" (E:345–346).

Having characterized Dewey's experimentalism, and identified the differences between natural and social sciences as he views them, let us revisit some topics of concern to today's philosophers of social science—interpretation, intervention, justification, and explanation.

Interpretation: Additional Issues

The stress on interpretation is part of the "linguistic turn" in the nineteenth and twentieth centuries—the recognition that language is not a transparent medium through which reality reveals itself, but a force shaping our understanding. Dewey, influenced by Charles S. Peirce and others, recognizes that human meaning is virtually coterminous with language (EN:Ch. 5). There are, perhaps, nonlinguistic meanings—in the form of visual images—but Dewey sees their reach as extremely limited. Human culture, especially its capacity to refer to the past and the future and transmit experience across generations, would be impossible

without language. Like analytical philosophers, Dewey frequently analyzes concepts, often probing their historical sources and vicissitudes.
But, for the most part, he is not explicitly concerned with, nor does he
articulate a method for, textual interpretation. He presents his interpretive method as a means for making sense of social situations (see HWT).

Dewey's writing contains no reference to the hermeneutic tradition of
interpretation in German philosophy. Nonetheless, he offers something
approximating the hermeneutic circle (HWT: 121–126). In a conflicted
social situation, one draws upon or formulates general concepts that capture one's inarticulate sense of the situation. These concepts become
tools for finding and highlighting salient features. Once identified, however, these features may resist being organized under the original conception. The concepts are then revised or dismissed, and new ones are
added until the features fit into a pattern. These new concepts, as tools
for exploration, permit the identification of still further details. More
features, formerly hazy or overlooked, are brought into focus. If continued use of the existing set of concepts does not bring coherence to this
new ensemble, the concepts are revised or replaced once again (HWT:
122–123; LTI: 113). Thus there is a circular interplay between organizing concepts and details—an hermeneutic circle. Dewey also identifies
a circle in which the self of the inquirer interacts with the material observed. "The formation of a self new in some respect or some degree is,
then, involved in every genuine act of inquiry" (EKV: 70). Dewey extends the hermeneutic circle to historical interpretation as well. Present
ideologies—such as Marxism and classical liberal individualism—are
explored in light of their contextual origins and their histories reconsidered in light of our present understandings and concerns (LSA: 74).

INTERVENTION

Interpretive approaches in social science are borrowed from literary
criticism, history, biblical exegesis, and history of philosophy. In all of
these fields, intervention in the material studied is precluded because
the artifact that is interpreted lies in the past. Anthropology has the potential for intervention, but renounces it on ethical grounds. This is not
to deny that interpretation changes the meaning of a text—in a sense,
changes the text. The artifact, however, is fixed; additional markings do
not appear on the parchment or stone tablet in response to the interpreter's queries. This does not preclude occasional quasi-experimental possibilities, as when an astute interpreter infers the existence of a missing

text which is later found. But this is strikingly different than vigorous intervention in current social situations—to restructure the production and distribution of commodities, for example, as in the Mondragon Cooperatives. It is such intervention that is crucial for Dewey's experimentalism. To be sure, interpretation is involved at every step of experimentation—construing the situation, conceptualizing the intervention, understanding the outcome—but the possibility of intervention and its repercussions is an additional element not accounted for in text-based theories of interpretation.

JUSTIFYING INTERPRETATIONS

The question arises—how is one to evaluate one interpretation or critique as better or worse than another? There has been much discussion of what constitutes a valid interpretation, involving considerations of coherence, independent non-textual evidence, the hermeneutic circle, empathy, and other issues. And there has been much questioning as to whether any such criteria can be sufficient and whether interpretation isn't radically underdetermined (Bohman 1991:104; Hiley, Bohman, and Shusterman 1991). This issue replays the positivist concern for validation in natural science. Dewey's Pragmatist answer is the same as his answer for natural science. The crucial test lies prospectively, in applying interpretation as a tool or working hypothesis, both for further interpretation and for practice. If interpretations are only evaluated in terms of their formation, the result will, indeed, be indeterminate. Dewey's view is akin to that of the early views of Habermas—that interpretation and critique are valid if they are emancipatory (Habermas 1971; Bohman 1991:196). Taylor, too, because he sees the problem of interpretation as a matter of guiding action, develops a "practice criterion" (Guignon 1991:87).

Given the complexity of social action, however, there will not necessarily be a direct or immediate link between interpretation and action, much less a clear one-to-one relation. Many interpretations are acted upon together. "We cannot take a present case of [a human practice, or social pattern] and cut it into section, or tear it into physical pieces or subject it to chemical analysis" (MW2:9). The fruitfulness of each interpretation for guiding action can only be sorted out over time, and often tacitly rather than explicitly. Furthermore, the evaluation of purposes is intertwined with the evaluation of results. Ethical inquiry and justification are also required. As Rorty points out, both our goals and our conceptions of success are, themselves, by Taylor's own admission, based on interpretations. And these are interpretations from within our own culture. To think that we can transcend this "buys into the old grand metanarrative of progress that is no longer credible" (Guignon 1991:89). Dewey insists, however, on the creativity as well as the continuity of inquiry. At his best, he avoids this "metanarrative of progress," without slipping into a relativistic or static position. He achieves this by insisting that standards emerge within experience, and evolve with continuing experience and inquiry—but not in some predetermined or uniform direction.

EXPLANATION AND UNDERSTANDING

Explanation is a primary category in positivist treatises on the philosophy of social science (Hempel 1965; Nagel 1961), and explanation remains the dominant focus in interpretivist and postempiricist approaches (Bohman 1991; Fay 1996; Rosenberg 1988; Taylor 1985; Winch 1958). Standards for the validity of explanations take center stage in all these traditions, suggesting a common preoccupation with epistemology. There is a retrospective focus on the formation of an idea, rather than a prospective concern for its use; justification of existing knowledge, rather than the search for new knowledge. Explanation as the answer to some particular "why" question implicates fixed ends, rather than open-ended exploration which raises new questions. Virtually alone among philosophers of social science, Dewey does not make explanation a central category. His key units are ideas viewed prospectively as guides to exploration and discovery. Dewey sees "understanding" not as the fruit of explanation so much as the byproduct of practical knowing and doing. Comprehension flows from applied science, which "is directly concerned . . . with instrumentalities at work in effecting modifications of existence in behalf of conclusions that are reflectively preferred" (EN: 161). Dewey characterizes the understanding which results: "events so discriminately penetrated by thought that mind is literally at home in them . . . comprehension" (161).

While it is important to stress the difference in language and emphasis between Dewey and most schools of philosophy of social science today, there is also convergence on particular issues. For example, Bohman (1991) argues that due to inherent indeterminacies of social science explanation, single factor and single level explanations are always inadequate and can be improved upon by taking note of macro-micro interactions, individual consciousness and social structure, multiple variables, thick description, and critical as well as interpretive analysis. Dewey's account of worker alienation and distorted consciousness, for example, has all of these attributes (HNC:272; ION:131–132; PP:175). It fits closely Bohman's ideal type account of a theory of ideology (Bohman 1991:192–197). If such complex and thick accounts of human behavior are to be made legitimate, however, positivist standards of justification must be relaxed, and this risks acceptance of explanations that are frivolous, shoddy, or simply wrong. Dewey's stress on the fruitful use of ideas for further discovery, and his account of justification in terms of reflectively accepted practices provide rigorous standards that avert this risk.

Like philosophers of social science today, Dewey reckons with the adequacy of "rational choice" explanations of human behavior. Dewey's criterion for fruitful hypotheses is that they promise to be effective in producing "modifications of existence *on behalf of conclusions that are reflectively preferred*" (EN:161, italics added). For Dewey, the (provisional) desired outcome is participatory democracy among citizens equipped with the highest possible degree of social intelligence. This means fostering the sort of reflection and inquiry which will change precisely the preferences which rational choice theorists accept as given. Thus even if rational choice theories are claimed as justifiable within their narrow domain, Dewey considers that domain of limited significance. This invites discourse among social scientists as to what aims are significant—a discussion Dewey would welcome, and for which he suggests fruitful methods, as discussed in Chapters 4 and 5.

Dewey applies a second criterion to rational choice theories. As indicated earlier, immature sciences have the opportunity, and the imperative to check their theories against everyday experience. The deliberately simplified model of transitive preferences, utility maximization, and, in some variants, psychological hedonism, does not match up with the complexity of human desiring and choosing—as noted, for example, in literature, and in thick description by interpretively inclined social scientists. Dewey's own account of unreflective human practices, with its attention to the role of custom, habit, impulse, and symbolic gratification is at odds with this simple model (PP:158–162, 175; HNC:222). "The fact that society acts from crudely intelligized emotion and from habit rather than from rational consideration, is now so familiar that it is not easy to appreciate that the other idea was taken seriously as the basis of economic and political philosophy" (PP:158). (Here, Dewey is a trenchant critic, if not a good prophet!) With regard to habitual behavior, Dewey continues, "the idea that men are moved by an intelligent and calculated regard for their own good is pure mythology. Even if the principle of self-love actuated behavior, it would still be true that the objects . . . which they take as constituting their peculiar interests, are set by habits reflecting social customs" (PP:160).

The sacrifice of verisimilitude by rational choice theorists is deliberate. Postulates are kept thin to make possible formal deductive theories, which are, ultimately, to be subjected to rigorous empirical test (M. Friedman 1953). This approach is designed, then, to meet positivist methodological standards. Whether such standards can be met, and whether looser ones don't amount to abrogation of any justificatory standards, are much debated (J. Friedman 1996; Bohman 1991). But if positivist criteria are unfulfilled or jetisoned, then the case for this description collapses. Dewey's alternative—justification, in the wake of discovery, as emergence of reflectively settled practices—provides a rigorous criterion of justification, without requiring simplistic theories which lack verisimilitude.

Conclusion: Values and Social Science

In this chapter, I argued that Dewey's experimentalism, with its stress on daring social inventions, offers exciting new possibilities for social science that are far removed from its mainstream pursuits. Dewey seeks social inventions which realize aims that are "reflectively preferred." Discussion of aims that are "richly and fully human"—ethical discourse—is deeply implicated in Dewey's account of social science. For analytical purposes, in this chapter ethical aspects were temporarily set aside in order to focus on empirical aspects of experimentalism. Now let us turn to Dewey's account of the method of deliberation and decision on ethical issues. Social scientists have eschewed such discussion, in part, out of a mistaken conflation of physical and social sciences, and an interpretation of physical sciences as value-free. Another reason for this is the sheer difficulty in reaching any determinate answer, any resolution to conflicts over values. Dewey offers a means to bring value conflicts to resolution in a way that does not depend upon questionable foundationalism in ethics. I devote the next two chapters to Dewey's account of ethical deliberation, decision, and conflict-resolution.

4 Ethical Deliberation as Dramatic Rehearsal; Ethical Decision as Conflict-Resolution

Introduction

At the heart of democratic community, in Dewey's view, is discourse about the means and purposes of policies and institutions. This view is also held in various versions of communitarian, deliberative, discursive, and participatory democracy. This chapter focuses on Dewey's account of individuals' deliberation and decision on values and actions. It is not my intent to overlook the social nature of ethical discourse and practice, but merely to simplify it for analytical purposes. Dewey writes of the kinship between, on the one hand, ethical deliberation in a community or society, and, on the other hand, the multivocal dialogue within a person. "An assembly is formed within our breast which discusses . . . proposed . . . acts. The community without becomes a forum and tribunal within" (HNC:315; also EEL:195). The account of individuals' ethical deliberation below is a step toward Dewey's account of public deliberation, presented in the next chapter. Also in Chapter 5, I present Dewey's account of the nature of ethical life—metaethics, and his account of good, right, virtue, and care—normative ethics.

Historical and Theoretical Background

The philosophical context for Dewey's approach to ethics, as for his philosophy of science, includes various countertraditions which existed well before the philosophical revolts of today. Mainstream ethics consist of Anglo-American utilitarianism and social-contract theory, along with Kantian ethical philosophy. These approaches prevail during the nineteenth- and well into the twentieth-century. Dewey is much influenced by this tradition and adopts many specific points, especially from Hume and Mill. He sees mainstream theory becoming divorced from practice, however, hence becoming prey to skepticism and responding with a quest for certainty. Dewey is not alone in rebelling against this tradition. There are threads of a communitarian ethics, running from Hegel, which ground ethical choice not in abstract reason but in inherited tradition. Kierkegaard, Nietzsche, and the early existentialists, especially Heidegger,revolt against the universalism and essentialism of mainstream tradition. They place responsibility back on the engaged agent, and call attention to the indeterminacy of general ethical principles when confronted with conflict situations. Critical theorists in the Marxian tradition also critique mainstream ethical philosophy as expressing the point-of-view and interests of the dominant sectors of society. These early countertrends anticipated the revolt against the analytical and Kantian mainstream in progress today. One branch of this revolt is the revival of communitarianism in response to John Rawls's (1971) dominating Kantian approach of the 1970s (MacIntyre 1988; Taylor 1989; Sandel 1996; Rasmussen 1990). A second branch revolves around today's feminist ethical theories (Held 1993; Noddings 1984; Ruddick 1989; Tronto 1994; Walker 1998), which extend and critique the seminal work of Carol Gilligan (1982). Feminist ethical theories return the emphasis to the moral agent and her moral sentiments, challenging the dominant position of analytical reason (Baier 1991). Feminist ethics emphasize the role of cultural and political critique of domination and subordination. Inquiry into moral psychology forms a third branch of the current revolt, reviving a pursuit rejected as unphilosophical by the mainstream tradition (Flanagan 1991; Johnson 1993; Lakoff 1996). The new moral psychology considers the role of empathy and moral imagination, reviving the theory of moral sentiments (Nussbaum 1996), and considering models of moral development. If Dewey's work is read in the light of these countertraditions, there will be a better chance of grasping his orientation and not reading into it the perspectives of the mainstream.

Dewey's challenge to mainstream ethics parallels his opposition to mainstream philosophy of science. In both cases, he rejects the fixed end of refuting skepticism. He reconstructs practice as a way to find both the goals and means of inquiry. In both cases, the emphasis shifts from

justification to discovery. In practice, moral deliberation is concerned
with emergent situations "where we need to discover what is good and
right" (E: 317). Stressing discovery in science seems more plausible than
emphasizing it in ethics—seemingly a realm of timeless standards, the
golden rule, the categorical imperative, and prohibitions against killing,
stealing, and bearing false witness. Discovery does have a place in ethics
for the following reasons. First, we must deal with emergent situations
and the dilemmas they pose—where past answers don't work, and our
great ethical injunctions conflict with one another. General principles
are never sufficient to determine the choice of action in a particular
emergent situation. Second, because society's transition from customary to reflective morality is incomplete, some general principles are always open to reconsideration. Third, in order to commit themselves
to moral principles and actions, individuals must recapitulate society's
movement toward reflective morality. Fourth, modern society is rapidly
changing and constantly posing new ethical challenges. Discovery, in
both science and ethics, is seen by Dewey as instrumental for the creative resolution of conflict. If ethical deliberation is about discovery,
Dewey reasons, then ethical principles are corrigible. As with science,
Dewey sets more store on what remains to be discovered than on our existing stock of moral "knowledge." He does, however, see all discovery
proceeding from existing knowledge, not starting with a tabula rasa. In
philosophy of science, discovery is a theme of today's postempiricism.
In ethics, Dewey's emphasis on discovery is more startling; even the recent countertraditions neglect this theme.

As with natural science, Dewey is by no means neglectful of validation, but sees it as following after discovery. Justification proceeds by
the achievement of reflectively settled practices and principles that are
fruitful for the exploration of novel situations. When he calls for making
ethics scientific—seemingly an outrageous proposal—he is referring to
the priority of discovery, the goal of conflict-resolution, and the attainment of reflectively settled practice. Dewey does not propose specific
means to predetermined ends, derive ought from is, or take a mechanistic view of human affairs—elements we are prone to attribute to him if
we read the conventional view of science into his proposals.

Reconstruction

Dewey begins his reconstruction of ethical life with an agent in a situation of moral conflict. Such conflict blocks our habitual responses and

forces us to puzzle over—to deliberate upon—what would be best to do. Not every situation calling for moral responses presents us with conflict. We often know what is right to do. Conflicted situations, however, cause us to ponder, to devise new solutions—to take responsibility for our inherited body of ethical principles, and to transform them. Dewey seeks to observe and understand what goes on in our minds as we struggle with ethical conflict. His ethical theory begins with the reconstruction of practice. Dewey's procedure can be called one of integrative reconstruction. It is reconstructive, in Habermas's sense, rather than merely descriptive. Like Habermas, Dewey extrapolates from observation to construct hypotheses about fuller functioning under facilitative conditions. In contrast to Habermas, Dewey's integrative approach does not isolate "reason," in the narrow sense, from the agent's other possible responses including emotion, motivation, desire, metaphorical thinking, tacit knowing, and esthetic sensing. Dewey respects the unity of human response to problematic situations, but his reconstruction is integrative rather than holistic, in that he analyzes various aspects and contributory processes.

Dewey's reconstructive method has some kinship with phenomenology, but phenomenological investigation can be directed at various aspects of ethical experience. Mandelbaum's phenomenology focuses on willed action, for which we can give reasons, and hence returns to mainstream preoccupation with judgment and justification (Dreyfus and Dreyfus 1990:239). Hubert L. Dreyfus and Stuart E. Dreyfus (1990) examine phenomenologically the skills of those capable of responding quickly and appropriately to situations of ethical choice as they arise. Virginia Held offers a feminist viewpoint, which builds theory on womens' experience. Held appears close to Dewey, mentioning inquiry, ethical dialogue, thick description, and the search for consensus (Held 1993: 28–42). The processes of deliberation and dialogue, however, do not receive sustained analysis. Held's emphasis is on "the transformation of moral concepts"—on critical and normative ethical theory (1993:Ch. 3). While each of these authors employs a phenomenological method, each focuses on a different aspect of experience. Dewey's Pragmatist approach to our engagement in the world, and our encounters with problematic situations, accounts for his emphasis on deliberation.

I have divided the following interpretation of Dewey's work in two major sections. The first section is devoted to Dewey's account of deliberation as dramatic rehearsal—how people mull over interests at stake, possible courses of action, and foreseeable outcomes. The second section covers Dewey's reconstruction of how deliberation culminates in decision and how the viability of an ethical decision is tested. Here, Dewey's account of harmonization, unification, or, if you will, conflict-resolution is presented. Finally, I explicate his account of how agents and observers recognize resolutions as genuine or spurious.

Dramatic Rehearsal

Dewey's point of departure—encounter with an ethical dilemma—is delineated as follows. A person is "confronted with situations in which different desires promise opposed goods and in which incompatible courses of action seem to be morally justified" (E:164). "In the presence of moral perplexity, of doubt as to what it is best or right to do, he attempts to find his way out through reflection" (164). As an example, Dewey gives the following account. "A critical juncture may occur when a person . . . goes from a protected home life into the stress of competitive business, and finds that moral standards which apply to the one do not hold for the other" (164). Another example is that of a young man torn between patriotic duty toward his country and religious nonviolence (164–165). These cases provide a vivid sense of the occasions for ethical deliberation—reference points for exploring Dewey's detailed account of deliberation. Neither these nor other cases reappear, however, in his subsequent analysis. I further develop the conscientious objector case later in this chapter, drawing on material beyond Dewey's writings. The primary example employed here is the widely discussed issue of abortion. In this chapter, I present a woman's deliberations about a problematic pregnancy, exploring the process of deliberation, not the justification of choices for or against abortion.[1] The public question of the legal status of abortion is taken up in Chapter 5.

Considering what would happen if certain options were adopted is essential to deliberation. Dewey writes of "a dramatic rehearsal in imagination of various competing possible lines of action" (HNC:190). Scenarios are formed and spun out in the mind. Choices of action are developed and followed through to their consequences. "Deliberation is actually an imaginative rehearsal of various courses of conduct. We give way, in our mind, to some impulse; we try, in our mind, some plan. Following its career through various steps, we find ourselves in imagination in the presence of the consequences that would follow; and as we then like and approve, or dislike and disapprove, these consequences, we find the original impulse or plan good or bad" (E:275).

The terms "rehearsal," "lines of action," and "dramatic," are used advisedly. Deliberation is dramatic in four senses, which are briefly stated here. First, deliberation is dramatic in its concern with character. As we ponder choices of action that have ethical import, "our dominant interest is the manifestation and interaction of personalities . . . [as] in the drama where the colorful display of incidents is, save in the melodramatic and sentimental, a display of the outworking of character" (E:176). This interest in character is central in Dewey's ethical thought and is discussed at length in the next several sections.

Deliberation is dramatic, second, in its concern for plot. Deliberation has a narrative quality, following "lines of action" through their appearance, developments, and complications. "We can judge [the] nature [of a course of conduct], assign its meaning, only by following it into the situations whither it leads, noting the objects against which it runs and seeing how they rebuff or unexpectedly encourage it" (HNC:192). For Dewey, such complex contextual elaboration of the plot is necessary for an accurate assessment of the consequences of action. Following some impulse or plan, Dewey writes, "through various steps, we find ourselves in the presence of the consequences that would follow" (TML:135). Furthermore, dramatic plot follows the narrative to denouements which pull together the various plot-threads, and resolve the dramatic tensions.

Dewey's stress on the dramatic quality of deliberation is, third, an attempt to distinguish his account from the utilitarian approach. Like utilitarian calculation, dramatic rehearsal is concerned with consequences. Dewey rejects, however, the quantitative reckoning of pleasures and pains—the psychological hedonism—of Jeremy Bentham and his followers. "Deliberation is dramatic and active, not mathematical and impersonal" (E:275). "Deliberation . . . no more resembles the casting-up of accounts of profit and loss, pleasures and pains, than an actor engaged in drama resembles a clerk recording debit and credit items in his ledger" (HNC:199). The values or ends at stake are not commensurable.

Dewey's objections to the utilitarians would apply, today, to decision theory. There is some resemblance between Dewey's dramatic scenario and the game theorist's decision tree—the branching set of alternative lines of development of moves and countermoves. For Dewey, however, alternative choices are qualitative and incommensurable, not reducible to the quantitative values associated with the branches of the decision tree. More fundamentally, as Dewey sees it, there are no preestablished rules of the game—no *a priori* specification of possible moves—from which a unique decision tree can be generated. In dramatic rehearsal, one must discover—through reflective inquiry—who the relevant actors are, what their tendencies are, and what external constraints apply before one can ascertain possible "moves." There is no single way to construe this. Scrap one plan of action and, by creative reconceptualization, you will generate another. As later discussed, it may be that such invention of new narratives, rather than being merely preliminary, is a crucial step toward resolution.

Dewey views these mental scenarios as "thought experiments." "The advantage of the mental trial . . . is that it is retrievable, whereas overt consequences remain . . . Moreover, many trials may mentally be made in a short time" (E:275). The term "thought experiment" alludes to the unity of inquiry, scientific and ethical. The metaphors of dramatic script and scientific experiment may seem to clash, but, as in his theory of natural science, Dewey is primarily interested in experimentation as exploratory, as promoting discovery, not for confirming a previously reached conclusion. Exploratory experiment—with its unpredictable unfolding, its suspense, its narrative development—has intrinsic dramatic qualities. This contrasts strongly with Rawls's (1971, 1993) use of thought experiment, based on the positivist account of formal experiment, for purposes of justification.

Fourth, deliberation is suspenseful. As in the drama—whether from the perspective of the playwright in mid-script, or the audience as the play unfolds—deliberation is open-ended. Even as we create our own scenarios, we don't know what the next event will be nor what new concepts we will next seize upon to reorganize our understanding. To deliberate successfully, we must open ourselves up to the unexpected. Dewey is keenly aware of this indeterminateness and the risk it involves. "The poignancy of situations that evoke reflection lies in the fact that we really do not know the meaning of the tendencies that are pressing for action. We have to search, to experiment. . . . Conflict is acute" (HNC:216). Concerning inquiry in general, Dewey speaks of risk and insecurity, reminiscent of existentialism. "Surrender of what is possessed, disowning of what supports one in secure ease, is involved in all inquiry and discovery; the latter implicate an individual still to make, with all the risks implied therein . . . unforeseeable result of an adventure. No one discovers a new world without forsaking an old one; and no one discovers a new world who exacts guarantees in advance for what it shall be" (EN:245–246). What enables us to endure such uncertainty, and how can we sustain deliberation in the face of it? Dewey's answer is "security" and "support": economic security provided by full employment at decent wages, cognitive security through successful methods of inquiry, and emotional support provided by local communities and communities of inquirers, and through respectful listening in conversation and negotiation (E:345; EBNS:309–311; see CD, PP).

Given these general attributes of dramatic rehearsal, let us explore it in detail, using illustrative examples. Although this analysis is made up of separate sections, each of which highlight particular features, these features are all part of an integrated process.

Inquiry into Tendencies of Others and Oneself

With regard to "the manifestation and interaction of personalities" and the "outworking of character" (E:176), dramatic rehearsal provides both a lens and a mirror. It is an occasion for exploring the reactions of others, as well as discovering our own tendencies. First, following out the narrative evokes anticipation of the needs, desires, and values of those involved. In Dewey's words, we can "put ourselves in the place of others, to see things from the standpoint of their purposes and values" (E:270).

Consider the case of an unmarried woman dealing with an unplanned and undesired pregnancy. Moral principles dominate most discussion about abortion—principles concerning the developing life (of the "baby" or "fetus," depending on one's perspective) and principles concerning the rights of the woman. Although these matters are taken up later in this chapter, they are not the only things at stake. In a Deweyan account, the issue is not only responsibility about the pregnancy, itself, but responsibility to all the other people in the pregnant woman's network of relationships. First, let us consider how the woman takes into account the responses of the biological father. In dramatic rehearsal, the pregnant woman may picture herself informing the biological father about her condition. In her mind's eye, she sees his face contort with anger and seems to hear his harsh, blaming words. Or, she sees concern and resolve. On the other hand, perhaps she sees worry and fear. She may speculate—will his main interest be his "freedom," or will it center on her and her needs in the situation? Will his focus be on the baby's birth as proof of his virility, carrying on the family name, or a genetic continuance of his existence via offspring? Will such interests and feelings lead him to insist that she "have *my* baby," or, "get rid of *it*," or that he will "support her in her decision, whatever that may be?" If he insists that she have the baby, will he provide and care for it, or simply boast of its existence and leave the care and cost to her? Associated with these images of the biological father and his emotional responses are the beginnings of plot lines: he supports or threatens, stays or leaves; and she reacts by giving in, or by asserting her needs. Although we can treat them separately for analytic purposes, character and plot are intertwined. Already the dramatic scenario has become quite complex, and we have not yet considered the pregnant woman's response to "her baby," if indeed, her belief is that the life developing within her is already a person. Nor have we considered her anticipation of the reactions of her parents, his parents, perhaps her other children, perhaps even his wife and children, or her minister or other religious authority.

Second, looking within, during the course of dramatic rehearsal, we come to know ourselves. "We shall have to discover the personal factors that now influence us unconsciously" (EEL:327). "The imagining of various plans carried out furnishes an opportunity for many impulses, which at first are not in evidence at all, to get under way. Many and varied direct sensings, appreciations, take place" (E:275). As the scenario unfolds, "every object hit upon reinforces, inhibits, redirects habits already working or stirs up others which had not previously entered in" (HNC:192). "The running commentary of likes and dislikes . . . reveals to any man who is intelligent enough to note them and study their occasions, his own character" (HNC:201). Returning to the example: the pregnant woman asks herself, "How will I react if he threatens to leave? Can I bear giving him up? Can I raise a child alone?" Alternatively, "If he offers to marry me, do I really want to make a life with this man? Am I unable to live without a relationship to this man—some man? Or, do I have the strength to be on my own, which I haven't yet called upon?"

Consider, too, a woman who always imagined that, should the situation arise, she would have an abortion with no qualms. Upon becoming pregnant, she may discover an intense caring for the child-to-be developing within her. This may drastically alter, or at least bring into question, her prior ethical beliefs. It may also motivate her to begin caring for herself, in order to be able to care for a baby, and thus leave behind a period of self-destructive behavior, of which the pregnancy was one consequence (Gilligan 1982:112). On the other hand, a woman who previously had strongly opposed abortion, upon becoming pregnant, may newly perceive it as a very real, even ethically preferable, option.

Considering having the baby, a woman will anticipate her response to both the joys and the burdens of motherhood—perhaps including the demands of single motherhood, poverty's effect on the child, and the absence of a father. These imagined scenes are the sorts of "manifestations and interactions of persons" that are the stuff of drama and explain the designation of deliberation as dramatic rehearsal. (We will later consider her weighing of internalized moral injunctions, which add still another dimension to the drama.)

As Dewey notes, new impulses, habits, and concerns not previously in evidence are brought into awareness by deliberation upon an ethical dilemma. Again, considering the case at hand, a woman may newly find herself deeply committed to religious teachings she formerly regarded casually. Conversely, she may discover that once strongly held religious beliefs now seem to take no account of her particular circumstances. They may even feel like an arbitrary and cruel imposition. Until we explore dilemma situations through dramatic rehearsal "we really do not know the full meaning of the tendencies pressing for action" (HNC:216). This sort of discovery is usually only possible in situations which combine the pressure of having to make a real choice, "the helpful exigencies of practice," with the time to reflect and carry out thought experiments (RPh:165–166). Access to such discovery explains Dewey's preference for studying ethical decision-making in actual situations rather than in more general, detached discussion, or through responses to hypothetical dilemmas.

Dewey's dramatic rehearsal, then, is complex and contextual, involving "thick description," not simple, general, and "thin." Universality of ethical principles is not neglected, but is built up from below. Broad principles are realized from the resolution of many specific cases (RPh:206). Having introduced the basic idea of dramatic rehearsal, let us now explore the ways in which Dewey elaborates upon it, and the various component features he identifies within it. The abortion decision case will again be used to illustrate some of these features.

The Roles of Sensitivity and Emotion

Our ability both to anticipate and to evaluate the responses of others depends upon "sensitiveness," an intuitive capacity (TML:124–132). Dewey explores this through analogy to physical sensing. "A keen eye and a quick ear are not in themselves guarantees of correct knowledge of physical objects. But they are conditions without with such knowledge cannot arise. . . . Unless there is a direct, mainly unreflective appreciation of persons and deeds, the data for subsequent thought will be lacking or distorted" (268–269). With sensitivity comes the vivid experience of real and imagined events and persons—"rendering vivid the interests of others and urging us to give them the same weight as our own" (270). Thus Dewey would hope that the pregnant woman, as she visualizes her parents' faces, for example, would perceive the full extent of their shock, concern, anger, sympathy, or disappointment. Reflection—following, in the mind's eye, the vivid images of others' reactions enables one to grasp underlying values, needs, and interests. For Dewey, the insights which arise from our sensitivity to persons and values, are accompanied by emotions. "There must also be a delicate personal responsiveness—there must be an emotional reaction" (1909:288). "Emotional reactions form the chief materials of our knowledge of ourselves and of others" (E:269).

To understand Dewey's particular usage of these terms, we may turn to his theoretical statements (EN:Ch. 7; AE:Ch. 1). In these works, sensitivity and emotion are viewed from an evolutionary perspective—that is, in relation to need-satisfying mechanisms in living organisms. For simple organisms, in which instinctive behaviors are hard-wired, specific stimuli elicit specific behavioral responses. In higher organisms, the individual may choose from among a repertoire of behaviors and capacities which can be deployed or developed. Fulfillment and action are likely to be separated by time and space. These organisms have developed the capacity to anticipate the outcome of a course of action, and intuitively, to sense the degree of satisfaction it will bring. This intuitive capacity, "sensitivity," is "actualized as feeling" (EN:257). In Dewey's words, "each preparatory response is suffused with the consummatory tone [i.e., feeling of satisfaction] to which it contributes [i.e., which will attend its successful outcome]." Emotional responses, then, become "premonitory" (257). In short, emotional responses serve to register in consciousness the intuitive predictions (premonitions) of the satisfaction of a desire or need. As culture develops, human desire and need develop beyond the simply biological into interests, purposes, ends, tastes, values, duties, rights, and virtues. Emotional responses, then, become premonitory as to whether a projected outcome fulfills a duty, enhances the virtuous character of the actor, and so on.

Dewey takes the evolutionary argument a step further. Satisfying a need—or several needs, purposes, values, etc.—Dewey suggests, brings resolution to a disturbed situation. A situation of conflict or disorder or incompleteness is rendered, for the moment, complete, whole, harmonious. "Only when an organism shares in the ordered relations of its environment does it secure the stability essential to living. And when the participation comes after a phase of disruptions and conflicts, it bears within itself the germs of a consummation akin to the esthetic" (AE:15; also 55–56). Human beings exhibit a sensitivity to complete gestalts, which we call esthetic, and which is registered in pleasurable emotion. Though evolved out of our desire to fulfill basic needs, Dewey sees esthetic sensitivity as a response to wholeness, to integrity, however remote this may be from satisfying particular biological needs or acculturated desires. "To every complex situation [there is] a sensitiveness as to its integrity" (HNC:194). These aspects of sensitivity—to fulfillment of desires and to integration of "elements of the scene"—are intertwined, as illustrated in the next passage. For Dewey, the following description of an employment interview is meant to be representative of any human encounter. "The employer sees by the means of his own emotional reactions the character of the one applying. He projects him imaginatively into the work to be done and judges his fitness by the way in which the elements of the scene assemble and either clash or fit together. The presence and behavior of the applicant either harmonize with his own attitudes and desires or they conflict and jar. Such factors as these, inherently esthetic in quality, are the forces that carry the varied elements of the interview to a decisive issue" (AE:43).

For Dewey, "emotional reactions" are not an incidental, but a constant and crucial feature of our deliberations. As we spin out our scenarios, there is a "running commentary of our likes and dislikes, attractions and disdains" (HNC:201; also E:274). Invention and evaluation are intertwined in this process of running-commentary. Sensing that one line of action will "clash and jar," we dismiss this option and are spared the waste of time and thought of pursuing it. This frees us to concentrate on inventing new possibilities and exploring further the more constructive ones. "Nothing is more extraordinary than the delicacy, promptness, and ingenuity with which deliberation is capable of making eliminations and recombinations in projecting the course of a possible activity" (HNC:194). This statement is reminiscent of accounts of skilled chess players projecting the course of various strategies (Dreyfus and Dreyfus 1990).

For Dewey, sensitivity involves vividly imagining other ways of life, as well as the immediate feelings and needs of other persons. Dewey quotes the poet Shelley: "'The great secret of morals is . . . a going out of our nature, and the identification of ourselves with the beautiful that exists in thought, action or person, not our own. A man to be greatly good must imagine intensely and comprehensively'" (AE:349). Individual sensitivity, like literary creation, functions "to perpetuate, enhance, and vivify in the imagination the natural goods" (EN:408). Here, Dewey, via Shelly, is referring to images of the good life. Thus he anticipates what Lionel Trilling, Putnam, and others speak of as the "moral imagination." In Hilary Putnam's words: "Imagining ways of living, or particular aspects of ways of living, is tremendously important in moral argument" (1984).

Principles

For Dewey, moral principles, rules, and commands—concerning the good, the right, and the virtuous—figure prominently in deliberation. As adults, we have been to a greater or lesser extent socialized by our communities and have acquired a store of moral principles and an awareness of when they apply (E:281–282). These principles represent the cumulative experience of a people or society—pooled, sifted, and crystallized through public discussion. Thus they will be, and deserve to be, taken very seriously. "Human history is long. There is a long record of past experimentation in conduct, and there are cumulative verifications which give many principles a well earned prestige" (HNC:239). Dewey's "verifications" here involve both the survival of communities and the hammering out of consensus in public discourse, both discussed in later sections. Any nontrivial dilemma situation will involve a clash of such principles—with each other, or with other values, habits, desires, and impulses.

A lay person's ethical deliberation will involve reasoning from principles, often in rather abstract fashion, not unlike that of professional philosophers. (This will, of course, vary depending on temperament and training, including gender-role socialization.) Reasoning from principles has a place in the context of dramatic rehearsal, but is not the sole means of deliberation. Furthermore, considering the very nature of dilemma situations, there is no higher or more general moral "key value" by which to adjudicate, or to "trump," the conflicting principles (HNC: 241). Given these complexities and indeterminacies, Dewey concludes that moral principles, like scientific findings, are best understood as instruments for examining the meanings of a particular ethical dilemma situation, not commands controlling the outcome of one's deliberations. "A moral principle, then, is not a command to act or forbear acting in a given way; it is a tool for analyzing a special situation, the right or wrong being determined by the situation in its entirety, and not by the rule as such" (E:280). Jennifer L. Hochschild's (1993) empirical study of citizens reflecting on controversial political issues is representative of recent work that resembles Dewey's on this point (see also Mansbridge 1993; Moon 1993b; Pitkin and Shumer 1982; Warren 1992; Wong 1994). J. Donald Moon sums up Hochschild's (1993) viewpoint: "If we consider the actual nature of moral reasoning in specific contexts . . . [it] tends to be informal, making appeal to a variety of ideas, beliefs, values, and principles, in which the reasons offered for a judgment often do not strictly entail the judgment, but lend varying degrees of cogency to it" (1993b: 216–217).

For Dewey, the role of principles in ethical deliberation parallels the role of scientific laws and theories in investigating a new phenomenon (HNC:242–243). When one explores, say, the outer reaches of the universe, newly accessible through improved telescopes, one assumes that the laws of gravitation and of the conservation of mass/energy will apply. This enables the scientist to make sense of data, and plan tests of hypotheses. The possibility is always present, however, that anomalous results will ensue, suggesting that these principles no longer apply. Dewey would have us see even the most settled scientific laws, not as certainties, but as principles that are instrumental for finding the meanings of new domains. He would have us, likewise, give up the quest for certainty in ethics (QC·277; HNC:223–237).

Dewey insists that to renounce a belief in immutable ethical principles is not, as many people fear, to court moral chaos (HNC:238). "The choice is not between throwing away rules previously developed and sticking obstinately by them. The intelligent alternative is to revise, adapt, expand and alter them. The problem is one of continuous, vital readaptation" (239–240). Dewey comes very close here to the common formula, "creative reappropriation of tradition," which has its origins in Gadamer's hermeneutics. Again, the analogy to physical science is helpful. Despite fears of relativism and nihilism in the wake of the postempiricism of Kuhn and others, physical and biological science continue to function fruitfully, indeed with immense success. The fundamental principles of physics prove remarkably durable, if by no means incorrigible. Even the "standard quantum mechanical model" of subatomic particles, though far less settled—indeed, plagued by anomalies from its outset—has survived test after test and has been immensely fertile in generating new research.

In the abortion case, principles concerning rights and duties are indeed prominent: "abortion is murder"; "a fetus is a human person"; "unborn persons have rights"; and on the other side, "a woman has a right to control her own body"; "there is a constitutional and moral right to privacy"; "individuals and society have a moral obligation to provide a decent life for children"; and so on. There are "duties to one's parents" and "duties to God"; and these are sometimes in conflict with "responsibilities to oneself." For some people, particularly adherents to certain religious creeds, the principle, "abortion is murder," has great force. But women faced with problem pregnancies, while feeling the weight of that principle, may find that it doesn't simply and conclusively determine their choice (Gilligan 1982:83–85). For the pregnant woman, "abortion is murder" may be weighed, for example, against an overwhelming sense that she is unprepared to care adequately for a baby and would do it harm. The original principle continues to remind her of the gravity of the abortion choice, but it does not preclude other urgent considerations and principles. Is not the prohibition against murder absolute? In courts of law there are extenuating circumstances, reduction of charges to justifiable homicide or manslaughter, reduced sentences, even acquittals. Some women will engage in this sort of legal reasoning in justifying to themselves their own private decisions, or will resort to authoritative casuistic interpretation of the moral law provided by their religious creed. Other women will go further, and reconsider the basis of the principle, itself, or question the authority of the religious leaders or texts which promulgate the principle. Some may focus on dissimilarities and discontinuities between a fetus and an infant, where previously they saw only continuity. Whether a given woman ends up accepting, mitigating, or rejecting the principle, and whether we observers find this justified, is not the theoretical concern here. Dewey's aim is to show that these principles serve deliberation but do not control it, and are, themselves, subject to reconsideration and possible revision.

Principles about that which is good also figure in deliberations on abortion. If single motherhood, perhaps with limited income, is the expected outcome, what will be the quality of life for the child, and for the mother? Principles about the good suggest what sorts of material and emotional provisions will be needed and desired in such situations. Safety, the child's education, the availability and type of playmates for the child, time spent at home versus on the job—all are matters of the good, along with material considerations of quality of nutrition, clothing, and shelter—as well as some degree of comfort and some means of entertainment. These principles about the good, in Dewey's terms, are instruments for ascertaining the meaning of the state of single parenthood. In deliberation about a fateful issue like abortion, principles about the good life may conflict with unquestioned ethical principles about the preservation of life. Such previously taken-for-granted considerations may need to be reexamined. Principles concerning virtue may also shape one's understanding of and inquiry into the dilemma situation. What sort of person will one be, and become, if one chooses to bear this child, or if one chooses abortion? Is this an act of courage or cowardice, responsibility or irresponsibility, moderation or excess? And how will one's character be shaped by the new environment and experience that follows in the wake of one's decision? In Dewey's words, "what kind of self is being furthered and formed?" (E:295; see also R. A. Putnam 1997:288, on the use of this criterion by William James). As a single mother, will one become more mature, responsible, and caring, or will one be crushed under the burden and become embittered?

Change in Principles: Reconceptualization and Critique

As we reconsider principles, such as "abortion is murder," we find ourselves scrutinizing concepts—such as "murder." Concepts, like the principles that employ them, are instruments for inquiry. They motivate and assist us in identifying, ordering, and interpreting facts—for example, aspects of fetal development. But they are also subject to revision as we consider other facts—such as the quality of life for both mother and child after a baby is born. Dewey, looking at inquiry generally, writes: "No conception, even if it is carefully and firmly established in the abstract can at first safely be more than a candidate for the office of interpreter. Only a greater success than that of its rivals in clarifying dark spots, untying hard knots, reconciling discrepancies, can elect it and prove it to be a valid idea in a given situation" (HWT:125).

In the abortion case, a host of concepts can come under question and reconsideration. These include "human," as in "human life"; "privacy," and "rights," as in "privacy rights"; "freedom of choice," "duty," "responsibility"; and so on. For some women, concepts that are entirely new to their thinking may emerge from deliberation. Gilligan notes, in

particular, the concept of "responsibility to self" as opposed to a blanket
notion of responsibility that refers only to obligations to others (Gilligan
1982, 94). The role of such reconceptualizations in the final outcome of
ethical deliberations is further discussed below. Exploration of concepts,
the daily labor of professional philosophers, emerges in the thinking of
anyone engaged in serious ethical deliberation. Nor is reconceptualization a special phase of the inquiry process. "There is continual apprais-
ing of both data and ideas" (HWT: 125). "Evolution of conceptions thus
goes on simultaneously with determination of the facts; one possible
meaning after another is held before the mind, considered in relation to
the data" (124). Charles Taylor is another theorist who has stressed this
element of reconceptualization, especially for its role in resolving the
most difficult ethical dilemmas. We must develop, Taylor writes, "readiness to receive any gestalt shift in our view. . . . any quite innovative set
of categories in which to see our predicament that may come our way in
inspiration" (1977:131).

Reconceptualization is akin to critique, and critique can play a large
role in ethical deliberation. Many of the values, habits, and ethical principles that we bring to deliberation were adopted, more or less unthink-
ingly, from the larger culture. Once they enter into an ethical dilemma,
however, they are exposed to critical reflection, by the individual engaged in deliberation. And that individual may choose to borrow the critical view of specialists—public intellectuals, critical theorists, philosophers, theologians (EEL: 134). Though we may be disposed, on the whole,
to accept the legitimacy of the ethical code, which represents the claims
of others upon our actions, "any particular claim is open to examination
and criticism" (E: 229). This position is analogous to the one in Pragmatist and postempiricist philosophy of science which rejects Cartesian
systematic doubt, but sees any individual proposition as corrigible.

In a discussion of ethics in *Experience and Nature,* Dewey identifies
as criticism the process of dramatic rehearsal, itself—the exploratory
discovery of the meanings of various courses of conduct (EN:Ch. 10).
Dewey also offers a critique of alienation, on the general ground, among
others, that it undermines people's capacity to deliberate about values
(HNC: 144, 156–159). For Dewey, critique is a task for philosophy—
distinguishable from, though intertwined with, empirical investigation
and moral imagination (EN: 408). But philosophical critique is only a
refined form of what takes place in ordinary ethical reflection (401), just
as science is a refined form of the empirical inquiry that arises in everyday experience and in the practical arts. Dewey also practices critique in

the contemporary political and analytical senses. That is, he examines both the political biases and the conceptual confusion involved in seemingly disinterested and unambiguous ethical principles.

In a more specialized sense of critique, Dewey offers a fairness or reciprocity principle as a standard against which claims about duty can be criticized (E:230). He observes that people are disposed to adopt and apply this principle, but he rejects the Kantian argument for it as the dictate of reason. Related to the general fairness principle is Dewey's critique of principles and values that confer advantages upon one party in a dyadic relationship, or upon the wealthy and powerful in the community as a whole (82).

Facts and Scientific Findings

Dewey is a crusader against the "error that has made morals fanatic or fantastic, sentimental or authorita[rian] by severing them from the actual facts" (HNC:296). Dewey calls for "physical, biological, and historic knowledge placed in a human context where it will illuminate and guide the activities of men" (HNC:296). "Physics, chemistry, history, statistics, engineering science, are a part of disciplined moral knowledge so far as they enable us to understand the conditions and agencies through which man lives" (HNC:296; also RPh:173; FC:154). Stuart Hampshire's (1971) view is similar to Dewey's: "Almost all previous philosophies [before Kant]—and most people without Kantian or other philosophical prejudices—have assumed that accumulating knowledge or changing beliefs arising out of the study of history, psychology, anthropology, and other empirical sciences to be relevant to their moral judgments" (54).

There are several kinds of relevant facts. Important but mundane facts, about the case at hand, are available simply by asking or looking. Facts about similar cases circulate in conversation, and through journalistic reports and popular books. Facts about the social, cultural, and historical contexts are also available without specialized training and research. There are scientific findings that take specialized skill to obtain, but are communicable to the general public, and ones for which consultation with an expert is required. Scientific findings include narrow determinations, and broad theoretical generalizations, rigorous natural science results, and more tentative results of social and psychological inquiry.

Scientific results do not automatically stamp the character of the particular case but are instruments for inquiry into that case: "We may recur to the case of the physician . . . in diagnosing a case of disease [he] deals with something individualized. He draws upon a store of general principles . . . but he does not attempt to reduce the case to an exact specimen of certain laws. Rather he uses general statements as aids to direct his observation of the particular case, so as to discover what it is like, they function as intellectual tools or instrumentalities" (QC:207; also RPh:168). All claims of fact are corrigible—from the most specific to the most general, the most mundane to the most technical. If a given fact fails to clarify the situation at hand, indeed, clashes with our understanding of that situation, we are entitled to reconsider the fact (HWT:122–123)—and to reexamine our construction of the situation. Thus facts, like principles, are instruments for exploring the meaning of emergent situations, not determinants of their meaning.

In the case of the pregnant young woman, a multitude of mundane facts become relevant. If she plans to raise a child as a single parent, for example, she needs to know about the burdens as well as the joys of parenthood; the financial, and physical, and emotional demands of nurturing infants and small children—the medical bills, the loss of sleep, the interference with social life, the liability to maternal depression, and so on. She needs to know about the availability and price of day care if she will be returning to work or continuing her education. The list goes on.

The role played by findings from psychology, for example, is particularly illustrative of using facts and theories as instruments for ascertaining meanings, not as determinants of meaning. When people attempt, by means of dramatic rehearsal, to understand the needs, desires, and likely responses of others, their intuitive appraisal cannot, in Dewey's view, be replaced by psychological generalizations. At best, such generalizations sensitize us to search for cues in specific areas of human personality which we might otherwise have overlooked. At worst, such generalizations, applied rigidly, override our own perceptions of the other people. We are blinded to their particular responses arising from unique combinations of life history, temperament, and character. Psychological findings may indeed be less well-established than those of physics, but that is not the issue here. Even the facts of physics are responses to established situations, and don't necessarily illuminate emergent situations. What matters in both cases is the applicability of the fact or theory to the case at hand.

On matters of public policy affecting large numbers of people, how-ever, face-to-face appraisal of each recipient is not possible, and general-izations become necessary. Were there an adequate scientific psychol-ogy, its generalizations would be preferable to those based on tradition, anecdote, and idiosyncratic experience. Even in this regard, several cau-tions are necessary. First, for Dewey, scientific findings are best used in conjunction with tacit knowledge rooted in experience, rather than overriding it. Second, Dewey's conception of a scientific psychology is not the mainstream one, in either substance or method. Third, findings from psychology, and from any other science, should be treated as hy-potheses, subject to close monitoring of their success in use. Their truth is viewed prospectively, in application, rather than retrospectively, ac-cording to some conception of formal experimental and argumentative validation. Psychological theories should be applied tentatively, experi-mentally, subject to "ready and flexible revision," not dogmatically.

The case of abortion also calls up many questions of medical science. For example, what is the effect of drug use (prescription and/or narcotic and stimulant) on the probability of fetal abnormalities? What does re-search reveal about fetal development and viability at various stages of pregnancy? What scientific information exists on spontaneous abortion, that is, miscarriage? How do advances in life-support technology for ex-tremely premature births change our conception of viability? What do abortion statistics show about chances of complications from the pro-cedure, or its effects on ability to become pregnant in the future—com-pared with the risks of carrying to term? What does social research show about its emotional complications? Scientific results are necessary but not sufficient to determine our choices. Dewey, were he alive to-day, would presumably endorse the common philosophical proposition: when human life begins is not decidable on scientific grounds alone, al-though scientific evidence is certainly relevant. Today's presentation of scientific reports that favor preconceived positions is clearly not what Dewey had in mind, however. He advocates adopting the spirit as well as the findings of science. This means seeking the most rigorous, com-prehensive, and impartial investigation possible, and committing one-self beforehand to accept the outcome.

Dewey at times appears to overstate the relevance of scientific find-ings to ethical decision. "Where will regulation come from if we surren-der familiar and traditionally prized values as our directive standards? Very largely from the findings of the natural sciences" (QC:273). Gir-

vetz, for example, uses this sentence to justify his rejection of Dewey's
ethical theory, despite his finding aspects of it instructive (1973:138–
139). Dewey's statement, however, refers to his concern with social problems generated by the rapid advance of science and technology, and their
use for "personal and class advantage" rather than the public good (QC:
274; also 9, et passim). As he states in an earlier text, "the crisis in which
man is now involved all over the world, in all aspects of his life, [is] due
to the entrance into the conduct of the everyday affairs of life of processes . . . whose origin lies in the work done by physical inquirers in
the . . . laboratories" (RPh:xxi; also SS:54–58). How much we curtail
the burning of fossil fuels, for example, renouncing the previously
unquestioned value of development without limit, depends heavily on
scientific findings about global warming. Even for such issues where
technology looms so large, in Dewey's view, scientific information is
necessary but not sufficient for ethical choice. There remain questions
about the environment's value, responsibilities to future generations,
and the value of life styles supported by use of nonrenewable energy
sources. "The question is not what a thing will do . . . it is whether
to perform the act which will actualize its potentiality" (EEL:361; also
367–368).

Tacit Thought

Dramatic rehearsal involves thick description of complex scenarios. The conscious, deliberate, categorizing, and calculating mind can
scarcely encompass all of this detail. Tacit thinking, however, which is
fluid and metaphorical, can better handle this complexity and indeterminacy. "We continually engage in an immense multitude of [tacit] selections, rejections . . . of the most minute, vibratingly delicate nature . . . Even our most intellectualized operations depend upon them
as a 'fringe' . . . They give us premonitions of approach to acceptable
meanings" (EN:300; also AE:50, 59; HWT:124, 280–283; RPh:88–89).
Some mental work will occur altogether outside of awareness during a
fallow period, or incubation process (E:271–272; AE:23, 56, 72; HWT:
284; also Poincare 1952; Hadamard 1996). Tacit thinking is a feature of
both the deliberation and the decision processes. Ethical decision as
conflict-resolution brings deliberation to its conclusion, as will be discussed below.

Decision

Deliberation as dramatic rehearsal is completed when the unfolding dramatic plot climaxes in a satisfactory resolution. "Deliberation has its beginning in troubled activity and its conclusions in choice of a course of action which straightens it out" (HNC: 199). Resolution in drama is often achieved by means of character development or maturation in the chief protagonist, and sometimes even by a shift in a community's moral standards. Ethical conflicts, too can be settled by creative choices that harmonize competing interests instead of simply picking the most pressing or weighty interest and foregoing the others. While emphasizing that side of drama that provides esthetic satisfaction and moral instruction through plot resolution, Dewey, surprisingly, neglects the tragic dimension in which characters are caught up in the anguish and dire consequences of irresolvable conflict. Later in this section, I propose how a tragic sensibility might be added to Dewey's account.

Throughout the deliberation process, according to Dewey's model, we have been trying out different courses of action via imagination. With each imagined scenario, we have used concepts and principles to grasp the meaning of events. We have used both scientific facts and our sensitivity about people to forecast the next step in the unfolding of these events. And at every step, there has been a "running commentary" of feelings of approval or disapproval, and an esthetic sense of either completeness or lack of fit. Negative reactions have alerted us to try out another scenario, to recombine elements of earlier versions, to reconsider our concepts, to critique the principles which have guided us thus far, or to reevaluate our own purposes. Implicitly, we are searching for a path that requires none of our conflicting goals to be sacrificed. We usually settle for far less. We yield to what appears to be necessity, letting the stronger aims predominate while the weaker ones are renounced. If there are richer possibilities, we lack the time, resources, patience, or tolerance of ambiguity to continue searching for them. Dewey is most interested, however, in that subset of cases in which, in a creative moment, we hit upon a new course of action that reconciles seemingly incompatible dispositions. He views these cases as the most significant, because such creative decisions can transform individuals and their society. Erik Erikson's (1993) account of "young man Luther" illustrates these possibilities at their most sweeping extent. The Theses of Wittenberg are, on the one hand, a creative response to Luther's personal conflict. On the other hand, Luther's conflict reflects cleavages in the culture as a whole, and his solution resonates with the populace. The resultant social movement transforms not only the church, but European politics as well.

Finally, in Dewey's ideal-type case, our searching leads to imagining a course of action that does not evoke emotional rejection. Our dispositions, urgings, needs, and desires have found "a way fully open. . . . energy is released" (HNC: 192). Dewey rhapsodizes a bit about this image of release. "As long as deliberation pictures shoals or rocks or troublesome gales as marking the route of a contemplated voyage, deliberation goes on. But when the various factors in action fit harmoniously together, when imagination finds no annoying hindrance, when there is a picture of open seas, filled sails, and favoring winds, the voyage is definitively entered upon" (HNC: 192). Dewey returns to the harmonization and release images, introducing the notion of sublimation: "The object thought of may be one which stimulates by unifying, harmonizing, different competing tendencies. It may release an activity in which all are fulfilled not indeed in their original form, but in a 'sublimated' fashion . . . which modifies the original direction of each [tendency] by reducing it to a component along with others in an action of transformed quality" (193–194). The initial positions put forward by the different voices within the self create a win-lose conflict, but moving from positions to interests has made a unifying resolution possible. The ethical dilemma has been transcended, or transformed, or resolved. "This implies . . . [the discovery of] a comprehensive object, one which coordinates, organizes . . . each factor of the situation which gives rise to conflict" (195). Here, "object" refers to an objective, a goal. This is not an abstract ideal goal, but a concrete one; an "end-in-view" that is the outcome of a particular, specified, feasible course of action. The specificity of this resolution must be emphasized, lest Dewey be misunderstood as suggesting the atomistic individualist notion of a completely unified, fully transparent self.

Let us again consider briefly the example from Chapter 1—the ethical crisis faced by the parents of a young man who announces to them his homosexuality (Griffin, Wirth, and Wirth 1986). These parents are torn between love of their child and cultural or religious teachings that press them to reject him. After agonizing deliberation, they reach beyond dichotomous choices: neither renouncing their beliefs, in order to accept their son, nor compartmentalizing their beliefs as still true but not applicable to their own family. Their prior moral and religious position, which rejected homosexuality, is not renounced, it is transformed.

They reach both a new, and arguably richer, sense of what is natural and good and a more complex understanding of God and God's love for humanity. In the resolution of their dilemma, they accept their son for who he is. In doing so, the parents also reach a deeper closeness with their child and a new level of self-awareness and self-acceptance, as well as an awakening of social awareness and social conscience. This is a resolution in the fullest sense—a win-win solution in which familial love and moral duty are both fulfilled, and a life richer in meaning is opened up. It is this sort of "harmonization" and "unification" that Dewey intends in his abstract account of the resolution of ethical dilemmas.

In Carol Gilligan's recounting of women's abortion decisions, there are cases that exhibit, concretely, Dewey's image of harmonization and self-resolution. In each of these cases, a reconceptualization which directs the imperatives of responsibility and care to include oneself, not just others, is crucial. Choices which meet the woman's own vital needs are no longer seen as immoral per se. A win-win solution is envisaged, in which care for oneself is a necessary condition of caring adequately for others. "Once obligation extends to include the self as well as others, the disparity between selfishness and responsibility dissolves" (Gilligan 1982:94). In the specific case of "Sarah," "confronting a choice between the two evils of hurting herself or ending the incipient life of the child, Sarah reconstructs the dilemma in a way that yields a new priority which allows decision. She recapitulates the sequence of development as she first considers, but then rejects as inadequate resolutions based on her feelings of loneliness or her wish to appear good in others' eyes. In the end she subsumes these considerations to concerns about responsibility for herself as well as for the father and the child" (Gilligan 1982: 91). Gilligan's themes of "reconstruction," "allowing," and "subsumption" are remarkably similar to features of Dewey's account.

Use of the word, "resolution" is not meant to imply that there were no regrets among the women Gilligan interviewed who reached a satisfactory closure in their deliberations. Gilligan's respondents did grieve for the road not taken, but were nonetheless confident that they had made the best possible decision under the circumstances. In Dewey's writings on ethical deliberation, on the other hand, the absence of any mention of grieving is one of his rare lapses of insight. To complete Dewey's theory, it is necessary to add the concept of tragic conflicts in which even creative solutions do not prevent the renunciation of a valued option. We are able to make the best choice and go on with our lives, in such situations, only because of our capacity to grieve. Martha Nussbaum (1990) and Bernard Williams (1973) make this point by examining moral decision in the Greek tragedies. Although Dewey overlooks this element, his theory does not preclude it. Adding Nussbaum's and Williams's perspectives to Dewey's extends his metaphor of deliberation as dramatic rehearsal to include classical tragic drama.

Dewey's theory of decision by conflict-resolution must answer the question: could an individual resolve conflicting motives into single-minded vengefulness, hate, fanaticism, racism? Through deliberation, can one resolve feelings of guilt about one's own destructive impulses by viewing others as persecutors, thus feeling justified in destroying them? In short, what about Hitler and the holocaust, Stalin and the purges, or Serbian "ethnic cleansing?" For Dewey, this sort of apparent unification of the self on behalf of a particular emotion is achieved only by compartmentalizing opposed emotions, such as sympathy and guilt. Opposed awareness of the humanity and dignity of others is suppressed; and opposed moral principles concerning human rights, and against killing, stealing, and bearing false witness are reserved for one's own group. This is the very opposite of full deliberation and conflict-resolution, which bring all such factors into play and resolve the conflict among them. "'Bad' impulses and habits . . . can be subdued only by being utilized as elements in a new, more generous and comprehensive scheme of action, and good ones can be preserved from rot only by similar use" (HNC:195). For example, frustration and rage at being discriminated against can be juxtaposed against values of fairness, love, and community, and resolved into a nonviolent campaign for liberty for everyone— as in the civil rights movement. Most humans appear to be equipped with pro social impulses—perhaps due to our evolutionary adaptation as a social species. (Apparent exceptions to that generalization are taken up in the next chapter.) Bonding and cooperation among members enhances the survival chances of the group (see 1937a). To take another example, rage at being denied desperately needed employment, could lead immediately to violence or, say, to membership in the Ku Klux Klan, but is likely to checked by deep inhibitions against hurting others, as well as by fear of punishment. That same anger, once checked and then given a place in a larger understanding of political life, can energize action, such as participation in politics and labor union activism. Rage can be transformed into righteous indignation, and previously unexpressed political beliefs and commitments can now be actualized (E:269). Dewey concludes that, "it is not that the emotional, passionate phase of action can or should be eliminated on behalf of a bloodless reason. More passions, not fewer is the answer. To check the influence of hate there must be sympathy, while to rationalize sympathy there are needed emotions of curiosity, caution, respect for the freedom of others" (HNC: 194–195). The clash of opposed passions, impulses, or habits is both what makes us stop and think, and what lends breadth to our reflections. Some inhibitory force "is required to stop the ongoing of a habit or impulse. This is supplied by another habit. The resulting period of delay [is when deliberation takes place]" (HNC: 197). Rather than being conducted in the narrowly focused sphere of habit or immediate impulse, action is mediated, and its horizons expanded. "Variety of competing impulses enlarges the world. It brings a diversity of considerations before the mind, and enables action to take place finally in view of an object generously conceived and delicately refined, composed by a long process of selections and combinations" (HNC: 197). Full resolution produces the opposite of fanaticism. It results in exactly the sort of decisions that we recognize as just and compassionate.[2]

One general reason why integrative resolutions to intrapersonal ethical conflicts may be possible is this diversity and balance of passions, interests, and values. A second general basis of resolution, in today's language of conflict-resolution, is the movement from (narrow, fixed) positions to (broader, more flexible) interests. For Dewey, the desire, say, for a particular narrowly defined object is a fixed end which rigidifies thinking and renders ethical dilemmas insoluble. Dewey's hypothesis that alternatives are possible is based on his concepts of broad underlying desires and alternative objects of desire (E: 248). "Even in the case of hunger and sex, where the channels of action are fairly demarcated by antecedent conditions (or 'nature'), the actual content and feel of hunger and sex are indefinitely varied according to their social contexts" (HNC: 153). Tastes and cravings with regard to food vary according to the diet and cuisine of our cultural niche. Sexual behaviors and preferences are similarly patterned by culture, in Dewey's view. Indeed, some current theories go far beyond Dewey's position, to assert that our sexuality is entirely socially constructed. If this can be said of biologically based needs, it holds all the more for interests in well-being, dignity, beauty, growth, justice, and virtue, with their substantial component of cultural construction.

Stepping back from the dramatic density of deliberation, the movement of emancipation from fixed ends, has these general aspects: (a) Each desire—or interest, or value—at stake in the conflict can be traced back to a broader underlying desire; (b) With regard to each broader desire, one can ascertain a range of objectives or acts that would satisfy it; (c) One can identify where these ranges overlap—can discover a course of action compatible with each of the broader desires. Although the initial narrowly focused desires have objects that are mutually exclusive, the broader underlying dispositions have larger sets of objects, some of which lie in an overlapping subset. Several additional principles suggest how these possibilities can be enhanced. First, the more desires and values at stake, the greater the possibility of combining these in an imaginative way, to foster all of them. This corresponds to the principle, in contemporary theories of negotiation, of enlarging the agenda to permit trade-offs. Second, given a long enough time horizon, a variety of needs can be met sooner or later—needs which clash when their fulfillment must be immediate. Ethical deliberation, by deferring immediate choice and action to consider a fuller set of possibilities, functions to open up these broader time horizons and issue spaces. In an attempt to illustrate these principles at work, I present below the complexities and ambiguities of an actual case.

In this example, I return to the issue of conscientious objection. Although Dick B., the person involved, narrated this account to me, it is paraphrased here from memory.

> Dick considered becoming a conscientious objector during World War II. He had a deeply felt ethical and spiritual obligation to nonviolence. On the other hand, he recognized both the appalling nature of Hitler's conquests, and the sacrifice so many young Americans like himself were making in order to stop Hitler by military means.

This was an inescapably tragic conflict, imposed by the fateful developments of world politics. Yet there was room for an element of creative resolution.

> An older friend of his said to Dick: "can you refuse to fight, knowing that so many others are fighting and dying to stop Hitler's war machine? The only way I could see you justifying not fighting would be by dedicating the rest of your life to working for peace." Dick found this point compelling, and spent time mulling it over. He ended up joining the Navy and serving in combat. After the war he found himself nonetheless, following his friend's injunction and dedicating the rest of his life to working for peace.

The friend's suggestion, as originally proposed, responded to the anguish of not fighting. In Dick's adaptation, however, it responded to the anguish of participating in military violence. In either case, the friend's advice placed the immediate action in a much longer time horizon. R. A. Putnam, contemplating another dilemma concerning pacifism, writes: "sometimes only within the frame of a whole life, and sometimes only within the frame of the life of a whole community can these decisions be evaluated" (quoted in H. Putnam 1992:224). This allows for accommodating both Dick's need to help stop Hitler now by fighting, and the larger interest served by his nonviolent position—working for a world without war.

A degree of unification was possible here precisely because the decision employs the general bases for resolution. It moves from the fixed end of never committing a violent act, to the broader underlying interest of building a nonviolent world. It has the breadth of scope and the duration to encompass the deeply divided ends of nonviolence and armed resistance to a tyrant. It is a lifetime commitment so profound as to approximate the profundity of the conflict. This did not save Dick from the tragic dichotomous choice of bearing arms in combat versus being a conscientious objector. Nor would everyone have made the same decision. Such a resolution is incompatible with the fixed end of never participating in violence under any circumstances, and some would find this an unacceptable sacrifice of principle. The moral and political force of completely unyielding nonviolence, as in the case of Gandhi, cannot be discounted. Nonetheless, this was an integrative solution for Dick, however imperfect.

Given this account of decision as conflict-resolution, we can now explore Dewey's approach to testing or justifying an ethical decision.

Testing

Beyond deliberation and decision in Dewey's theory, but strongly linked with it, lies the testing of one's decision through experience. To the limited extent that ethical choice is a straightforward matter of selecting the means to a single end, the testing of its success would be an empirical/interpretive procedure of matching criterion and actual result. This is indeed part of the test of an ethical decision, especially in public policy decisions that involve sophisticated social theories about the effects of particular interventions. Testing for causal means-ends connections, however, is often seen as all that Dewey meant by testing an ethical decision. For Dewey, however, ethical decision involves the

choice of ends as well as means. The new chosen end harmonizes conflicting dispositions—resolves the conflicts among desires, values, and
ethical principles. The test, therefore, is whether this resolution is a genuine and stable one. "The unification which ends thought in act may be
only a superficial compromise, not a real decision but a postponement
of the issue. . . . Or it may present, as we have seen, the victory of a temporarily intense impulse over its rivals, a unity by oppression and suppression, not by coordination. These seeming unifications which are not
unifications of fact are revealed by the event, by subsequent occur-
rences" (HNC:210–211). That is, when the precipitating situation next
occurs, the old doubt, uncertainty, and ambivalence may be reawakened.
Needs, interests, and values within the self, which were shunted aside
in the rush to spurious unification, may reassert themselves. The quiet
voice of conscience, which was drowned out by some urgent passion,
may be heard again. The mental walls, behind which certain principles
or desires were compartmentalized, may be breached. New encounters
with the environment may evoke suppressed dispositions in spite of
the recent decision. Upon further consideration, perhaps one will reaf-
firm one's choice, but in some cases the doubts persist. One finds oneself, again, in an ethical dilemma situation, and action is once again sus-
pended. The apparent resolution of the ethical conflict has been tested
and found wanting. By contrast, if the unification is genuine, doubts may
arise, but are dispelled. Quiet confidence in one's choice may emerge
and remain stable—until a changing environment poses new dilemmas.
The case of Dick B. exemplifies this positive outcome.. Forty years after
his decision to devote his life to working for peace, Dick was still pursuing that path, assured that it was the best course for his life.

In contrast, consider another case of opposition to war that led, not to
assured unification, but to regret and repudiation. A young man, Phil J.
(a pseudonym), known to this author, refused to fight in Vietnam—
which, unlike World War II, he thought unjustified by any standard. As
a selective objector, Phil did not feel legitimate in claiming conscientious objector status. And to dramatize his protest, he wanted to refuse
alternative service. As a draft resister, he risked going to prison for up to
three years, although most sentences in such cases were considerably
shorter. He did decide to defy the draft openly, and, as it turned out, was
convicted and sentenced to the full three years. He came out of his jail-
term burnt-out and cynical. Phil said he scarcely knew the person, his
former self, who had chosen the actions leading to his imprisonment and
the loss of three precious years of his youth. He was bitter against that

former self for its naiveté' both about prison conditions and about his own human limitations. This is a case in which the agent, himself, concluded unequivocally that his decision had failed the test of genuine unification.

In addition to a feeling of harmony, and absence of nagging doubt, successful decisions may be accompanied by a sense of power, of strength, and of freedom (Gilligan 1982:112–123; Griffin, Wirth and Wirth 1986: 18). In Gilligan's study of abortion decisions, some of the women found new energy and resolution for going on with their lives. They took care of health problems, gave up drugs, returned to school, and settled into steady work—dramatic changes! They had survived a crisis and had emerged from it strengthened, with a new feeling of responsibility for self and others that manifested itself in many areas of their lives (1982: 115). Conversely, "for the women whose choice signified, in their own terms, a retreat, this was the time when things fell apart" (113). Decisions both to have an abortion and to carry to term can equally well pass the test of genuine unification. Which decision will unify depends upon the circumstances, and the life-history, beliefs, and character the particular woman brings to the situation. This is far from saying that anything goes. Although decisions may vary from woman to woman, there can certainly be a better and a worse choice for a particular woman in a particular circumstance. That this sort of deliberation gives no single right answer for all moral agents, will, obviously, have consequences for community-wide discussion and decisions on government policies on abortion.

Dewey is well aware that such testing of the unification associated with ethical decisions is not foolproof. In ethics, as in science, all tests— all validity claims—are corrigible. In ethics, as well as science, the individual is subject to blind spots. Indeed, the more committed we become to a spurious resolution, the more difficult it becomes to examine our dispositions and behaviors. "It is one of the penalties of evil choice, perhaps the chief penalty, that the wrong-doer becomes more and more incapable of detecting these objective revelations of himself" (HNC:211). This is not to say that there is a philosophical flaw in Dewey's account of the way ethical resolutions are tested. Rather, individual finite humans are not always capable of carrying out these tests. Correction of individual errors is possible, however, within a larger community, for ethics as well as for science.

If an individual is blind to the inconsistency of his own thought and behavior, the observations of acquaintances become important. Observers may note contradictions between speech and action, and observe irritability and defensiveness that suggest unacknowledged ambivalence. Observers are not privileged over the agent in judging the unification in his behavior and thought, nor are they entitled to overrule the agent. Dialogue between agent and observer, however, offers a fuller understanding than either can achieve alone. The failure of an individual agent to recognize her incomplete resolution of an ethical dilemma is analogous to the failure of an individual scientist to recognize discrepant evidence. She may be so deeply committed to her experimental result that it takes critique and attempts at replication by other scientists to reveal her error. Thus, in both science and ethics, validation is ultimately achieved by the community, not the individual.

It remains possible, however, that a whole scientific or ethical community, wedded to a particular paradigm, will persist in errors. This possibility raises the specter of unfalsifiable claims, therefore, of relativism and nihilism, and perhaps thence to facism. Habermas's search for universal grounds of validity appears to be motivated by this fear (Strong and Sposito 1995:264–266). History suggests that persistence of error in science, though it certainly occurs, does not endure (Kuhn 1970). The constant encounter with new experience—indeed, the systematic search of scientists for new experimental and theoretical configurations—ensures that anomalous results will appear. The mutual criticism intrinsic to scientific communities keeps these anomalies on the agenda. Accumulation of anomalies will eventually result in a paradigm crisis, despite dogged defense of the paradigm with ad hoc explanations. Dewey sees the same process of crisis and transformation occurring in the ethical sphere. Humans are immersed in an environment that constantly challenges their decisions. We are faced with moral exigencies, despite our efforts to evade them and escape into abstract ideals. There is enough plurality among individuals, groups, communities, and nations that alternative perspectives and critical commentary are inescapable. If ethical thought were deliberately modeled on science, however, the process of acquiring new experience and deciphering its challenges would be more methodical and persistent. Consultation between opposing viewpoints would be sought out, not shunned. Ethical theorists—unlike scientists, but like philosophers of science—have often been more interested in defending established principles, than in using them as tools to confront new ethical choice situations. The difference between the quest for discovery and that for validation is as crucial for the theory and the practice of ethics, as it is for science.

If the resolution of an ethical dilemma is experienced as stable, over time, by the agent, this particular resolution can be said to be reflectively settled for the individual. It passes the first test of its validity. If, furthermore, this particular decision instantiates a principle that can be applied in a number of other cases, and these resolutions also prove to be sustained, then a reflectively settled practice has been established. This provides an additional test of validity. Third, if the new principle proves helpful in exploring and lending meaning to novel situations, then it is fruitful as well as settled. Fourth, if observers do not detect ambivalence in the individual, a step has been taken toward validation by the community, not just the individual. Finally, if the new principle becomes for others in the community, not just the original agent, a settled basis for choosing actions in familiar situations and for exploring the meaning of novel ones, then a fifth and more difficult test of validity is met. These tests of an ethical decision correspond closely to the ones required of a scientific finding, in Dewey's Pragmatist account of justification in natural science.

This discussion of testing an ethical decision expands the focus beyond the single episode of deliberation. It suggests that, for the individual, an ethical decision is followed by a time of reflection in which the decision's viability is assessed. Since such assessments are fed back into subsequent decisions, there is a continuing cycle of deliberation, action, and reflection. Furthermore, one reflects on the principles implied, the process by which these were reached, and their relation to additional cases of ethical decision by oneself and others. Reflection renders subsequent deliberation more conscious and systematic, and more informed by personal and collective experience. Deliberation passes over into informal theory worked out by ethical agents, a step toward the refined theories of philosophers. Philosophical theory of ethics is taken up in the latter part of the next chapter. The process of reflection on and testing of ethical decisions extends across individuals, as well as over time. Individual deliberation becomes a component of public deliberation, a topic discussed in the next chapter.

5 Public Ethical Deliberation and Ethical Theory

Democracy for Dewey is about citizens having a "share in forming and directing the activities of the groups to which [they] belong" (PP:147). Indeed, public communication, for Dewey, is the necessary means for the creation of community and results in communion, a deeply cherished end (EN:184, 202). In discussing individual deliberation, then, Dewey's goal is to move toward an account of public deliberation on issues of society-wide concern (FC:128, 160). "Communication alone can create a great community" (PP:142; also PP:152–155, 184; RPh:206; AE:334–335). He addresses this subject at scattered points in his later works, but not as fully as one might wish (E:Part III; also FC; CD). In this chapter, I attempt to fill out Dewey's account of public deliberation by bringing to the foreground his allusions to communication and conflict-resolution, and by extrapolating from his more detailed account of individual deliberation. Chapter 3 on social science, addressed the empirical aspect of public discourse. Here, the focus is on the ethical aspect. I present Dewey's views on public discourse in three main sections: the process of public deliberation; the abortion rights controversy; and the fostering of deliberation. I summarize his views on ethical theory in two main sections: the nature of the ethical life—metaethics; and substantive ethical principles—normative ethics.

Public Judgment and Conflict-Resolution

Dewey is concerned with the broad range of citizen conversation, in informal settings, in formal meetings, and via electronic media—in response to direct experience and to journalistic reports. Conversation topics include daily events, trends, policy issues, electoral campaigns, governmental proceedings, and protest actions. Given Dewey's focus on communication/community, he is less concerned with the specialized deliberations of legislatures and courts, though these feed into and are influenced by citizen discussion (cf. Rawls 1993; Habermas 1996). Public discussion occurs in the context of political organization and action but can be treated separately for analytical purposes.

Daniel Yankelovich (1991), following Dewey's lead, carried out a reconstruction of public deliberation. Yankelovich studies the actual conduct of public discussion on issues, and extrapolates from it to develop an ideal-type model. Where public deliberation is thorough and well-informed, there may be a "coming to public judgment" (Yankelovich 1991:5; MW13:15; PP:177–179, 203). Citizens, in discussions with one another and in responding critically to mass media, may develop complex and differentiated views on what is at stake. They may weigh multiple values. Though short on facts and theory, they may choose responsible experts to help them grasp broad parameters. Citizens may embrace creative solutions offered by experts. And in the end, they may resolve their conflicts on issues, and reach stable, reflectively settled commitments. Public judgment is reached gradually: social experiments unfold over time; information gradually filters out among the electorate; and people intermittently focus their divided attention on different issues. Experts may have formed judgments early and concluded that the public is hopelessly adrift—only to find responsible public judgment emerging when they least expect it. Public judgment, when finally achieved, has all the attributes of well-conducted individual deliberation and decision.

There is considerable difference in degree, though not in kind, between deliberation on public issues and individual deliberation on personal behavior, addressed in the last chapter. More complex links between action and consequences require theoretical prediction and empirical exploration of cause and effect. Actual social experiments replace the thought experiments of dramatic rehearsal. Public discourse is more impersonal and has a greater place for expert testimony. It favors the ethical perspective of the judge over that of the agent. A consensual social goal—such as full employment, literacy, equal opportunity, freedom of speech—is often presupposed, rather than making the goal itself the subject of inquiry. Dewey reminds us, however, that reconsideration of goals will occur when conflict between them occurs: when economic, technical, and social changes pose new challenges; when social experiments raise questions of ends as well as means; and when critics expose biases and distortions underlying widely held social values. In public discourse, analysis and critique of social ethics also tend toward the impersonal, and are often conducted by expert theorists.

Not only is public deliberation analogous to individual personal deliberation, it also interacts with it, and this brings an agent-oriented, self-critical perspective into public deliberation (E:317–319). When individuals take a stand on complex public conflicts, conflicts among their own values and interests are evoked, setting personal deliberation in motion. Experts and public officials, though they seek objectivity, are not exempted from personal conflict and the need for individual deliberation. One's personal ethical decisions help to form the perspectives and general ethical principles one brings to questions of social ethics, and vice-versa. In both public and personal deliberation, the empirical and the ethical are inextricably intertwined.

Since there is an element of reasonable and thoughtful deliberation in coming to public judgment, a politics of transition can be built on the existing democratic process. Nonetheless, the defects of today's judgment-formation process must be recognized in order to envision a more effective one. Discussion is often arrested at the level of slogans, symbols, rigid positions, and polemical attacks. Stuart Klawans, quotes a virtuoso of negative campaigning, who, "with a touch of real sorrow," says that "'governance is about forming a consensus; but politics in present-day America is about dividing people'" (Klawans 1996:36). Furthermore, citizens incongruously demand both more government services and less taxes. Powerful groups manipulate the representation of issues remote from citizens' experience (PP:169). (On some issues, however, citizens have direct experience and are less vulnerable to manipulation—abortion, public education, women's rights, and aspects of the enivironment, for example.) Citizens today are ill-prepared by their schooling for productive deliberation. Furthermore, they are distracted by the stresses of work life and the seductions of mass consumption and entertainment. They lack experience and information on remote and complex issues (PP:131–132; Edelman 1964). Agenda setting, framing of issues, and information sources are skewed according to the relative wealth and power of the interest groups involved. Both concentrated ownership of the media and misconceived journalistic philosophies act to deprive citizens of the materials they need to form reflective judgments (FC:149; LW6:166; MW15:42; PP:168–169, 177, 180–182; Yankelovich 1991). A politics of transition involves, therefore, popular mobilization—using people-power to offset the power of wealth and position—in order to create a more level ground and more facilitative institutions for public deliberation. Second, a politics of transition involves promoting conflict-resolution, including formal mediation as a form of public discourse, and the spirit of conflict-resolution as an influence on informal discussion and media presentation.

Conflict-Resolution in Public Discourse

Dewey's broad account of public communication has all the components included in today's conflict-resolution theory. "Different interests . . . have to be harmonized in any enduring solution" (FC:73; also MW8:443–444). This involves "sympathetic regard for the intelligence . . . of others, even if they hold views opposed to ours" (E:329; also CD/LW14:228). It involves the search for "things which unite men in common ends" and "the integration of . . . divided purposes and conflicts of belief" (DE:98; QC:218, 252; also RPh:203; MW10:216). Dewey implies that the spirit of conflict-resolution should permeate all public discussion. In today's times, this also implicates the professional theory and practice of mediation, conflict-resolution, and common ground dialogue (Moore 1996).

The principles of conflict-resolution are already apparent in some segments of public discourse. Some speakers and writers take pains to show their awareness of their adversaries' concerns, even as they present their own. Rather than adhering to fixed positions, they explore broader interests, and inquire into creative solutions. Speech that is conflict-resolution-oriented does not necessitate compromising away one's objectives; it includes firmly voicing one's interests and beliefs. A striking feature of such principled speech is that it can be introduced unilaterally! It does not require general agreement on norms governing discourse. Initiation by one party is an invitation and challenge to other parties to reciprocate. The speeches of Martin Luther King Jr. (1986) exemplify this approach. They make forthright and passionate claims for King's constituency, but also call for community and liberty for all. Calls for justice are rooted in the common values of the United States Constitution and Declaration of Independence. The recent truth and reconciliation process in South Africa is another example of the spirit of conflict-resolution in public discourse. In this example, judicial processes are adapted, not for a win-lose adversarial contest, but for a collaborative effort to ascertain the truth and heal wounds.

Formal, mediated conflict resolution may be introduced into the mix of public communication on many issues: from interstate negotiations on water resources and public-private conflicts over land use, to common ground discussions on abortion rights; from interracial and interethnic dialogue groups, to labor-management negotiation. In formal conflict-resolution, all the aspects of public judgment are present, but as explicit parts of an agreed-upon process, supervised by a skilled mediator. Inquiry into creative solutions is stressed—with the assistance of expert consultants. Formal negotiations reach the broader public when representatives report to their constituencies, and publish their agreements. In this way, citizens learn about new policy options, participate in new social experiments, and witness the changing perspectives of opinion leaders.

The temptation is great, however, to win short-term political victories by appealing to the fears and hatreds of one's constituents, by manipulating symbols, polarizing issues, and escalating conflicts. As Hickman points out, Reinhold Niebuhr argued, against Dewey, that mobilization can flow from "the right dogmas, symbols and emotionally potent oversimplifications" (Hickman, 1990:186). This is all the more true in U.S. electoral politics of today, when vast congressional districts increase the influence of broadcast media and reduce the impact of face-to-face campaigning. In Dewey's view, manipulative popular mobilization will miscarry; "democratic ends demand democratic means for their realization" (FC:175). Instead, looking to the long run, citizens must be educated to resist such emotional and symbolic appeals, whether from the left or the right. Given this account of the theory of public deliberation, let us now consider a concrete example.

Abortion Rights: Social Conflict, Public Judgment, and Conflict-Resolution

Let us examine the discourse on abortion: in today's public debate; in experimental common ground dialogues, and as might be found in the future. Today's abortion controversy reflects the historical experience of legalized abortion after *Roe v. Wade,* and the attendant conflict and political struggle. Yankelovich—using less-stringent criteria than Dewey's—argues that the present abortion discussion is a "coming to public judgment" (1991:26–27). He sees a settled majority opinion based on experience of the legalized abortion quasi-experiment at two levels—

personal and historical. A substantial portion of the electorate has direct, or close second-hand experience with personal abortion decisions. More than a million women have abortions each year, and many others consider abortion and reject it. Their deliberations and decisions on abortion as a personal choice are also participated in by family members and close friends. How all of these people evaluate the decision and its aftermath will greatly influence their stance on the public policy issue of the legality of abortion. A large number of women find this experience morally and medically unproblematic, and of benefit to their health and their family's well-being. Politically, they form a strong constituency in favor of legal abortion with minimal restrictions. Some remember, furthermore, how problematic and dangerous abortions were before legalization (Gold-Steinberg and Stewart 1998), and are fervently pro-choice. Some, who are personally untroubled by abortion, however, are indifferent to the public issue, taking its availability for granted. Others, due to exceptional circumstances, consider themselves entitled to such services, but do not support abortion rights generally. On the other hand, there are women who decide to have abortions and later grow to deeply regret their choice. Some of them will not oppose legalized abortion though they now reject that choice themselves. Some will decide that other women need to be protected from such fateful choices, and will become actively pro-life. Similarly, many women who reject abortion for themselves join pro-life ranks politically, but some eschew political involvement, some support choice of abortion for other women, and some, regretting their decision, shift both their personal and political stances. All of these varied reactions to direct personal experience contribute to the overall public deliberation and judgment formation.

Citizens, generally, have access both to information and to persuasive appeals about the consequences of legal abortion. The media report that more than a million legal abortions are performed each year. There are also widespread anecdotal accounts of some women having multiple abortions—allegedly using abortion as a means of birth control. Statistics and anecdotes about teenage pregnancy, unmarried motherhood, and welfare dependency form a larger context in which this information is evaluated. People hear claims from the pro-choice side that complications from abortion procedures are extremely rare, and less than the rate reported for pregnancy; and from the pro-life side that a woman runs a significant risk of compromising her fertility if she has an abortion. These data and claims are juxtaposed with reports of womens' injury and death due to illegal abortions before *Roe v. Wade*.

Citizens are exposed to the direct action of the pro-choice and pro-life movements—the clinic protests and defenses, the rallies, demonstrations, and public speeches—and the press coverage these generate. Despite the polarized, inflammatory debate, activists have raised public awareness and initiated deliberation processes. Citizens hear arguments about fetal viability, sentience, constitutional rights and so on. Perhaps more important is the way the issues are framed, especially the images and metaphors used—the pictures of fetuses, the symbol of the coathanger representing unsafe abortions, and so on (Woliver 1996). The intensive direct action of Operation Rescue, with its shouting and blockading, mobilizes and energizes some pro-life constituents, but simultaneously produces a backlash, mobilizing pro-choice sympathizers and raising disturbing questions for moderates and those on the fence (Ginsburg 1998:232, 235, 239). (These effects on public discourse are aside from the intimidating effects on providers and patients, and resulting clinic protection legislation.) In viscerally rejecting extreme tactics, moderate citizens discover that they are unpersuaded by the arguments that justify them. Violent actions, bombings and murders, and other tactics push the abortion-is-murder thesis to its extreme consequences and chillingly demonstrate the logic of certain arguments, in a way words never could. Revulsion against antiabortion violence prompts many citizens to renewed deliberation and revision of their positions (Ginsburg 1998:239).

Many people experience conflict and dissonance due to cross-pressures arising from their group memberships and roles, and due to clashes in principles they have internalized (Sutton et al. 1961). A parent may continue to love and support a daughter whose choice on abortion is contrary to the parent's values. One's moral commitment may clash with the compromises required to build a political coalition to achieve another moral goal. People are often pulled in one way by religious ties and in another by the values of their professional community. Social mobility may move people into neighborhoods with very different values from their community of origin. People deliberate over such conflicts, often with the result of moderating or complicating their prior beliefs.

Over many years of such experience, exposure, conflict, and deliberation, people tend to form considered judgments on the policy of legalized abortion. They report to interviewers that their positions are stable, and this self-assessment is confirmed by aggregate data, over time (Yankelovich 1991:26–28). Only a small minority opposes legal abortion under any circumstances, and only a minority accepts legal abortion without restriction. Most survey respondents accept some constraint, like waiting periods or parental consent for teenagers. Many are shocked at the sheer number of abortions performed, and are offended that some women have multiple abortions. Yet most people stop far short of banning abortion, indicating that, whether consciously or not, they don't accord the status of full human personhood to the fetus. A strong majority approves of legal abortion where the mother's life is at stake, where there will be serious birth defects, and where the pregnancy is a consequence of rape (Yankelovich 1991:28). These stable, middle-of-the-road majority views are what Yankelovich takes to be public judgment.

Will this rough public judgment on the abortion issue continue to be stable or will it change in predictable or unpredictable ways? Murders of abortion providers in 1994 led to a sharp increase in support for pro-choice groups, from 29% to 38% (Ginsburg 1998:239). On the whole, however, since Yankelovich's 1991 report, there appears to have been a modest shift toward more restrictive views on abortion, reflecting continuing efforts of the pro-life movement and a conservative shift on a range of issues. Opinion also seems to have been unresponsive to new scientific information (Yankelovich 1991:28). Taking a longer term view, the present *modus vivendi* can be upset by generational and demographic effects; by forgetting the human costs of illegal abortion before *Roe v. Wade;* by new impacts from science and reproductive technology, by overall shifts in ideology; and by changing socioeconomic circumstances. In Dewey's view, the possibility of such changes does not undermine the meaningfulness of present public judgments. Moral issues are not settled once and for all, and judgments should, indeed, be responsive to changing conditions.

Assuming that these expressions of public opinion are indeed considered decisions, are they moral decisions, and if so, are they adequate moral decisions? If one distinguishes between a narrow range of moral reasons and a larger range of deliberative or prudential reasons, then these decisions do not qualify as moral ones (Maffetone 1998; Williams 1973). If one defines "moral" more broadly, as Dewey does, including such considerations as the health consequences of illegal abortion, and the overall drift of society's sexual and reproductive mores, then these are clearly moral decisions. Are they good moral decisions? If one insists that good reasons are limited to valid logical deductions from universal moral principles, then these decisions would not qualify. Applying Dewey's criterion of deliberation as dramatic rehearsal and decision as conflict-resolution, the evaluation is a mixed one. Citizens appear to have entered upon such deliberation, but not, in most cases, to have carried it out to the full extent that Dewey proposes.

Dewey imagines a future public, much better equipped to conduct personal and public deliberations along the lines presented in this chapter and the previous one. A more democratic polity would institute many forums for formal and informal dialogue on the issue of legalized abortion.

Common Ground Dialogue

A social experiment of dialogue on abortion has been in progress since 1989 (Gorney 1998:526). After pioneering efforts in St. Louis, Buffalo, and Madison received national news coverage, common ground dialogues were developed in a number of other U.S. cities, and a national network was formed—the Common Ground Network for Life and Choice (Jacksteit and Kaufmann 1995; Arbogast 1994; Kelly 1994). These efforts were motivated by dismay at the escalating incivility in clinic protests and public debates, and violent attacks on clinic property and personnel. They also reflected a perceived stalemate in the courts and legislatures. After the 1989 *Webster* and 1992 *Casey* decisions by the U.S. Supreme Court, legalized abortion was neither going to be revoked, nor made more easily available (Gorney 1998:486–496, 518–520). Pro-life and pro-choice representatives met and discovered shared concerns about, for example, prenatal and maternal health care, and opportunities to act upon them. Common ground dialogues got under way.

Specific procedures of common ground dialogue include the following (Jacksteit and Kaufman 1995). The first phase in a typical structured common ground dialogue has participants introduce themselves with biographical information. This establishes the common humanity of the participants and dispels stereotypes. Membership in each group is more diverse than the other group expects. Second, participants tell each other the stories of how they came to their views—with those on the other side committed to listen actively and not pass judgment. These distinctly individual personal narratives further undermine stereotypes and evoke empathy, if not agreement. They also provide material out of which broader interests may be articulated. A third phase may be brainstorming on values, concerns, and issues on which both sides can agree. Fourth, policy initiatives may be considered, to achieve these common goals. A fifth and final phase, for some groups, is joining together to work politically to enact these policies—an outcome achieved for a time in St. Louis, and, on an enduring institutionalized basis, in Buffalo.

Some of the substantive outcomes of common ground dialogues are now presented. Pro-life participants in St. Louis pressed for adoption as an alternative. The pro-choice representatives had neither seen adoption as part of their responsibility, nor as a desirable option for most women. They were persuaded, however, to think of it as an aspect of choice, and they opened an adoption service in their clinic office (Gorney 1998:526). In many dialogue groups, the idea of reducing abortion by preventing unwanted pregnancies arises (Webne-Behrman 1996:19). There is some agreement that teenage girls are subject to peer pressure for early sexual activity, making it neither a voluntary choice, nor a healthy one. Teaching young people to resist peer pressure is acceptable to both sides (Jacksteit 1996:1). Creating wholesome, supervised group activities for teenagers is another point of common ground. Some of those opposed to legal abortion have also opposed sex education in the schools, or insisted on abstinence-only sex education. But this response has been in the context of sex education programs designed by experts, and experienced by many parents and interested citizens as imposed upon them. In Wisconsin, a sex education program which stressed parent participation was worked out together by representatives of pro-life and pro-choice groups. The joint planning group discovered that when parents are present during sex education presentations, and can discuss the issues with their children on the spot, the parents are open to hearing views with which they disagree (Maggi Cage, personal communciation, May 1998). Of course, disagreement still arises in common ground discussions regarding some of the means to pregnancy prevention, such as abstinence and contraception. Again, common ground groups have found it more constructive to leave core commitments off the table and to search for areas of agreement.

RESISTANCE TO DIALOGUE; CHANGE IN BELIEF; WEB OF BELIEF

People are not exactly lining up in droves to join common ground dialogue groups. This is hardly surprising. Mainstream schooling puts a premium on having the right answers. The quest for certainty, which Dewey critiques and struggles against, is still firmly ensconced in education and culture in the United States. The schools, the news media, entertainment, and everyday lives socialize us for adversarial debate.

Few models of dialogue are offered, much less experience and skills. Add to this picture the ordinary human propensities to demonize adversaries, to fear the new, to take opposed views as threats to one's own identity (ION: 54–55, 162; 1936: 133–134; PP: 59). The response to these obstacles has been to develop a social movement for conflict-resolution, mediation, and common ground dialogue, as discussed in the next chapter. Formats are designed that maximize support and safety for individuals and facilitate successful problem solving. Skilled mediators and discussion leaders are trained, the idea of dialogue is promoted, and participants are recruited. People who have positive experiences with the process often join this movement and recruit others.

Resistance to common ground dialogue is not only driven by inexperience and anxiety. There are believers who are certain about their positions and see no point at all in talking with those who disagree with them. There are political and organizational activists who approach the abortion issue strategically, finding polarized debate and escalated public action to their advantage (Kelly 1994). Polarizing tactics are, unfortunately, very effective, but they also produce a backlash. Indeed, it is just such a backlash that generated the current efforts at common ground dialogue on life and choice. No doubt some believers will never consent to dialogue. Common ground movements must begin with those more amenable, and not stand or fall on their ability to reach the hard-core. Furthermore, not everyone who claims unshakable belief is immune either to dialogue or to change.

Both as citizens and theorists, we tend to take believers' claims of the fixity of their views at face-value. Among friends and acquaintances, we have seen principled and just plain stubborn resistance to change. The classical liberal view tacitly assumes fixity by taking people's preferences as given. The associationist model of cognition takes each tenet to be held independently, not subject to the pressures of dissonance among ideas. If we examine the matter reconstructively, however, we see that people do change their views. They move, for example, from religious denomination to denomination, and in and out of active church membership. Churches change their doctrine over time, and contain factions. Within the pro-life movement, there are conflicts over strategy, and organizational schisms (Risen and Thomas 1998). People and institutions have complex webs of interconnected beliefs, including inconsistent tenets and vague leanings (Quine and Ullian 1970). Cross-pressures and dissonant beliefs—"disjunction and ambivalence," in

Hochschild's (1993) terms—provide opportunities and incentives for change.

Views on core issues are part of larger world views and political programs, and this creates dialogue opportunities. For many feminists, freeing women to choose or reject abortion, is part of empowering women for choices about relationships, careers, and public life (Solinger 1998; Kaplan 1998; Luker 1984). For many social conservatives, preventing abortions is part of a general restoration of traditional values, including reducing the divorce rate, reintroducing prayer and bible reading in public life, controlling pornography, reducing federal government regulation and social welfare provisions, and so on. A common ground dialogue can be envisioned in which these broader views and programs are discussed productively. Though there is a vast difference between these positions and communication would no doubt be fraught with difficulties, there is still an opportunity to search beneath the opposed positions for underlying interests on which there may be some overlap.

A Hypothetical Outcome

Suppose a multifaceted common ground program to reduce unwanted pregnancies was started, and succeeded in drastically reducing the teenage pregnancy rate. The salience of the legalized abortion issue would likely decline for the electorate as a whole, and even for many one-time activists. The core members of pro-choice and pro-life groups would, presumably, maintain their beliefs, and continue their electoral, legislative, and legal struggles. But other interest groups that sought to make their electoral fortunes by linking up with these movements, would lose interest. The issue would, for all intents and purposes, be settled—settled, as so many issues are—by attrition and obsolescence, and by generational change, not by clinching arguments, or full consensus (1910; Kuhn 1970). That is to say, a successful social experiment on pregnancy reduction would be a major force for reorientation of moral emphases.

Faye Ginsburg (1998) compares today's struggle over abortion with the controversy over teaching evolution in the pre-World War II era. Though that struggle is seeing a minor revival today—illustrating that no issue is ever settled with certainty—it was largely settled in the manner just described, by attrition among activists and a gradually coalescing public judgment among citizens generally. In Dewey's view, such an outcome would indeed represent a public moral judgment and a valid one. This perspective on morality is sharply at odds with the mainstream tradition, which would likely view such an outcome as expedient, not moral, principled or reasoned. On the contrary, Dewey would argue that it is by just such political struggle, dialogue, social experiment, and coming to public judgment that our moral principles and our entire moral system have been formed. Losing sight of their origins, we mistakenly see these judgments as eternal moral truths. This is analogous to the positivist misconstrual of scientific truth.

It is unlikely, however, that unwanted pregnancies would decline a great deal due to the narrowly focused programs suggested above. The question of more fundamental determinants in the socioeconomic structure, therefore, would, sooner or later need to be faced. Common ground dialogues—which have been confined to issues of pregnancy and birth, and offer specific solutions adapted to existing economic conditions—would need to expand their horizons. A narrow focus, to be sure, offers a great advantage; enabling participants to devise actions that they themselves can implement. Once rapport has been built up around common ground and joint action, however, it should be possible to tackle broader, less tractable issues—to ask about transformation, not just adaptation. Participants might begin by asking why a single wage-earning parent today has so much difficulty supporting a family. Why have the real wages of many working people declined? How is this related to technological change, union busting, high interest rates, ongoing high rates of unemployment, globalization, and the like? What shifts in economic policies and systems might alleviate these conditions, providing for a closer approximation to full employment at a living wage? If enough rapport and trust has been established in earlier discussions, it might be possible to examine sensitive questions of social class and social mobility, as experienced by the participants themselves—for example, the sense of powerlessness of the majority of single women who do not have the skills, education, or professional credentials that command jobs, adequate wages, and respect. How equality of opportunity could be achieved in the United States, in fact instead of in fantasy, might be addressed. It is Dewey's hope that some day informed discussion of the basic organization of production and distribution will characterize the political participation of ordinary citizens. And growth of such discussion out of narrower concerns, out of initially polarized and fractious debate, is one way he envisages this occurring. Conflict-resolution and common ground dialogue are the means that make such a transition possible. As shown in

Dewey's theory, and in this case study, public deliberation is essential for democratic life (CD:228). Let us now consider Dewey's program for fostering deliberation.

Fostering Deliberation

In ethics, as in science, Dewey is less concerned with any particular substantive output of deliberation/inquiry than he is with fostering the process. He would increase the occasions and opportunities for deliberation, by creating communities in which people have power to make significant decisions. People in self-governing communities encounter urgent ethical dilemmas and have strong incentives to resolve them wisely. In Dewey's view, membership in such communities should be provided as early as possible in childhood, and continue throughout adulthood. Thus, the heart of progressive education is creating a small community within the school, and the heart of democracy is creating both the Great Community, and smaller communities on the shop floor, in the voluntary association, the neighborhood, the house of worship, and so on (see PP; 1909:272; EBNS). For people to be free to deliberate fully on ethical choices, there must also be relief from the crushing burden of economic insecurity and alienating work in a cyclic economy and a hierarchical workplace (EBNS:319–320). Dewey envisages a benign circularity in which structures which foster deliberation lead to deliberations which endorse and advance such structures.

In conjunction with opportunities for deliberation, Dewey advocates training in the skills and habits of inquiry—through education for adults, as well as children. Skills should be taught through hands-on work, guided by teachers and mentors who foster the student's problem-solving rather than dispense answers—encouraging them to articulate their thoughts and feelings and to sustain deliberation despite the unease of lacking an answer. Part of such training would be in the natural sciences, where Dewey sees the highest development of methods of inquiry. Science would also be taught in a hands-on way, with students rediscovering classic findings. The goal would not be to create budding scientists, so much as to emphasize broad aspects of scientific inquiry readily applicable to diverse fields and enterprises, including ethical deliberation.

Scientific inquiry involves imagination, as well as deductive reasoning and methodical gathering of data, and this too must be fostered. Similarly, Dewey promotes the development of moral imagination. He suggests the arts as the best pedagogical resource for exemplifying and developing the ability to imagine other ways of life, other specific lives, needs, and purposes (AE:Ch. 14). History and anthropology also serve this function. Some things, however, must first be experienced before they come to be desired (HNC:22–23, 53). Dewey advocates field placements and apprenticeships to expand people's range of experience (see ST). In this way, many desires, capacities, and meanings of the individual are evoked, and the likelihood of discovering novel options that harmonize conflicting tendencies is enhanced.

Deliberation is fostered by encouraging people to tell each other their stories of ethical dilemmas, deliberations, and decisions. Dewey would foster a gradual transition from narrative into reflection—articulating and critiquing the process of deliberation, and the substantive considerations deployed within deliberation. Deliberation becomes, then, one phase of a larger ongoing process of moral development. Philosophical theorists bring further articulation, critique, and organization to that process. Drawing on public experience, they also introduce their conclusions back into public deliberation, through books, courses in moral problems, lectures and sermons, and editorial essays. "It is not the business of moral theory to provide a ready-made solution to large moral perplexities. . . . The function of theory is not to furnish a substitute for personal [deliberative] choice but to be an instrument for rendering deliberation more effective and hence choice more intelligent" (E:316). At best, ethical theory can clarify and organize the tangle of considerations that arise in ethical dilemmas. But ethical theory all too often raises its own confusions, leaving us stranded in interminable debates, on issues that cannot be settled by argument. At worst, ethical theory, like science when misused, can become a new authority to replace the older customary world view. Substituted for awareness, its abstractions imposed on the situation, it can blind people to their own experience.

As we turn, in the next section to Dewey's normative and metaethical theories, we should bear in mind that which Dewey considers primary— the deliberation process itself. In narrowing our focus, we risk inviting interminable debate on specific tenets; although Dewey offers these not as demonstrable truths, but as hypotheses, testable only in experience. Nonetheless, in order to thoroughly review Dewey's writings, and also compare them with mainstream accounts, I present these theories here. Again, it must be emphasized that Dewey encourages us to embrace the open-ended quality of ethical deliberation. Dewey, as philosopher, provides the intellectual rationale for staying with uncertainty and bringing resolution out of it. As political theorist, Dewey calls for a society that provides the material support and educational fostering that maximize citizens' opportunity and capability for ethical deliberation. Let us now briefly consider Dewey's views on theoretical issues.

The Nature of Ethical Choice: Metaethics

The theoretical work of philosophers of ethics is, for Dewey, the same as that for any moral agent, differing only in intensity of pursuit and refinement of analysis. The agent looks back over past decisions and begins to articulate the processes and principles involved, in the hope of conducting future deliberations with more awareness and wisdom. "What is called moral theory is but a more conscious and systematic raising of the question which occupies the mind of any one who in the face of moral conflict and doubt seeks a way out through [deliberation]" (TML: 5). Dewey's reconstruction of the process of deliberation suggests answers to questions about the nature of the moral enterprise—metaethical questions. Thus several metaethical positions have already been articulated. First, ethical principles are hypotheses which are instruments for exploring new ethical dilemma situations. Second, discovery is primary, and justification follows in its wake. Third, ethical judgments are tested and justified when they become reflectively settled practices and fruitful principles—when the unification that yields them proves to be genuine and enduring. Fourth, these principles are common to both ethics and science. My analysis continues, now, with the classic question of presumed conflicts between self-interest and duty. This opens the way to an analysis of Dewey's conception of duty, which, in turn, suggests the question of moral motivation. I claim, with Dewey, that human ethical motivation is virtually universal. Possible exceptions to this generalization are taken up and refuted. In this context, I propose a Deweyan dialogical as opposed to an argumentative approach to ethical discourse. Next, I apply this approach to the question of encounter between distinct ethical traditions, and end by comparing Dewey's account with several mainstream theories.

Duty: Conflict of Self-Interest and Duty

To explore further the metaethical implications of Dewey's theory of deliberation, let us consider a classic perplexity: how to resolve the conflict between self-interest and duty, or love and duty. Dewey criticizes

the manner in which this question is framed. There is no self existing in
isolation from others. We become selves in a social medium, the family.
Thus, the interests of other individuals, and of the family group, are internalized as concerns of the self. Later, our social environment expands
to larger groups and society as a whole, and these contribute to our identity. Thus the very idea of conflict between the atomic individual and society is a misunderstanding (PP:186–191; E:323–325). Different roles,
different aspects of our social self, however, pull us in different directions. Nonauthoritarian families and societies foster individuation, even
as they place their stamp upon us. As we become increasingly reflective,
conscious, and intentional in our choices, explicit conflicts will arise between broader duties and interests, and narrower loyalties and desires
(E:228–229). Such conflicts are not understood as morality versus self-
interest, or individual versus society. Duties can be interests of the
self—not simply external impositions of authority, or disembodied commands of reason. And one's narrower concerns are not necessarily
"mere" self-interest, but can be intimate responsibilities to others and
to one's self. The resolution of such conflicts, then, is not a special case;
it coincides with ethical deliberation and decision, generally. It requires
identifying broader underlying interests and working out options that
lie in the overlap among those interests (E:248).

Contrary to Bernard Williams's (1973) separation of the "deliberative
ought" and the "moral ought," for Dewey they are one and the same.
The right and the good, the moral and the ethical—these are not taken
as distinct spheres. There is no "priority of right," or "supremacy of the
moral" (Rawls 1993:6, 173; Williams 1973:185). Each pole of the conflict involves both interests and responsibilities, and one seeks out the
overlap between broader underlying conceptions of these objectives.
Dewey points out, for example, that if one is to be in adequate physical
and emotional condition to take care of others effectively, one has a responsibility to take care of oneself, and vice-versa (E:294). There is also
the poetic formulation: "I could not love thee half so much, loved I not
honor more." Let us examine in detail Dewey's general conception of
duty underlying this analysis.

Dewey is convinced that duty is indeed an independent factor in ethical deliberation, not merely a proxy for the good, or enlightened self-
interest, or imposed authority (E:216; see also 1930b; Edel and Flower
1985). Duty certainly begins, in childhood, as an externally imposed parental command. But the authority of that command is inseparable from
a child's feelings of affection, belonging, and gratitude. These feelings

contribute to the constitution of the child's self (E:218). As children grow up, they are introduced to the larger communities and society to which their family belongs, and their sense of duty broadens. Duty to country is also suffused with affection and gratitude. In adulthood, when a command of duty comes into conflict with other values, it is subjected to articulation and reformulation. The underlying feelings and the sense of self that give duty its motivating force are brought to consciousness, and duty is reaffirmed on a voluntary basis. The specific content of duty, as understood in childhood, however, is open to revision. Some specific duties will be seen as illegitimate, because they cause harm or distribute responsibilities and benefits unfairly (E:225–231). Duty to country, for example, may change from obedience, to an obligation to dissent on behalf of a nation's ideals, against current policies. If a society and its government cease to be just and viable, duty is strained, and the legitimacy of the state is questioned. Duty then obligates the individual to speak and act politically for reform. If this effort is futile, duty to this state—but not the sense of duty—is renounced, and one withdraws or emigrates (Hirschmann 1970).

One corollary of the above analysis of "self-interest versus duty" is that the problem of moral motivation in mainstream ethical theory is not a problem for Dewey. The typical ethical dilemma is between one ethical motivation and another. Selves are social; the interests of others and of the group are internalized. Perhaps this is because human evolution, both biological and cultural, is the evolution of social animals adapted to living in groups (1927a). "No community could endure in which there were not, say, fair dealing, public spirit, regard for life, faithfulness to others" (E:255–256; also 1927a:22; Johnson 1993:237). The moral sentiments of sympathy and affection, and the concept of duty are, therefore, likely to be recognizable across cultures. "But no two communities conceive the objects to which these qualities attach in quite identical ways," so the specific content of sympathy and duty will vary from one place to another (E:256). Thus by adulthood, if not innately, we have built-in prosocial dispositions. There are important exceptions and margins of this universality of ethical motivation, however, that are revealing of the nature of morality.

First, we may be fully socialized persons, but fail to give considerations of duty their due weight, because we avoid deliberating fully. We shunt the promptings of duty off into separate compartments of thought (PP:191). This may free us to pursue a particular duty, or interest, or narrow gratification, but it exacts a price in vague but nagging feeling of disunity—perhaps of guilt or shame. Dewey would challenge and support us in overcoming our compartmentalized thinking, through dialogue, as discussed below.

Second, socialization is a matter of degree. Some families are less effective at developing a sense of duty in their offspring. Perhaps there are sequential stages of moral development, and some people reach higher stages than others—though lower attainment is a matter of opportunity, not of potentiality. Dewey alludes to moral development from customary to reflective morality, in the individual and in the culture (E: 12–14). He sees each episode of moral conflict and resolution as contributing to development. He does not, however, prescribe a single line of development, characterized by specific stages, and irreversibility, such as one finds in Lawrence Kohlberg's (1981) moral development theory. This reflects Dewey's pluralism; he acknowledges the uniqueness of individuals and the immense complexity and variety of ethical values and courses of action. Nonetheless, Dewey sees the fully alive, engaged person as developing throughout life (HNC:208). Dewey agrees with Plato that the full moral meaning of a life can only be known at its end. Dewey points to development through adult socialization—education in its broadest sense. One grows in ethical maturity, and toward self-unification, for example, through the demands and challenges of work and the admonishments and guidance of supervisors, mentors, and fellow workers. "Morals means growth of conduct in meaning—in that kind of meaning which is consequent upon observing the conditions and outcomes of conduct—it is all one with growing. In the largest sense of the word [education], morals is all one with education" (HNC:280).

Third, powerlessness, actual and imagined, has an extraordinary negative impact on the ethical life. When there is no chance of influencing events, there are no dilemmas. One's capacity for making ethical decisions withers or never develops at all (1928a:108; DEA:223). People who numbly or resentfully comply, under the compulsion of illegitimate authority, may act with utter irresponsibility if the constraints are ever weakened. Powerlessness "results in apathy and indifference; a deflection into evasion and deceit; a compensatory over-responsiveness to such occasions as permit untrained preferences to run riot" (1928a:108; also HNC:142). On the other hand, where there are genuine opportunities for influence, individuals may use claims of powerlessness as a rationalization for evading responsibility. Like the existentialists, Dewey points out that responsibility brings with it the anxiety of uncertain outcomes of fateful choices (HNC:216; EN:245–246). We evade that responsibility and anxiety, however, only at the cost of retreat from living (ACF:25; LSA:57; RPh:119). The powerlessness excuse is ubiquitous. Above all, it affects citizen participation in democratic life. Powerlessness occupies a far greater space in personal moral deliberation than it does in mainstream philosophical theory of ethics. Dewey, however, is acutely aware of powerlessness and anxiety, as expressed in "the quest for certainty" (QC), and the retreat into fantasy (LSA:57). Dewey's entire philosophy of ethics, education, and democracy is meant to empower citizens for ethical deliberation and choice—to foster deliberation, as discussed above.

Fourth, in some tyrannical or discriminatory social systems, a countermorality develops. It is considered honorable to disobey laws and defraud institutions; and dishonorable to break solidarity with one's fellow resistors. Behavior, therefore, that is criminal or traitorous from the official perspective, is not amoral, but expresses duty to a different group. This is a problem in social integration and government legitimacy, more than in ethical motivation (PP:147–148).

Fifth, there are individuals with a strong sense of duty toward their kin, friends, and, perhaps, local community, but who deny any responsibility beyond these bounds. These individuals are not amoral, given their sense of duty to those close to them. The limited range of their sense of obligation may be due to feelings of powerlessness, failure of moral imagination, feeling overwhelmed by the immensity of suffering and injustice in the world, resentment against injustices toward themselves, reaction against the hypocrisy of do-gooders, or other reasons and dispositions which reconstructive inquiry would reveal (HNC:294; RPh:206; E:251).

For those concerned with human rights, poverty, and racism—with universal justice and humanitarian issues—the various departures from and exceptions to the expected moral engagement of average persons pose a practical and theoretical problem. We are challenged to reach out to such people and reengage them in the ethical community. Typical responses are: to redouble efforts to justify universalistic ethical theories; to exhort recalcitrant individuals to adopt "the moral point of view"; to issue stern judgments on the immorality of the act; and to blame and punish the person. According to Dewey, argument, exhortation, praise, blame, and punishment are themselves actions to be evaluated on ethical grounds, hence to be chosen or rejected based upon their consequences (E:304). Dewey's evaluation of those consequences is largely negative (HNC:324). He finds exhortation usually futile, abstract rea-

soning incapable of tapping the springs of moral motivation in many
people, and judgment, blame, and punishment often provoking rebellion
(E:254, 316).

Hence, for convicted criminals, Dewey advocates rehabilitative not
punitive justice. More importantly, for average citizens who evade responsibility, Dewey would create positions which would bring them
face-to-face with the consequences of their indifference. The "exigencies of practice" are a far more powerful corrective to moral blindness
than logical argumentation. As for persuasive efforts, Dewey prefers a
dialogical to an exhortative approach. One tells one's own narrative of
engagement in the moral conflicts and decisions of the larger community, and encourages the other to offer the narrative of his withdrawal
from such engagement. One listens receptively to the reasons and feelings that emerge in that narrative—encouraging further articulation and
reflection in the other—and remains open to learning and changing oneself (E:345–346; CD:228). Several social scientists, in their role as interviewers, offer models of respectful listening to views far removed from
their own (Klatch 1987; Luker 1984). A heroic example of empathetic
understanding given to those whose beliefs and behavior one condemns
is the interviews with neo-Nazis conducted by Rafael Ezekiel for his
book *The Racist Mind* (1995). Beyond listening, one communicates one's
own sense of the obligatory nature of ethical injunctions. One appeals to
the person's moral imagination through metaphor and anecdote, through
literary and artistic references, as well as argument. One suggests scenarios that highlight the consequences of not acting. All of this provides
challenge, but also support, which counters the anxiety of responsibility experienced by the other. Thus one may facilitate another's return to
an unfinished deliberative process.

This dialogical approach suggests an answer to the question of encounter between two complete and distinct ethical traditions. The problem of entering into a different perspective, rooted in an unfamiliar
culture, is addressed through presentation that employs narrative, metaphor, and artistic expression, and through listening that employs empathy and moral imagination (AE:286, 332). Once the challenges of
the alternative view are felt, the process of deliberation and conflict-
resolution are initiated—just as for dilemmas within one's own tradition. No overarching norm is required to permit one to judge between
the traditions. An explicit statement as to how one tradition accounts
for the different approach of another may be a by-product, but it is not
the necessary condition for resolution that Alasdair MacIntyre (1988)
suggests. It bears repeating that, in Dewey's view, moral reasoning is but

one aspect of moral deliberation, and one aspect of reflection on the outcome of deliberation. Dewey's deliberative and dialogical approach, and his criterion of reflectively settled practices, suggest how his ethics can be pluralist, but not parochial, relativist, or nihilist (cf. Kekes 1993; Moon 1993a). That is, there can be dialogue across cultures and ethical traditions, nonarbitrary decisions can be made in response to the challenge, and these decisions are justifiable prospectively as they are incorporated into practices that stand up under continuing ethical scrutiny.

Finally, there are those few individuals, presented in the chronicles of psychiatry and criminality, who appear to have no moral compunctions whatsoever—who are designated "sociopathic." Apparently, these people do not experience guilt or shame. Do such people represent an alternative to, and implicit critique of all moral stances? Or are they less than completely human, the exception that proves the rule that morality is an expected aspect of developed human selfhood? Dewey does not dwell on this question, but would likely be in sympathy with the analysis offered today by Peter Singer (1993). Singer sees this largely as an empirical question, as would Dewey, and one to which present-day psychology and psychiatry offer only incomplete and tentative, though tantalizing answers. The alleged sociopath appears to live only for the moment. He is incapable of forming projects, incapable of giving life purpose and meaning. This would be an individual incapacitated for fulfilling the potentiality of human life as Dewey, as well as Aristotle, sees it (H. Putnam 1992:182).

Types of Ethical Theory

Having reviewed Dewey's position on several metaethical questions, I now summarize, and compare and contrast his conclusions with those of mainstream schools of ethical theory: consequentialism, pluralism, Kantianism or deontology, and virtue ethics (E:154–156). Dewey employs concepts and principles drawn from each school, but rejects a presupposition common to all of them—his reconstruction of deliberation yields primarily an ethics of the agent focused on discovery, while these schools presuppose an ethics of the judge concerned exclusively with justification. Deliberation as dramatic rehearsal is concerned with consequences. We follow a scenario out to its outcomes, and decide if these are acceptable or not. This is acceptability, however, for the particular agent engaged in deliberation resolving conflict among a number of incommensurable values, including justice and virtue. It is not, as in typical consequentialist accounts, acceptability for the judge applying some universal criterion of the good. Utilitarianism—a particular form of consequentialism—is rejected by Dewey, as incompatible with his account of deliberation as dramatic rehearsal. He criticizes both its psychological hedonism, as noted earlier, and its distributive standard of the greatest good for the greatest number, discussed below under normative ethics. In assessing consequences, Dewey assumes a plurality of goods, virtues, and duties with no *a priori* or context-free hierarchical ordering among them (RPh:162; E:212, 257–258; see also Kekes 1993; Moon 1993a). Deciding among them is a matter of conflict-resolution. As with duties, the goods humans tend to choose are not arbitrary, but influenced by our biological and cultural evolution as social creatures.

In taking a consequentialist and pluralist path, Dewey opposes the Kantian, or "deontological" type of ethics in which certain acts and principles are known—through reason—to be right, independent of their consequences. Dewey appreciates the Kantian stress on human beings as ends, not means. He is aware of the pervasive appearance of the principle of fairness in people's deliberations. What he rejects is a separate faculty of reason and judgments that acts are right or wrong solely on the basis of reason (E:216–217, 223). Deliberation is seen by some deonotologists as being conducted incessantly and hastily, by fallible and ill-informed people, with capricious results (Pettit 1993:234). Some have concluded that there must be certain actions and orientations that are not on the deliberative agenda—that are simply forbidden. Recall, however, that Dewey's theory includes extant moral principles and habitual responses to established situations, which do prohibit certain actions. (This resembles what Pettit calls a "restrictive," but not a "restricted or rule-consequentialism" [1993:236].) As for emergent situations, general rules are insufficient to determine action, and deliberation is the appropriate response. If well-conducted, it can produce finely tuned responses. Dewey criticizes "the idea that adherence to standards external to experience is the only alternative to confusion and lawlessness" (QC:278). He notes that this view "was once held in science. But knowledge became steadily progressive when it was abandoned" (QC:278). Again, he is stressing discovery as a common thread at a general level in both ethics and science. This is by no means an invitation to moral laxity. Deliberation, as Dewey reconstructs it, is governed by a rigorous coherence standard, in efforts toward unification and conflict-resolution.

In reflective ethics, there will always be a pull toward generalization, but, Dewey claims, this must proceed from concrete cases, through public deliberation. "Communication, sharing, joint participation are the only actual ways of universalizing the moral law and end" (RPh:206). Dewey sees universalization as being in constant tension with the unique qualities of particular people and situations—with no easy resolution. Arguments among feminists, for example, over universal human rights versus policies specific to oppressed groups, cannot be settled by reasoning alone. This conflict must be worked out in practice, through political action, and experimentation, public discourse, and conflict resolution—until public judgment and reflectively settled practices are achieved, or until social change and progress render the conflict obsolete. Dewey observes that principles essential to Kantian ethics, fairness and universalizability, routinely enter into these deliberations but are not the overriding consideration.

In Dewey's account of dramatic rehearsal and conflict-resolution, the Kantian idea that reason and will should overcome passion is at best, a misunderstanding of the process, at worst, a subversion of it. In Dewey's view, there is no independent faculty of will, and even if it did exist, it would have no motivational force since motivation comes from desire (E:175, 221). Ethical choice is a resolution of the conflict between different desires, including ones that are other-regarding. Will, for Dewey, is single-minded pursuit of a course of action, due to the unification of the self achieved by conflict-resolution (176, 256). While rejecting Kant's primacy of reason, Dewey also rejects literal interpretations, or rather misinterpretations, of the Humean notion of reason as the "slave of the passions." Dewey believes that deliberation can transform desire, and lead to more intelligent, more reasonable desires (189–190).

The process of deliberation does not produce an ethics of virtue, in Dewey's view, because the focus of each deliberation is on the needs of the situation and the action appropriate to these needs. Deliberation is not directly concerned with developing a good self. If that objective enters in, it is one among many. Nonetheless, the result of successive deliberative choices in dilemma situations is to develop enduring commitments and life plans, hence character and virtue (E:168–173). Finally, Dewey rejects the "non-cognitivist" position—the notion that ethical statements and choices are mere statements of preference. Ethical choices are the result of painstaking deliberation. They are persuasive to both oneself and others, but corrigible in the light of criticism and further experience. Dewey is not, however, a "cognitivist," in the narrow sense that ethical choices are the outcome of strict logical deduction from principles—much less principles that have authority outside of experience. What we take to be authoritative principles are the product of a long historical and individual process of sifting, in the course of mak-

ing many decisions in specific situations. They are embodied in reflectively settled practices. In summary, Dewey's ethical theory incorporates some features of most of the traditional metaethical approaches,
but is not closely identified with any one of them.

Conclusion: Pluralism and Consequentialism

As reflective morality replaces customary morality in the actual practice of everyday life in complex, diverse society, particularisms tend to
yield to broad pluralism. Systems of moral rules tend to yield to broad
consequentialist approaches. Concern for the physical and emotional
well-being of others, and of the self, tends to replace specific behavioral
rules. This gradual evolution toward pluralism and consequentialism is
contested in each generation by theorists, clerics, and lay people who
would have us return to more traditional rule-bound approaches to ethics. Dewey's debates with Lewis Mumford, Jerome Frank, Robert Hutch-
ins, Mortimer Adler, and others in the late 1930s and early 1940s are a
classic example (Westbrook 1991:515–521)—to say nothing of today's
social conservative attacks on secular humanism. This is a conflict between two approaches to ethics, not between morality and amorality, as
one side would have it (Lakoff 1996). Should one of these orientations
finally prevail in public judgment, after a long period of social experimentation and discourse, one of the great historical dramas will climax,
with significant political consequences. This conflict is complicated,
however, by other tendencies simultaneously at work. A consumption-
oriented capitalism exploits the breakdown of community to sell material goods and sensational forms of entertainment as substitute gra-
tifications (PP:214). Consumerism deflects us altogether from moral
deliberation, even as it undermines authoritarian morality (Barber 1995).
It is the enemy of ethical engagement. Ethical liberals and conservatives
often blame the effects of consumerism on each other, rather than joining to oppose amoral tendencies, based on their shared concern with the
ethical life.

Right, Good, and Virtue: Normative Ethics

Normative ethical theory offers general principles which answer the
question, "what is right, or good, or virtuous." In particular, it indicates

how government should form policies on issues of collective concern. Dewey offers a fairly detailed normative theory, but with a major reservation: this is a descriptive account of the results of public deliberation—results which will be fed back into future deliberation as hypotheses and instruments of exploration. The purpose of normative theory, then, is articulation, clarification, and critique, but not justification—in order to lend clarity to deliberation, but not to supersede it. As in Dewey's—and post-empiricist—philosophy of science, this normative account is offered as "case law," not "statute law."

Based on the examples in the previous chapter, a sense emerges of the sort of substantive ethic produced by the Deweyan deliberation/conflict-resolution process, both in the individual and the community. In the example of parents of a gay son, a religious ethic is transformed to prohibit exploitative and irresponsible sexuality, but not a particular sexual orientation. In the abortion example, an ethic of responsibility is generalized to include responsibility for self as well as others. In the conscientious objector example, a nonviolent ethic is enlarged from the opposition to violence, to working for a nonviolent world. The posture that emerges is an ethic that rejects unalterable principles and narrow prohibitions, not for moral looseness, but for broader, more integrative, and more responsive conceptions of the good and the right, the just, the caring, and the virtuous.

Justice and Rights

Human rights are high-ranking values for Dewey, but he rejects the view that rights exist in nature apart from historical experience, and that rights are inherent in individual personhood. These positions, he argues, are based on the fiction of individuality as complete prior to and independent of society. Dewey argues for civil liberties, for the Bill of Rights, on three grounds. They are necessary for a democratic society, they follow from considerations of fairness, and they advance the good of individuals. Since Dewey sees individuality as a relationship to community, he is not positing rights against society. The logic of arguments for rights does not explain, however, how they have come to exist. Rights have come to exist because the disadvantaged struggled for them, against dominant groups, through political and military action. Citizen action has created space for public deliberation on rights claims. Over time, these rights become established in public judgment. In retrospect, we

may see these rights as dictated by reasons. But such reasons did not determine the social practices. Like crucial experiments in physics, these
reasons are honored after the fact. This is not to say that reasons are
empty, but that they are not sufficient. Principled leaders, like Jefferson,
may have seen beyond their contemporaries in understanding the logic
of fairness and rights against slavery, but still made political compromises or yielded to atavistic tendencies in themselves. Today, when so
many groups have successfully staked a claim to rights, the universality
of such rights might seem evident. But the boundaries are still unset-
tled. One of the latest claimant groups, gays and lesbians, has had to
fight the political battle all over again. Also remaining to be settled is
whether the rights now accorded to human persons extend to fetuses,
animals, and ecological systems.

On the question of justice, Dewey sees the criterion of fairness as inescapable. It is clearly part of our historical inheritance in a democratic
society. It is affirmed, and becomes even more prominent, as customary
morality is replaced by reflective morality. The centrality of fairness is
limited, however, by two considerations. First, fairness is a criterion for
compromise in zero-sum games; it is crucial for dividing a fixed stock
of goods. For Dewey, however, the good and the right are discovered
by transforming zero-sum games to cooperative games where a greater
stock of good is available. Second, like the communitarians, Dewey believes that judgments of fairness cannot be made independent of judgments of good. "The classic conception of justice is derived from Roman
law, and shares its formal legalistic character. It is 'rendering to another
that which is his . . . property, repute and honor' . . . But in its wide meaning the formula only raises a question: What does belong to man, as
man?" (E:252).

Why is fairness a criterion at all? For Dewey, it is sufficient, at least
for the present, that fairness is a reflectively settled principle that has
survived countless tests. If one wishes, however, one can speculate, with
Dewey, on its ubiquity. Concern for fairness arises for children early in
their development (MW5:526). Conceivably, it is an innate propensity.
Perhaps it has some evolutionary survival value. Perhaps the insistence
on fairness has to do with our built-in capacity for esthetic appreciation,
our sense of balance and symmetry, as much as our capacity for inferential reason (E:271). Perhaps some concept of fairness is necessary for the
survival of social groups, and is socialized into each new generation. In
any case, it is the coupling of emotional sympathy and sensitivity to context with abstract fairness that motivates ethical behavior; this keeps

sympathy from being partial and capricious in its objects and justice from becoming harsh and cruel (E:249, 270).

Distribution

   Dewey's approach to distributive ethics begins with critique of the distinction between production and distribution, which tends to produce grinding work and frivolous leisure. If one broadens the question of distribution to include nonmaterial values, and those that can only be attained by doing meaningful work, then a Deweyan analysis can proceed. Distributional issues, in Dewey's view, should be worked out through conflict-resolution. First, this means emphasis on creative solutions which increase the satisfaction of all stakeholders—increasing the "pie," rather than dividing a fixed pie according to a particular formula. This approach contrasts with the mainstream zero-sum view, represented by Moon, who writes: "in a world in which desired positions and social goods are relatively scarce, we can only alter the forms and distribution of disadvantage" (Moon 1993a:176). Second, it means distribution that is context-sensitive—ascertaining the interests at stake for particular individuals and groups, and the options available in the particular situations. (Cumulative experience with specific situations permits the extraction of general principles.) Third, each value at stake in distributional conflicts also calls for critique. Before principles of ownership, entitlement, and duty can be agreed upon, for example, the concepts and the frames within which they are understood must be examined. Dewey critiques the notion that each entrepreneur creates, and rightfully owns, the wealth that he or she appropriates (PP:211). The fruit of the activities of individuals is conditional on the society's fund of technology, infrastructure, resources, regulations, and cooperative relationships. Fourth, as does Rawls, Dewey seeks not only fair distribution of existing income, but consideration of how distribution affects investment and thus future income, and how distribution affects opportunity and democratic participation. Fifth, not one, but many principles should be fed into the discussion—as perspectives that clarify what is at stake in each case. These include the utilitarian greatest good for the greatest number, Pareto optimality, meritocracy, Rawls's difference principle, Walzer's (1983) pluralistic idea of different principles for different spheres, and "from each according to their ability and to each according to their needs." In Dewey's view, however, outside of action and deliberation, none of these principles can be established as fairer than the others in all cases, simply on the basis of argument. Whether desires are satiable, and whether there can be distributions that increase everyone's share, depends on what sorts of material and nonmaterial goods are valued. Let us now consider Dewey's account of the good.

THE GOOD AND SELF-REALIZATION

A person's notions of what is good are transformed through deliberation and conflict-resolution (Rosenthal 1986:191). If we start by seeking the immediate satisfaction of particular impulses and desires, we soon encounter conflict among these. If the conflict is creatively resolved, we form more "inclusive and enduring" ends, in which the separate desires become part of a larger purpose (E:185, 189, 205–206, 308; HNC:156, 195; also MW11:36, regarding enduring ends in the ethical theory of Hobbes). Conflicting impulses block each other, and this accounts for prudent restraint on impulsive acts. It produces an ethic of moderation comparable to Aristotle's. The image of moderation and integration that emerges should not, however, be confused with one of sour constraint or mediocrity (E:258; HNC:160). The integrated self is capable of spontaneity, creativity, and, when appropriate, the free play of impulse. We resolve conflict creatively, "sublimating" simple desires under more complex and long-term purposes (HNC:141, 156; also 195; E:270); this accounts for the choice of so-called "higher" pleasures—such as those obtained from cultivation of the intellect, and from appreciation of or participation in the fine arts (E:197, 200).

This observation avoids the difficulty of importing some external standard to certify that certain kinds of pleasures are intrinsically higher than others. Referring to John Stuart Mill's view, Dewey writes: "Mill's argument points not so much to a different quality in different pleasures, as it does to a difference in quality between an enduring satisfaction of the whole self and a transient satisfaction of some isolated element in the self" (E:197). Dewey suggests that "inclusive and enduring ends" and unification and expansion of the self (E:197, 270; HNC:210, 212, 283)—growth or self-realization—are two sides of the same coin. If people, under favorable circumstances, tend to choose goods that are nonmaterial and satiable, as Dewey hypothesizes, then the problem of distribution is greatly eased. Furthermore, the possibility of mutual self-realization in a cooperative community obviates the zero-sum struggle over fixed stocks of material goods, and scarce amounts of prestige in a competitive culture.

For Dewey, growth, or self-realization, is a by-product of individual ethical deliberation, but is an explicit goal of social policy and the design of institutions. It is a goal embedded in tradition: "an essential part of the creed of liberalism," "the cause for which liberalism enduringly stands" (LSA:91, 93). Dewey's account of the self and its growth can be stated briefly. The self is constituted by meanings and capacities. Meanings are sensed and understood interconnections between aspects of experience. Self-realization, or growth, involves unification and increase in meanings: "increase of present meaning, which involves multiplication of sensed distinctions as well as harmony, unification" (HNC:283). Dewey takes for granted a common understanding of the term capacities and gives no definition. He takes a pluralistic view of capacities, as he does of virtues (E:257–258). Capacities are extraordinarily diverse; there is no obvious short list or conventional catalogue. Particular capacities are abstractions from the integrated acts required to achieve goals. They should not be reified by treating them as distinct self-sufficient faculties. Self-realization involves the development and actualization of capacities. "The ultimate aim of education is nothing other than the creation of human beings in the fullness of their capacities" (LW5:297). Growth enriches life and increases one's capacity for ethical deliberation; it becomes both the goal of and a means to an ethical community. Dewey conceives this goal of growth from egalitarian, pluralist, and Pragmatist viewpoints. He intends the opportunity for growth to be open to all people, regardless of class, race, creed, gender, or other group attribute. Growth is an extremely general goal, leaving great room for variation in actual content. Dewey critiques the atomistic individualist model of growth, which unreflectively mirrors the practices of men in a market-dominated public sphere. Dewey's image of growth toward increased meaning, integration, and fulfillment of capacities, within an interdependent community, approximates the conceptions of higher stages of development in Gilligan (1982), Loevinger (1976), Maslow (1954), and C. Rogers (1961). Maslow and Rogers, however, have been criticized, whether fairly or not, as "expressive individualists" (Bellah et al. 1985; Taylor 1989; Lasch 1979). Dewey, on the other hand, takes a communitarian view. Perhaps a new category, expressive communitarianism, might be coined for his approach. This is a broader conception of human flourishing than Kohlberg's Kantian conception of higher stages of moral reasoning, trenchantly criticized by Habermas (1992).

Self-realization is a by-product of ethical deliberation, which challenges us to new awareness, evokes previously unrecognized dispositions, stimulates inquiry, and culminates in unification. Dewey speaks of "the identity of the moral process with the processes of specific growth" (RPh:186). Growth is the "end" of deliberation in the sense of end-as-outcome. For the most part, however, self-realization should not be the end-in-view of deliberation, since this blinds us to the needs and potentialities of the situation (E:302). One could easily substitute the term, "self-realization," for the term "happiness," in the following sentence. "Happiness is fundamental in morals only because happiness is not something to be sought for, but is something now attained . . . whenever recognition of our ties with nature and with fellow-men releases and informs our action" (HNC:265).

Though Dewey counsels against making growth the end-in-view of our deliberations, he hypothesizes a disposition toward, or need for the development and expression of our potentialities. "Human nature must have present realization"; in its absence there is an enduring "sense of misery" (HNC:274). "The capacities which constitute the self demand fulfillment" (E,1908:331; MW5). Dewey understands the self as process, selfhood exists through change. "Life is development, living, growing is life" (DE:49). "In the strictest sense it is impossible for the self to stand still" (E:306). Therefore, he answers his own question, "what is owed to man?" with: "the opportunity to become all he is capable of becoming" (E:252). This becomes the explicit goal, the end-in-view, for social ethics—for the design of public policies and institutions. "The true significance of 'the greatest good of the greatest number' is that social conditions should be such that all individuals can exercise their own initiative in a social medium which will develop their personal capacities and reward their efforts. That is, it is concerned with providing the objective political, economic, and social conditions which will enable the greatest possible number because of their own endeavors to have a full and generous share in the values of living" (E:251–252). But Dewey is not simply calling for self-fulfillment for atomized individuals. Dewey's broad social goal, his democratic commitment, is that individuals be able to deliberate fully and decide wisely and thus contribute as much as possible to each other and their community. "The best guarantee of collective efficiency and power is liberation and use of the diversity of individual capacities in initiative, planning, foresight, vigor and endurance" (RPh:209). This is tantamount to saying that the goal is self-realization for citizens, since, in a benign circularity, capacity to deliberate is a product of self-realization, and self-realization is a product of well-conducted deliberation. "When the identity of the moral process with the processes of specific growth is realized . . . it will also be evident

that the test of all the institutions of adult life is their effect in further-
ing continued education" (RPh:186).

If growth be the goal for elites, it should be, as a matter of fairness, the
goal for all. "To say that the welfare of others, like our own, consists in
a widening and deepening of the perceptions that give activity its meaning, in an educative growth, is to set forth a proposition of political import. To make others happy except through liberating their powers and
engaging them in activities that enlarge the meaning of life is to harm
them and to indulge ourselves under the cover of exercising a special
virtue" (HNC:293). Elites, in the act of deciding to dispense material
goods to the poor, avail themselves of the good of deliberating and deciding upon values. But if this is a good for them, then the same good
should be available to all—by engaging all citizens in public deliberation, and by developing their capacities to participate effectively (H. Putnam 1992:184).

Matthew Festenstein (1997:61, 99) asserts that the ideal of growth is
the normative basis, the foundation, for Dewey's theory of democracy.
He criticizes Dewey's conception of growth as biased to certain forms
of individuality, without providing a moral justification. The repudiation of the idea of a normative basis, outside of experience, however, is
central to Dewey's philosophy of ethics. He offers his image of human
growth as a hypothesis about how people tend to develop in democratic
communities, not as an ultimate destination known and approved a priori. Likewise, he accepts democracy as a value, enshrined in American
tradition, which becomes a provisional goal for the future. Democracy,
he hypothesizes, will be freely chosen in the long run; it will remain a
reflectively settled practice.

CARE AND VIRTUE

The transforming effect of deliberation and conflict-resolution also
works on sentiments of pity and sympathy. If sympathy is understood as
an impulse, then acting upon it directly and unreflectively may express
our good will, but may not be best for the person we seek to help. Deliberation allows us to inquire into how best to serve the interests of the
other person. "A union of benevolent impulse and intelligent reflection
is the interest most likely to result in conduct that is good" (HNC:163).

Deliberation and conflict-resolution also have transforming effects on
conceptions of the good self, or virtue (E:255–260). Different virtuous
traits and strivings toward virtue can conflict with aspects of the good

and the right. When such conflict is resolved, there is movement away from extreme traits toward the Aristotelian mean. Since deliberation is occasioned by particular situations, the traits appropriate to that particular exigency are called up and developed. Virtuous traits become resources for responsiveness, not fixed modes of behavior. Finally, conflict-resolution leads to the interpenetration of traits, the integration of character, rather than a collection of unrelated attributes or separate faculties (E:257). Thus Dewey's conception of an "inclusive and enduring" good merges with his notion of the "unification and expansion" of the capacities and meanings that constitute the self.

Conclusion: Care, Virtue, and Justice

The substantive ethic that emerges can be summarized briefly. It is democratic and egalitarian. A hierarchical ethic of nobility and baseness, honor and shame, is transformed into one of mutual recognition and universal dignity. Though Nietzsche saw democratic ethics as a cloak for resentment by the powerless, a participatory democratic ethic flows from the empowerment of all citizens—responsibility is fostered rather than resentment; creativity rather than conformity. This is an ethic of responsiveness and responsibility, a progressive or humanistic ethic (H. R. Niebuhr 1963; Fromm 1947; R. May 1953; Norton 1991). Though not strictly pacifist, it is an ethic that stresses the nonviolent working out of conflict. A customary ethic of revenge is transformed into a reflective ethic of restitution, rehabilitation, and reconciliation. Dewey's normative ethics stresses growth in meaning, realization of capacities, and the attempt to integrate these into more unified selves and more viable communities.

If an ethic of care is defined, as it is by Joan Tronto (1994), narrowly in terms of succor for the suffering of others, or provision for their unfulfilled needs, then Dewey's progressive ethic is that and more. It promotes the flourishing of the other, not merely amelioration of deficiencies, not merely the other's survival. If an ethic of justice is a matter of treating persons as ends in themselves, and treating all as equals, Dewey's progressive ethic meets these requirements; but also devotes more attention to others as unique individuals, from diverse groups, with whom we are actually or potentially in relationship. If an ethic of virtue stresses the achievement of particular excellences, this progressive ethic more than fits the bill, because it understands virtues not as concrete entities, but as abstractions from unified courses of action and integrated character. Finally, if ethics is understood as a special sphere of life, Dewey's ethics is more than this. He understands ethics as intertwined with life practice—with one's livelihood, one's behavior in the market, one's creative activity in science and the arts, one's intimate relationships, and one's participation as a citizen. Above all, individual and public ethical deliberation are bound up with political action. These two aspects of life were separated here only to facilitate close analysis. The next chapter is devoted to a discussion of ethically motivated social invention and political action by individuals and by social movements.

6 Progressive Political Strategy

Dewey's philosophical labors are all undertaken to improve the human condition—to solve the "problems of men," by creating democratic community (LW15:154–169). Reflective and analytical thought contribute to democratic politics, but only in conjunction with political action. Dewey calls for vigorous, organized social/political action by liberals and progressives (LSA:91; FC:162). Dewey has been taken to task for failing to offer a concrete progressive political strategy (Westbrook 1991). Building on Dewey's occasional mention of programmatic and strategic ideas, however, I synthesize a Deweyan political strategy. In this effort I return to and complete the account of participatory democracy with which this book begins. The discussions and examples used earlier—on social invention and experiment, and ethical discourse that seeks common ground—foreshadowed the ideas for political and social action considered here.

Dewey's commitment to building democratic community, before specific electoral and governmental institutions implies a broad definition of politics (PP:147). This includes (a) the personal as political, as in consciousness-raising; (b) the politics of social movements, as in identifying interests, forming interest groups, and developing and exerting political power; (c) a politics of process, as in promoting and perfecting the instruments of conflict-resolution; intercultural communication, and consensus decision-making; (d) a politics of social experimentation, as in progressive schooling, workplace democracy, deliberative forums, and the like; (e) a politics of communication, as in civic journalism, and teledemocracy; (f) a politics of theory, as in emancipatory conceptions of politics, science, ethics, esthetics, and education; (g) a cultural politics, as in democratizing the arts, improving the esthetic quality of daily life, and using artistic style to foster moral imagination and political engagement; and finally, (h) politics in the familiar narrow sense of electoral and party politics (PP:183–184; see AE). All of these aspects, though sometimes pursued in isolation, can contribute to a coherent Deweyan progressive political strategy.

Let us begin this thorough examination of strategy with Dewey's views on electoral politics. This is followed by a social movement case study, and next, by a broad social movement and coalition program.

Electoral Politics and Social Movements

Dewey's most explicit proposals for electoral action are offered during the 1930s, in response to the economic and social crisis of the depression. Let us first consider program, then strategy, and finally, a critique of this approach. Part of Dewey's program, is social-democratic (EBNS: 309–313). Government is the guarantor of full employment, and provides support for the unemployed during economic downturns. Government provides social insurance, regulates work conditions, and so on. A second program aspect is economic democracy (EBNS:313–314)—with government supporting the formation of producer cooperatives, and planning for production for valued uses, not just for profit. A third aspect is experiment sponsored by and conducted by government—the "planning society," not the "planned society" (EBNS:321).

The vehicle for achieving this program is third-party politics. Dewey believes that in the United States the two major parties are too committed to the status quo to ever lend themselves to thoroughgoing progressivism. The goal of a new party is winning an electoral majority so that it can implement progressive programs. This new party should be a coalition of a broad range of disadvantaged groups and social classes (LW6:407). Dewey envisions this not as a homogeneous universal party which subordinates all particular interest, but a diverse, pluralistic one which nonetheless unites around a progressive program. To organize such a party, much less win a majority, Dewey sees that there needs to be a single common goal (Lawson 1971:116). This goal must be the basis, first, for unifying educated middle-class liberals— those most able to recognize and implement it—and then the larger public, which could be persuaded to vote for it. Interestingly, Dewey does not propose democracy as that central goal, despite its pivotal role in his political theory. He concludes that only an economic position would have sufficiently wide, immediate, and potent appeal: a goal of economic security and justice—a more stable economy, committed to realizing the ideal of equal opportunity. This program has the simple but powerful negative emotional appeal of identifying an enemy—corporate wealth—but also includes a positive program of building toward a cooperative and just economy. Dewey envisages a coalition of disadvantaged groups forming around this appeal. During the depression, the middle class too, though relatively better off than farmers and workers, recognize the harm done to their interests by the unregulated market system. More specifically, Dewey embraces national economic planning as the means to achieve the broader goals. He naively believes that the idea of (democratic) state control and (democratic) planning will have a wide and visceral appeal. In his view, the depression demonstrated the collapse of the system, its inability to mend itself, and the necessity of adopting something drastically different.

During this crisis, Dewey responds with a hasty attempt at assembling a loose coalition based upon a single, simple, powerful idea—a slogan. This approach is hardly novel: it is compounded of populist, progressive, and democratic socialist themes, evident in late nineteenth- and early twentieth-century politics—and revived in the New Left of the 1960s. These themes so far have failed to pull together an electoral majority. The mutual distrust, and the clashing interests of immigrant and U.S.-born, labor and middle class, Catholic and Protestant, white and black were not overcome by these appeals (Kazin 1995). In states where a near majority was mobilized by progressive era grassroots activists, through slogans propagated by mass media, the support turned out to be soft. Opposing forces learned to use the same techniques of mass appeal, and the progressive blocs melted away (Clemens 1997). Dewey and others have greatly overestimated the possibility for success of such a strategy.

Nor, in the unlikely event of a victory at the polls, would the difficulties be over. Vested interests opposed to the new program would remain entrenched, and would do their best to undermine it—using persuasive appeals in the media, deploying their capital in the economy, and wielding their employment power and elite status in local communities. An aroused and informed citizenry would be needed to preserve the electoral gains. But the real work of building citizen participation and informed commitment would occur after the hasty electoral victory. This would necessitate active citizen partners in social experiments promulgated by the new, progressive administration and Congress. Lacking an already developed cadre of citizen activist-experimenters, however, it is an illusion to imagine that this could be done easily or quickly. The temptation for top-down reform would be great, leaving the citizens as marginalized as ever, and directing their resentment at the new, progressive elite instead of the old conservative one.

If this were Dewey's primary thinking about political strategy, it would indeed be disappointing. Fortunately, this is not his prevailing view, but one adopted only during a brief crisis period, and at odds with his thinking both before and after. Throughout his career, he rejects the politics of slogans, the appeal to citizens' fears and resentments, the shortcuts that do not involve developing a much higher level of social intelligence. "Democratic ends demand democratic methods for their realization. Authoritarian methods . . . owe their seductive power to their claim to serve ideal ends" (FC:175). Though democratic methods are painfully slow and difficult, the seeming shortcuts only serve to undermine democracy. Reinhold Niebuhr's impatience with Dewey's approach, for example, has overtones of a Leninist vanguard-approach to political mobilization, discredited by subsequent historical experience. Alan Lawson notes that Dewey, "in his deepest considerations . . . drew back from supporting any sort of dramatically doctrinaire program. Intelligent campaigns educating the public to realize its long-term interests seemed to Dewey the only tolerable weapon to use against those who would exploit mass delusions" (Lawson 1971:123). But such a strategy calls for a patient, long-term effort. The decisive failure of third-party strivings in the 1930s, in Lawson's words, "called for a reappraisal of the time needed to educate the public into readiness for significant political reform" (118). This does not mean abandoning electoral politics, which is itself a means for political mobilization and education. It means an interplay between electoral politics and citizen development through participation in social movements, social experiments, public forums, civic journalism, cultural expression, and conflict-resolution. It means, perhaps, contesting for office at the local level, if not yet at the national level. Dewey would likely be sympathetic if cautious about today's nascent third-party movements, such as the Green Party, the New Party, and the Labor Party (J. Rogers 1996; Kazin 1996). These groups have taken account of historical experience, set modest local initial aims, and have collaborated with social movements rather than rivaled them.

LONG-TERM PROGRAM: EDUCATIVE SOCIAL MOVEMENTS

Central to a Deweyan program, then, is the commitment to building a high level of citizen awareness, involvement, skill, and sophistication—

cultivating a constituency immune to demagogic appeals. Education, communication, participation, and conflict-resolution are the watchwords of his approach. Dewey advocates instructing directly through the progressive adult education movement, and progressive education in the schools. He is committed to fostering improved communication of social inquiry to citizens through the mass media. But education is far more than a matter of schooling and communication. Participation in public life is essential for political education (RPh: 209). Dewey is aware of and sympathetic to Tocqueville's idea that voluntary associations— the building blocks of civil society—educate citizens in the skills essential to democratic life. Dewey endorses the effort to rebuild local civil society and form functional networks across localities (FC: 160–161; PP: 212–219). For any progressive activist, however, this is just a beginning. Dewey, like theorists today, recognizes social movements as the primary building blocks of a long-term progressive movement.

Social movements articulate and represent citizen interests, and mobilize and educate citizens as participants (Mansbridge 1996). They give a voice to groups excluded from public spaces and discourses (Young 1996). They gain a place for dissenting views in the ongoing discussion and inquiry that identifies public interests, and a seat at the table when formal, mediated conflict-resolution is undertaken (Smiley 1990). Dewey, himself, was active in social movements for unionization of labor, civil liberties, world peace, women's rights, and so on. He would identify with the lively and skilled progressive politics of today, manifested in the issue-oriented relatively "new social movements" of environmentalism, feminism, minority/ethnic liberation, grassroots community organizing, peace, human rights; union democracy, and consumer protection.

Let us now examine an illustrative case of a democratic social experiment, one which achieves the Deweyan goals of citizen participation and education. Later, I place this one case in the context of numerous other examples, and of broad political strategy.

A Case Study: The School Development Project

The School Development Project originated in New Haven and is now being propagated nationwide. This is a progressive schooling experiment, but the emphasis here is not on the students, but on the parent's involvement and their ensuing development as citizens. The project's founder and director, James Comer, of Yale University, describes it in his book, *School Power: Implications of an Intervention Project* (1993). The discussion here concerns intervention in an underperforming school in the poorest part of the city, a neighborhood school, without the advantage of selective admissions—the severest test case. The project claims success in improving morale, reducing absenteeism and disciplinary problems, enhancing the social development of students, developing higher-level thinking and communication skills, increasing parent satisfaction, and simultaneously substantially raising standardized test scores (Comer 1993:287). This is achieved through a more or less progressive, but not permissive pedagogy, and a curriculum that stresses basic skills including phonics (233), but also social development, critical thinking, and arts education. Success was by no means immediate. It is more difficult to transform an existing institution than to build a new one, but this approach may be crucial for saving public education. Orderly progress came after several years of conflict and confusion, dealt with through organizational development and human relations methods—including conflict-resolution. Progressively inclined educators regard the School Development Project (SDP) as an exemplary achievement. Which is to say, it provides many fruitful avenues for replication and further experiment, not that it is the complete and definitive solution to educational problems.

The SDP draws heavily on social science expertise, yet, paradoxically, involves lay people in making crucial decisions on curriculum, pedagogy, and personnel. I direct my attention here to the manner in which the tension between experts and citizens is overcome. I examine the implications of this successful local experiment for nationwide dissemination and for use in national public discourse on education reform. Both the potential and limits of an educative participatory politics are here explored.

SOCIAL SCIENCE EXPERTISE AND PARENT PARTICIPATION

Comer does not present his approach as Deweyan, nonetheless, it is very much in the spirit of Dewey. Comer is deeply committed to the use of social science in social experimentation—"the application of social and behavioral science principles to every aspect of a school program" (Comer 1993:60; also 111). In particular, he draws upon theories from the fields of "human relations, child development, and organizational behavior" (223). Comer's "social and behavioral science principles" are taken more from clinical than from experimental traditions. They are formulated qualitatively, not quantitatively, and they are applied interpretively, not formally operationalized (xiv-xvi,24). This too is congruent with Dewey's approach (see PESE). Comer is convinced these theories are powerful instruments that can generate successful practices (60, 111). "We attempted to demonstrate that the improvement was due to the theory we set out with, and subsequently enlarged and applied (with the insights and help of parents, teachers, and administrators) . . . and that the theory applied anywhere . . . could make school improvement possible" (xi; also 50, 111).

In this case, dependence on expert knowledge did not result in top-down imposition of a preestablished design. Comer argues that for the clinical social science disciplines, collaboration between expert and client is essential to successful practice (1993:xv). Clients always have information and perspectives which the experts lack but which are necessary to them in their work. Clinical work involves change in organizations and persons, and requires both their assent and their active participation. "Theoretical and clinical knowledge in . . . many of the social sciences requires a mutually satisfying relationship with . . . clients. Each group needs the cooperative involvement by other" (Comer 1993:xv).

Like Dewey, Comer is sensitive to the complexity of social interaction. "Human problems are the result of multi-determined, interrelated factors" (1993:23). In response to such complexity, like Dewey, Comer calls for interpretive and qualitative methods: "Systems analysis, naturalistic study methods used in anthropology and human ecology, clinical diagnostic methods used in medicine, and the case study method used in business would permit a qualitative analysis of the interacting, interrelated forces at play in a school" (24; also PESE:268). Awareness of complexity leads to a rejection of "single treatment" interventions. Particular isolated changes in curriculum or teaching methods are easily subverted by other processes in the school. A systems approach to experimentation in education is needed. Comer calls for "comprehensive system analysis; the study of the interactions and impact of people, programs, and procedures among and upon each other" (23). Like clinical approaches, the systems approach, with its awareness of the interaction of people and programs, requires informed participation. School reform success depends on the "overall climate and management of the school" (24), and parent involvement is essential to creating the desired climate.

COLLABORATION

Collaboration is stressed on two levels—between expert consultants and teachers, and between the experts and teachers and the parents. (Collaboration with students is also built into the project [Comer 1993: 39–40].) I first explore the expert-teacher relationship, foreshadowing features of the relationships between school people and parents. Comer reports, "We planned to learn together and from each other by allowing clinicians to work together with teachers and educational administrators in the school setting, with agreement and involvement of the parents" (xvi). But cooperation between experts and teachers is by no means automatic. "American teachers tend to be intimidated by scholars as they simultaneously tend to mock them as 'just a bunch of theorists.'" (xvii). This attitude handicaps the teachers. "Denigration of theory left teachers disarmed in the face of the cascade of unordered phenomena, of the unpatterned facts they encountered daily." Thus experts had to find a way to impart their skills. "In this program, teachers searching for solutions learned to 'theorize' to seek patterns and the deeper meanings of overt behavior" (xvii). In other words, teachers were trained to become "reflective practitioners" (Schon 1983, 1991). The experts found that they could not succeed by talking down: "teachers learn best when scholars are colleagues rather than instructors" (1993:xvii, also 164).

Like Dewey, Comer recognizes that individuals must change in order to achieve this kind of collaboration, and that challenges to received beliefs and habits evoke insecurity and rigidity. He stresses, therefore, the need for support, respect, and solidarity. With systems and organizational development theories in mind, Comer seeks to establish responsive leadership by the school principal. "An increase in the principal's ability to understand the dynamics of student, staff, and parent behavior . . . will reduce the number of crisis situations and will give the principal time and energy to serve as an educational leader" (Comer 1993:69).

Collaboration between parents and school personnel is vital for several reasons. Comer observes that "the sharing [by parents] of insights and ideas can give school people a better understanding of local community needs and opportunities" (Comer 1993:39). Furthermore, children learn better when they see that their parents trust and support the school, when the parents are actively involved in the school, and when the parents themselves are engaged in learning (33, 126, 143). Participa-

182 Dewey on Democracy

tion is educative; parents involved in school decision making acquire "organization and planning skills" and improved self-esteem, and they pass these on to their children (126, 143). Conversely, when parents convey a message that "school is the enemy," childrens' learning suffers (13, 30, 126). Antagonism between parents and schools is a frequent occurrence in inner city school districts, due to a past history of neglect, false promises, and condescension from officials. Parents active in civil rights and antipoverty struggles may have enough negative political power to stifle those reform efforts which they don't trust, but not enough positive power to bring about desired changes (29–30).

Getting some parents to even set foot in the school building, however, is difficult. One truism in educational circles is that you can invite and urge parents to participate, but, except for a hardy few, they won't turn out. Comer finds, nonetheless, that when parents are given genuine decision-making power and real educational functions, their involvement rises dramatically. In the SDP, "parents and teachers are involved together in planning and implementing programs" (Comer 1993:207). Gaining parent participation, however, is just a first step. Stereotypes can easily become self-fulfilling prophecies and must be overcome on both sides (29–30, 35, 127–128). Parents need new skills and knowledge to function effectively in these positions. Without such capability, they experience themselves as inadequate and drop out. This confirms the teachers' prior stereotypes of parents as unable and unwilling to participate. At the same time, any sign of condescension from the teachers confirms the parents' stereotype of teachers as arrogant.

In conflict-resolution terms, there exists an initial situation fraught with conflict, and a theoretical potential for mutually advantageous collaboration. Inquiry, experimentation, and social invention are required to provide novel solutions which resolve the conflict and realize the potential. Skill development must be provided for the parents, but not in a way that intimidates or humiliates them. Parents cannot be treated as students, nor can they be addressed as colleagues in the unfamiliar language of educators. The resolution comes when, "social workers and staff arrange to share their expertise with parents through participation in the planning and implementation of parent-sponsored programs rather than in didactic teaching sessions." "In unobtrusive ways, social workers and teachers share their skills and expertise with parents" (Comer 1993:132, 133; also 135–145). Some parents, heartened by the learning they were engaged in, decided to pursue further formal education. As the School Development Project unfolded, new leaders emerged among parents and teachers (143, 241). Later, a formal leadership development program was instituted (128, 144).

Difference in knowledge, expertise, and social status is only one of the sources of conflict. Differences in ethnicity, race, religion, and social class between teachers and parents are frequent in inner city schools. Value-laden adversarial discussions on ethnic identity issues in textbooks, on skills needed for social mobility, on the content of sex education, the type and severity of rules and punishments, and other issues arise. The goals, not just the means, of schooling are also subjects for democratic deliberation. In Comer's experiment, the strategy is to maintain a continuous dialogue in which these issues can arise in a less confrontational way. "Because there were regular ongoing working and discussion sessions, differences of opinion could be talked about and resolved" (Comer 1993:207). Conflicts could be identified early, and timely response proved to be important. "When there was real or potential conflict in the system over group and individual interests, the governance and management board acted to resolve the issue before disappointment or a sense of being cheated or abused led to serious intergroup and interpersonal difficulties" (242).

Issues were discussed extensively with an effort at mutual understanding, problem solving, and reaching an eventual consensus. Comer hints at the conflict-resolution approach of separating the person from the problem, and positions from interests. "Our strategy of responding to confrontation without reacting as if the criticism and attacks were personal, while at the same time addressing the real problems [underlying interests, not positions] as quickly as possible, proved to be productive" (Comer 1993:243). Value conflicts are worked out in practice, experimentally, not only in discussion. Curricula and pedagogy reflecting certain valued goals are developed and implemented, and the school community decides if the results turn out to be ethically desirable. Experiments, ideally, not only measure up to previous value positions, they reveal new, valued possibilities, leading to value evolution and transformation. The goals of the experiment, too, should be regarded as hypothetical, not final, not as fixed ends. In Dewey's words, "ends-in-view are of the nature of hypotheses" (LTI:497). Thus they, too, are subject to revision. Dewey writes: "knowing is fully stimulated . . . [only when the] end [continues to be] developed in the process of inquiry and testing" (RPh:146).

The SDP avoids the facile assumptions either that collaboration is impossible, or that it can be had merely by attempting it. In this case, collaboration proved possible, but it was hard won; achieved by thought-fulness and effort. Whatever the cost in resources invested, many con-sider the results in improved school morale and student learning amply worth the investment. A by-product of this effort to build democratic community within the school is the empowerment of parents for self-government within the neighborhood community. Their involvement in the SDP has implications beyond the field of education. The methods of unobtrusive sharing of skills and knowledge, of collaboration on proj-ects between experts and lay people, and of democratic governance by a "representative management group" are models for all democratic and educative social experiments.

LOCAL POLITICS

The results of the SDP school reform effort are not limited to the school or even the neighborhood. The work in New Haven, in particu-lar, was initiated at the behest of the New Haven School District, and it remained dependent on the district for authorization and resources. The SDP had to learn how to communicate with and influence the school board, the school administration, several service delivery agencies, and the electorate behind all of these (Comer 1993:244). "We made sporadic efforts to improve communications so we would be perceived more ac-curately by people outside the program. . . . One of the major reasons there was little interest in our program at the end of the first five years was that we did not do a very good communications and public relations job with people outside" (229–230). Comer concludes, "Had there been careful planning . . . to utilize the expertise of people with communica-tions and public relation skills, we might have avoided some of our pro-gram difficulties" (230; also 244). In contrast to the neighborhood level, communication at the city level involves less participation, group delib-eration, and transformative experience for individuals, but these aspects are not wholly lacking. Site visits and participant observation are avail-able modes of face-to-face communication. Comer built alliances with union leaders, political leaders, political parties, and social movements (240, 244). These, too, are necessary political tasks for school experi-menters who would build and preserve public support for their projects.

Quantitative measures of performance play a larger role in communi-cation in the broader arena. Indeed, an intensive formal evaluation effort was mounted for just this purpose. The SDP initially kept evaluation in-formal and "low profile." Comer identifies two reasons for this. They feared that the teachers and parents would react negatively to full-scale evaluation as the sort of hit-and-run research of previous academic experts. Furthermore, some of the consultants, themselves, doubted the meaningfulness of traditional measurements of pupil and school success (Comer 1993:275). Informal day-to-day assessment seemed sufficient for formative purposes of ongoing adjustment and improvement. "All aspects of the curriculum, [are] continually assessed and modified by the staff to meet the needs of our particular children" (233). Ultimately, it was their desire to transmit news of their emerging successes to a broader public that led the project team to build in more summative, formal, and quantitative procedures. "What amounts to a formative evaluation was done during the first two years of the program . . . A baseline study was conducted [the following year]. Summative evaluations were done during the next two years. . . . Ultimately a variety of evaluative methods were employed, including consumer evaluations (by staff, parents, and to a lesser extent by children), reports of outside evaluators, studies of children's academic achievement," and so on (74). Narrative presentation, however, remains an important means of conveying a sense of the experimental school environment and its more nuanced accomplishments.

DISSEMINATION

Comer and his associates saw their work in the New Haven school as a demonstration program. In 1978, they began field testing the program in three schools in different states. In 1988, they set out to package the approach, and disseminate it nationwide—to over six-hundred schools by Fall 1995 (Comer et al. 1996:20–21). The SDP crafted "a professional development model" which employs written materials, training workshops, and "a variety of telecommunications strategies" (23–24). With foundation support, an institute was established at Yale, which brings school personnel in for training and sends consultants to SDP schools and school districts. It features a research department, and curriculum development and training components (Comer 1993:292–297). Comer's group at Yale has formed alliances with groups in other universities and has proposed changes in university curricula for teacher training (248–250, 292). The SDP has worked collaboratively on curriculum development with other progressive school change movements, including Theodore Sizer's, Coalition of Essential Schools, Howard Gardner's multiple intelligences approach, and the Educational Development Corporation (298).

The challenge of propagating the SDP on a national scale far exceeds that of working, by invitation, with one school in one's own community. Political and educational leadership changes from election to election. Community crises erupt, and economic cycles and shifting national moods affect support for school experiments. A dissemination project must acquire new political and sociological knowledge and skills for this complex and shifting environment. Theory and expertise in "planned change" must be developed (Sarason 1996). Even with the best of will and skill, it is safe to assume that there are many communities in which the SDP will not take root. The verdict is not yet in on the success of efforts in the hundreds of schools currently enrolled in the Project. Occasional news reports suggest that some are thriving while others are experiencing difficulties, but on the whole it is too early to form reliable judgments (e.g., P. Bush 1997).

If continuing and more widespread experimentation by Comer and other progressive educators is to occur, more support must be generated from the social sciences. Early in Dewey's career as a philosopher and educator, he sees religion and tradition as powerful obstacles to the adoption of social science approaches to schooling and society. By the mid-1930s, Dewey recognizes that the social sciences themselves, developing on positivist lines, are becoming a major obstacle. They form a diversion from, if not an outright opposition to, the value-laden exploratory experimentation Dewey advocates. Today, clinical social sciences—also action research and reflective practice—such as Comer relies upon, are considered, at best, as soft social science by the mainstream. They are relegated to the margins of academic endeavors. The limitations of positivist science have, in turn, provoked an anti-science backlash equally uncongenial to Dewey's approach. Part of Dewey's strategy is to win support for clinical/experimental approaches through his critique and reformulation of philosophy of social science. In today's more open and searching climate, it is possible that Dewey's project for a reconstruction of philosophy and social science will yet take hold, and that this will foster an expanded program of social experiment and invention.

Neither Dewey nor Comer forgets that schooling experiments are profoundly impacted by the social environment. As long as children and their families are in desperate poverty, learning is greatly handicapped. Comer disputes, however, the fatalistic conclusion that nothing can be done to reform schools and save children. He also calls for national efforts to address these tragic and unjust conditions. Schooling experiments cannot replace a politics of social justice and equality. Indeed, it is possible that, by creating an informed and empowered body of parents/

citizens, schooling experiments can foster, rather than conflict with, progressive politics.

NATIONAL PUBLIC DISCOURSE

Comer goes beyond the neighborhood and the city to address nation-wide audiences through a variety of communication media. His book, *School Power*, is in its second edition and a video on Comer and his work "has been shown on public television stations across the country" (Comer 1993:294). A profile in the *New York Times* (July 1, 1998, B1:2) described him as "a hero to many education advocates, not the least of them Hillary Rodham Clinton." *Scientific American* featured a lengthy report of the SDP in New Haven (Comer 1988a). This also serves as an example of the sort of social science journalism that Dewey strongly advocates (PP:183).

Comer's views, having achieved public visibility, have not gone unchallenged. Chester Finn, former Undersecretary of Education, answers Comer by citing the ideas of "Thaddeus Lott, a Houston principal recently profiled in *Policy Review* magazine who uses ability grouping, intensive drill, rote learning, and other traditional teaching methods to extraordinary result at his Wesley Elementary School" (*New York Times*, July 1, 1968, B1:2). How can such dramatic claims of success, from two seemingly diametrically opposed educational approaches, be judged by citizens who follow and participate in the national discussion? One option is to examine critically the appropriateness of the research methods upon which claims are based. A second posture is to wait to see how each experiment stands the test of time. Let us suppose, for the moment, however, that both claims are justified. Given the complexity of human beings, there are surely more ways than one to teach and learn successfully. The dedicated personnel and the consequent high morale of these schools may be as important a variable as the pedagogy. One might accept both approaches uncritically—adopting a pluralist laissez faire approach, or a vulgar pragmatism which endorses "whatever works." More is at stake, however, than improving test scores, and the basic skills they purport to measure. Comer is claiming to teach higher-level thinking skills and social development, which are not so easily measured, and to empower parents. Likewise, Finn and Lott are concerned with character education. Citizens are entitled to ask what sorts of development and character are being fostered here, and whether they fit one's concepts of the good citizen and the good life? That is, the discussion of schooling techniques barely masks a debate about values. The debate could be conceived, in George Lakoff's (1996) terms, as one between a strict father model of morality, and a nurturing (but not permissive) parent model of morality. By what method is such an opposition of sweeping and fundamental moral views to be discussed and assessed? It seems we have left behind the method of social experiment and empirical verification, and returned to a thorny question for democratic theory: how is moral discourse to be conducted? But we should not give up so easily. For Dewey, experiments are inquiries about values, as much as they are about means. The SDP already involves ongoing discourse, conflict, and conflict-resolution about what sort of human development is preferred. Value issues that seem impossible to resolve in abstract debate are worked out in day-to-day decisions on specific value-laden schooling practices and in judgments about the kinds of learning that result (see also Jonsen and Toulmin 1988). Parents whose position is authoritarian child-rearing, may change their views if their interest—in safe and orderly classrooms where learning can freely take place—is achieved by a more nurturing approach. Many inner city parents believe that only strictly disciplined children have a chance in their hostile social environment (Rubin 1976). They may discover that the SDP school climate—and the work environments it foreshadows—is not a hostile one, and that children who think critically and raise questions have both academic success and improved survival chances beyond school (Comer 1993).

If value conflicts are best settled by participation in social experiments and the conflict-resolution they engender, then discourse will proceed locally and slowly, site by site, and year by year. But this is not such a poor alternative to a national debate in the news media that tackles the issues directly and dramatically, but in an adversarial style that hardens positions, overlooks complexities, ignores common ground—and, in the end, leaves issues unresolved. National discourse can be reconceptualized, however, as one component of a process in which general public discussion feeds into local experiments, the results of which are taken back up into general conversation. As citizens grow more informed, they demand more complex reporting. Experimenters can report their work in ways that take note of common ground as well as difference—as Comer does when he points to the basic skills component of his curriculum and disavows permissiveness. When public discourse is not charged with the impossible task of adjudicating the correctness of abstract value positions, there is more room for narrative which stirs moral imagination and admits complexity through thick description. For example, Comer frames discussion of SDP with a narrative of his family's rise from a sharecropper background in Mississippi, through blue collar labor, to university education—itself, a valuable contribution to the public conversation on education (1988b).

The public discourse revolving around the SDP exemplifies the interweaving of experimentation and public discussion that Dewey advocates. Discussion without experimentation is indeterminate—and interminable (LSA:70–71, 73). Experimentation without discussion lays false claims to scientific certitude. Taken together, however, they enable citizens to reach public judgment. Above all, this experimentation/discussion process incorporates citizens as active participants and decisionmakers, and helps them acquire the knowledge and skill to participate effectively.

EXAMPLES OF EDUCATIVE PARTICIPATION

Far from being unique, the Comer project is exemplary of many democratic progressive experiments stressing citizen development. Jeffrey Isaacs's (1999) case study of "The Algebra Project" depicts a process of community involvement in education very similar to the SDP. Numerous other progressive educational efforts can be cited (e.g.: Meier 1995; Sizer 1992; Edwards, Gandini and Forman 1993; Rose 1995; Wood 1992). Beyond the field of education are the cases of the Mondragon Cooperatives and Common Ground Network for Life and Choice, discussed earlier, and the various types of social invention mentioned in Chapter 3, which also exemplify the highest levels of citizen involvement. Several of those social inventions deserve specific mention here. The Dudley Street Initiative for redevelopment in a deteriorated Boston neighborhood blends vigorous grassroots organizing and advocacy with participatory planning and highly professional housing development (Medoff and Sklar 1994). Citizens are involved at every level—public demonstrations; organizational decisionmaking, leadership, and administration; hiring of staff and consultants; project design; and presentations to public bodies and foundations. Citizen participants learn skills on the job, apprentice themselves informally to professional staff, and then go on to formal academic training. Specialists in participatory planning provide neighborhood residents with the skills to contribute to the design process.

For more than sixty years, The Highlander Center in Knoxville has offered workshop education in which citizen activists learn from each other (Adams 1975). Staff members unobtrusively impart skills and approaches, without invalidating the special knowledge and capabilities of less formally educated people. Highlander has pioneered participatory research, empowering citizens to conduct inquiries formerly reserved for university-trained social scientists (Merrifield 1989).

Other progressive examples include The Center for Living Democracy in Brattleboro, Vermont, which has gathered an archive of cases of grassroots citizen activism, and distilled principles for effective democratic organizing (Lappé and Dubois 1994). It offers introductory workshops to entice citizens into activism, and training workshops to increase their skills. Its American News Service supplies reports to the mass media on grassroots citizen action. Among other community organizing groups, the Industrial Areas Foundation (I.A.F.), headquartered in New York, sponsors projects around the country. It mobilizes citizens in particular neighborhoods around bread and butter issues, and goes on to develop indigenous leadership and a broad base of awareness among constituents (Boyte 1989). Theorizing is built into the I.A.F. approach—both discussion of political philosophers and reflection on grassroots experience.

These examples of movements that emphasize citizen education, participation, and public discourse can serve as models for other progressive social movements. Grassroots action alone, however, cannot transform society. Local and issue-specific movements require supportive policies from the state (Stiefel and Wolfe 1994:204). Along these lines, let us return to the broad spectrum of progressive political action and a Deweyan strategy for building it into an effective political force.

From Social Movements to Political Strategy

Absent any single broad political movement getting constant media attention—such as the New Left of the 1960s—it is easy to underestimate the significance of today's social movements. We fail to recognize the sheer number of participants, the magnitude of resources deployed, the amount of information disseminated, the participants recruited and trained, and the successes in fighting rearguard actions against a resurgent conservatism. Though far from constituting a unified political movement, or a majority electoral coalition, today's progressive social movements, taken together, provide a sturdy basis for building such a political force. In the 1960s, there was a progressive movement without

an infrastructure; today, there exists an extensive infrastructure await-
ing the right historical conditions to undergird a broad movement. If that
opportunity is to be seized, however, a higher level of coalition and concerted action among social movements must be achieved. Before discussing coalition though, let us first take a closer look at several types
of social movements.

TYPES OF SOCIAL MOVEMENTS

Going beyond familiar advocacy movements, Dewey implies a second
category: movements for social experiments and inventions that reform
the school, the workplace, the press, the public forum, and myriad other
institutions. These movements, too, both mobilize and educate citizens.
Social invention and experiment build new social forms and produce
both material and ethical goods—adding a whole new dimension to social movement activity, and fulfilling a key aspect of Dewey's program.
Consider the growing movement for worker ownership and control
of businesses, of which the Mondragon Cooperatives are exemplary.
This is just the sort of industrial democracy Dewey advocates (AE:243;
EBNS:313–314; LW6:226). Since the reach of these efforts is still tiny
compared to private and hierarchical businesses, a Deweyan progressive
politics must show how they can be the precursor of a much wider movement (Bowman and Stone 1996). It must demonstrate how such a movement can avoid being watered down, for example, by compromise versions of worker participation which involve ownership but not control,
or limited self-management on the shop floor but not ownership (P. Bernstein 1976). Recently, there has been a modest movement, in a Deweyan
spirit, to promote "civic journalism," or "public journalism" (Charity
1995; Rosen 1996). Indeed, there are movements to propagate all of the
various social inventions mentioned in Chapter 3—an urban agriculture movement, a community development banking movement, a community land trust movement, a local currency systems movement, to repeat but a few examples.

A third category, which also often goes unrecognized, is process-
oriented social movements. A nonviolent political action movement
carries on the legacies of Gandhi and Martin Luther King Jr. and con-
ducts extensive nonviolence training for activists in other social movements. Consciousness-raising and feminist process movements are
found among feminists and other kindred groups. There is a movement
for intercultural sensitivity and dialogue and a related movement for

common ground dialogue. There is also a movement for consensus decision-making, the constituency of which is progressive political and counter-cultural organizations (Avery et al. 1981; Saint and Lawson 1994). Efforts within academia strive for more participatory forms of research, as well as more collaborative and dialogical, less adversarial scholarly discourse. The progressive education movement may be listed here, since its curriculum stresses inquiry, group collaboration, communication, and deliberation. Although individually, each of these is a modest effort in the vast, complex society of the U.S., each penetrates many venues and touches the lives of a wide variety of people. Collectively, they constitute a significant and growing social force.

Most important among the process movements, from a Deweyan point of view, is today's rapidly growing movement for mediation and conflict-resolution. Conflict-resolution calls for high levels of citizen participation, as parties to negotiation, or as lay mediators. It educates participants in the essential democratic skills of communication, inquiry, and problem solving. Conflict-resolution provides a constant stimulus to and a laboratory for social invention. It can aid overburdened courts and administrative agencies, and thus restore legitimacy to government. It can, at times, help bridge the gulf between those with opposed ideologies, joining them together in a search for concrete solutions. It advances the goal of deliberative democracy by creating major public spaces and "discursive designs" (Dryzek 1990). Conflict-resolution offers a means toward healing deep gulfs of race, class, and ethnicity, and deep disagreements over sexual and gender roles, which cleave our culture and prevent the formation of a broad progressive coalition. It offers an urgently needed tool for resolving the debilitating conflicts that sometimes arise both within and between progressive social movements. In seeking to forge genuine mutually satisfactory solutions, conflict-resolution provides a model of democratic community—a community of mutual self-realization. A Deweyan political strategy, therefore, calls for vigorous efforts to propagate the method, to hold the practice to its highest standards, and to prefigure within the progressive community, the ubiquitous use and development of conflict-resolution. The goal is not to substitute conflict-resolution for politics, but to incorporate it within the broad realm of politics, in cooperation with other strands of political strategy.

Indeed, the practice is already becoming institutionalized in research and training bodies, codes of practice, and organs of communication. In this adversarial and litigious culture, there is much resistance to conflict-resolution. Its use appears to be growing, nonetheless, as the need for it and the logic of it grow more apparent. The danger is less that conflict-resolution will be marginalized than that it will be coopted. It could easily become a mere technique, hastily applied for narrowly defined purposes—limiting its participatory, educative, and transformative effects. Conflict-resolution advocates have already identified and are working to combat that tendency (R. Bush 1989).

AGAINST THE ODDS: SOCIAL INTELLIGENCE

The goal of long-term citizen education poses a paradox. Educated citizens are required for effective electoral politics on this model, even as electoral victories are necessary to open spaces for communication, education, and participation. Dewey's response is to transform the vicious circle into a virtuous one. "There is no possibility of complete escape from this circle. . . . It is a matter of accelerating momentum in the right direction, and of increasing the effective energy of the factors that make for removing obstacles" (LW3:39). "There is a circle, but an enlarging circle, or, if you please, a widening spiral" (1928a:104). Conventional electoral and lobbying politics can win more space for experimental and educative politics, while educative participation can provide a sophisticated constituency for the electoral work. Dewey would also bring social invention and experiment into the electoral and lobbying effort. In this Deweyan mold, a political party, interest group, or social movement would aspire to be open, nondogmatic, multi-tendency, and experimental. But Dewey is not a philosophical anarchist; he recognizes that any such organization still requires stable leadership, program, and strategy (1936:136).

Despite all the activity reported above, progressive political action, in the industrial capitalist world, is always action against the odds. Political movements expressing Dewey's ideals and methods are today dwarfed by consumerism, global markets, and media-driven politics. Progressive movements must compensate with skill and inventiveness for their disadvantage in resources. JoAnn Wypljewski expresses this need for innovation: "The recognition that there is no *one way* . . . opens the way to risk, to experimentation . . . flexibility and . . . creativity. . . . The role of the imagination is at least as important in the organizations people build . . . as in the society they envision" (1997:18). Social movements must mobilize citizens and groups to make up in numbers what they lack in wealth. Movements must develop "social intelligence," in-

venting novel solutions to social issues, and communicating these vividly to citizens. Social researchers must be persuaded of Dewey's core
thesis on social science—to experiment with creating democratic communities would enhance science as well as realize human values. Like
other resources, intelligence is, to some extent, for sale. Experts can be
hired by wealthy elites and shaped by dominant discourses. Progressive
social movements must provide a different set of incentives—moral and
intellectual challenges and supportive community.

Progressive politics must use means consistent with its ends, and
in its internal democracy, prefigure the society it envisions (DE:316;
FC:175). This requires supportive and challenging communities within
organizations—capacities for mutual understanding and respectful criticism. Internal community must support task-orientation and vice-
versa, not become an end in itself. Awareness and creative adaptation to
changing environments must replace denial and rigidity. Social movement groups have not always upheld these standards (Warren 1995:189–
191). But movements for processes of conflict-resolution, dialogue, and
consensus-building offer skills and leadership for making the difficult
changes required.

Dewey, more aware of daunting obstacles in his later years, is far from
the facile optimist (PP:58–59, 185, 209; ION:54–56; FC:146; 1936:133–
134). Yet, for him, the struggle for democracy is the only game worth
playing and must be pursued, whatever the odds (1936:144–145). In
times of ascendancy of conservative politics, it must be remembered
that history is not static. There will be pendulum swings and crises,
bringing new opportunities which progressives must be prepared to
engage. Prospects for effectiveness depend upon: first, expanding particular social movements, moving them into public visibility and influence; second, in combining "retail" with "wholesale" politics; and
third, building coalitions and creating unifying themes—bringing the
concerted power of many diverse organizations to bear. Many of the activities mentioned above, scarcely known even to the educated public,
are near the threshold of wider recognition. Once these alternatives
become visible, dissemination and advocacy can widen awareness and
build support, until a place on the public agenda is assured.

RETAIL AND WHOLESALE POLITICS

The strategy of educative participation is a retail strategy, involving
individuals in face-to-face relationships. Most politics today is whole-

sale, reaching citizens en masse through electronic and print media. Dewey, with his awareness of the Great Society and local communities, both understands and seeks to bridge this dichotomy. He advocates a progressive politics that integrates the national and local levels, wholesale and retail approaches. He seeks a progressive politics of mass communication that does not succumb to the lure of sloganeering. He seeks a retail politics that achieves national significance, because it is pursued at countless sites, in many different spheres of life. And, importantly, he seeks an interplay between these levels. Gaining access to mass media now dominated by giant corporations requires electoral and legislative actions to return to management of the public airwaves as a public trust. Progressives must also exploit the more anarchic and populist possibilities of new communication tools such as websites and pirate radio. A second challenge for progressives is not to succumb to the mindlessness and polarization that seem inherent in today's mass communication. Public or civic journalism, although still in its infancy, is a step in this direction.

A mass movement cannot be held together by theories alone, nor, for very long, by direct action alone. It requires the development of both culture and institutions (Rogin 1983:115; Flacks 1988). The counterculture of the 1960s was both the strength of and the undoing of the New Left. It provided unifying styles, rituals, and commitments, but its naive conception of personal liberation led to general disillusionment and individual tragedy (Rogin 1983:116). Earlier, the American Communist Party, in its popular front period, revived American folk culture and fostered political theater and fiction, as well as developing schools, summer camps, and housing cooperatives. Despite the vitality of this movement culture, its democratic qualities were undermined by the dogmatism and authoritarianism of the Party itself. Dewey develops a basic orientation for a democratic culture of graphic and performing arts, which could serve the cultural needs of a mass political movement (see AE). His account of progressive schools can be seen as a key part of a democratic culture. Conflict-resolution, itself, involves styles of communication and inquiry that amount to a cultural pattern, not just an instrumentality. Finally, Dewey's theory of the self and its development (see HNC) offers a more sober but no less transformative alternative to the ecstatic politics of personal liberation in the New Left, and the postmodern radical esthetic refashioning of Foucalt (Shusterman 1997).

Each separate social innovation, or element of an overall progressive politics, will have a narrow constituent base. Above all, diverse progressive groups must work together—must achieve more cooperation, coalition, and conflict resolution.

COALITION

The universalist ideology of the progressive movement of the 1960s cloaked its insensitivity, or even outright hostility to the needs of particular groups (Evans 1979; Young 1997). As groups discovered their unique identities and agendas, inevitable differentiation among social movements ensued (Evans 1979; Mansbridge 1996; Young 1997). There can be no turning back to seek unity on the old basis, but fragmentation means powerlessness. New possibilities, however, are emerging. Broad movements recognize their earlier insensitivity and become more inclusive. Particular groups realize that alone they can't win legislative or electoral victories. A first response is tactical coalitions (Simmons 1994; Delgado 1986; Reagon 1983). Despite differing interests, cultures, and values, there are win-win opportunities. Several groups can work together to reach a critical mass. Tactical joint action is appealing for its modest achievable goals and absence of threat to group identities, but it may leave no residuum of deeper ties. If conflict-resolution principles are applied, however, increased understanding and enduring respect can be built.

A progressive movement that can shape public opinion or win electoral majorities, must eventually forge a grand coalition. Integrative principles must include rather than override the particularity of constituent groups (Young 1997; cf. Gitlin 1995). Not only group interests, but social class concerns need to be addressed. Dewey envisions a very broad coalition: "the professional labor group; retail merchants; the white collar proletariat, male and female; farmers; laborers. . . . All these classes . . . stand to gain by [working together]. Yet to win their united and vigorous support [is a visionary project]" (LW6:406; also 225). They are "kept from uniting politically by divergence of immediate interests," (FC:60), exacerbated in lean times, when groups fight over scarce resources. The problem of building a progressive coalition is the problem of conflict-resolution (also 100–101).

Conflict-resolution methods for coalition-building do not promise instant success. Discussions may have periods of stalemate and be impeded by historical events. As with science and ethics, an entire generation may pass before new ideas are able to be accepted. Conflict-resolution may require new ways of thinking, perhaps emerging from

some other discipline. Progressives must not evade conflict or compromise away principles; but strive for innovative, mutually satisfactory solutions. Those active in the conflict-resolution movement must offer
their services as facilitators, and urge groups to join in discussions. From
this, cooperative exploration follows into novel programs which em-
body or create common interests. Progressive think tanks, independent
public intellectuals, and university-based scholars can all contribute.
Enduring coalition arises out of unanticipated new unifying visions and
programs, not by compromise among old ones.

Many today are keenly aware of the need for unifying themes and theorists have offered: "radical democracy" (Laclau and Mouffe 1985; Boggs
1995; Boyte 1989; West 1989); "politics of meaning" (Lerner 1996); "new
populism" (Boyte and Riessman 1986); "new progressivism" (Lind 1995);
"green politics" (Milbrath 1989; Rensenbrink 1992; Capra and Spretnak
1984); and "transformational politics" (Schwerin 1995: Woolpert, Slaton
and Schwerin 1998). Dewey, himself, offers a unifying approach organized around Pragmatist philosophy and participatory democracy—
though one addressed to reflective thinkers, not designed for visceral
impact and popular appeal (Ryan 1995). Despite the imaginativeness,
responsiveness to change, and generous intentions of these programs,
none has yet become a force for unification, so deep are the cleavages
among progressive groups. Conflict-resolution is needed on program
and theory as well as on tactics. While the search for unifying themes
must continue, actual coalitions will likely be forged out of practical
responses to historical contingencies—as with the Social Democratic
coalition in Sweden and the New Deal coalition in the United States.

The shared value of conflict-resolution could become a unifying factor around which diverse groups unite—a key concept and key institution in a unifying vision of participatory democracy. Agreement, rooted
in experience, on both the efficacy and desirability of this method could
help overcome centuries-old divisions within the progressive left, for example, over the role of violence in social change. This is possible only
if conflict-resolution is not allowed to become an instrument of co-
optation of the weak by the powerful. The integrity of the practice must
be preserved if its promise is to be fulfilled.

In addition to principled disagreement on progressive visions, the left
seems riven by factionalism and personal rivalries among its leaders, as
has been the case since its origins. To the extent that the educative experience of conflict-resolution can be self-transforming, divisions on the
left, rooted in the ambitions and insecurities of movement leaders may

yet be overcome (Colburn and Rogers 1996:11). This would demand a great deal of the educative potential of conflict-resolution, but this may be a necessary condition for moving toward unity. Under new circumstances, engaged persons may, unexpectedly, be capable of the change and growth required.

Conclusion

Having presented an overview of a Deweyan progressive political strategy, I can now situate his accounts of Pragmatism, social intelligence, social invention, and conflict resolution in a concrete politics of transition to a more participatory democratic society. There is no call here for a new party, a particular campaign, a riveting new slogan; only a long, adventurous yet slow process of movement and coalition-building. Nonetheless, the Deweyan progressive strategy sketched here offers enough concrete projects and enough new directions to provide specific tasks and fresh inspirations for political activists. There is much work to be done in movements for social experiments and inventions, towards use of new communication and organizational processes, and in traditional advocacy and electoral pursuits. Conducting conflict-resolution for coalition building and synthesizing unifying theory out of that experience are monumental steps. There are no guarantees of victory in this politics of transition. There are, however, many ethical and practical reasons to engage in the effort, and take the next step. Immediate rewards of such efforts may be found in the seemingly small political achievements and the day to day learning and growth that accompany creative effort. If hope for the long-term journey is needed, it can be found in Dewey's belief that ideas like democracy, community, inquiry and experiment, and the Pragmatist understanding of human experience can triumph in the long run—because they are so deeply in accord with human capacities, needs and ethical strivings (1927a:22; CD:228; FC:126–127, 162). "The foundation of democracy is . . . faith in human intelligence and in the power of pooled and cooperative experience. It is not belief that these things are complete but that, if given a show, they will grow and be able to generate progressively the knowledge and wisdom needed to guide collective action" (DEA:219).

Political strategy cannot determine the course of history; it exists in a political environment subject to vast forces beyond its control. Though a progressive movement cannot be insulated from these vicissitudes, it can learn to survive in lean times, to hold its ground, and build for the future. And in times of opportunity, it can learn to mobilize its forces for a resurgence of progressive organizing and action. Thus in spite of the many roadblocks on this path, Dewey's programs offer us sober hope for the eventual transition to a participatory democratic politics and a democratic Great Community.

Abbreviations

ACF (1934), *A Common Faith*
AE (1934), *Art as Experience*
CD (1939), "Creative Democracy"
DE (1915), *Democracy and Education*
DEA (1937), "Democracy and Educational Administration"
E,1908 (1908), *Ethics* (1st ed.)
E (1932), *Ethics* (completely rev. ed.)
EBNS (1939), "The Economic Basis of the New Society"
EE (1938), *Experience and Education*
EEL (1916), *Essays on Experimental Logic*
EKV (1939), "Experience Knowledge and Value: A Rejoinder"
EN (1929), *Experience and Nature*
EW (1882–1898), *Early Works*
FC (1939), *Freedom and Culture*
HNC (1922), *Human Nature and Conduct*
HWT (1933), *How We Think*
ION (1930), *Individualism Old and New*
LSA (1935), *Liberalism and Social Action*
LSS (1947), "Liberating the Social Scientist"
LTI (1938), *Logic: The Theory of Inquiry*
LW (1925–1953), *Later Works*
MW (1899–1924), *Middle Works*
PESE (1928), "Progressive Education and the Science of Education"
PP (1927), *The Public and Its Problems*

QC (1929), *The Quest for Certainty*
RPh (1920, 2d ed. 1948), *Reconstruction in Philosophy*
SS (1931), "Science and Society"
SSSC (1931), "Social Science and Social Control"
ST (1915), *Schools of Tomorrow*

Notes

Introduction

1. James T. Kloppenberg (1986), for example, argues that Dewey and other progressive thinkers were unable to resolve a contradiction between democracy and scientific expertise in the service of bureaucracy. "The question . . . is whether such expertise by shaping the alternatives to be discussed, slides imperceptibly but necessarily into control" (384). Kloppenberg also points to inadequate solution to problems of value discourse. "Intoxicated by . . . faith in democracy, Dewey . . . did not see clearly the difficulty cultures faced in . . . construct[ing] . . . standards to achieve harmony in a disenchanted world" (407). Kloppenberg concludes, "the persistence of power has corroded the political institutions and the civic virtue [Dewey] trusted to secure [his] ideals. While [his] victory has thus proved uncertain, [his] dream of democracy should survive" (407).

Despite positive response to Robert Westbrook's major biography (1991), reviewers damned Dewey with faint praise. In one of the gentler critiques, Edward Schwartz writes, "To honor Dewey as a powerful democratic voice with the liberal political tradition is appropriate . . . To suggest that Dewey can now help us transcend the limits of this tradition is problematic" (1991: 49). David Hollinger states: "Lippmann's misgivings about democracy are answered more directly by Westbrook than by Dewey himself. . . . For a more complete vindication of . . . radical democracy . . . one must go beyond both Dewey and Westbrook" (1991:155). Even Robert Westbrook, who has done so much to win recognition for Dewey as a theorist of participatory democracy, notes vague, unfinished, and contradictory aspects of his theory. In discussing *The Public and Its Problems*, Westbrook notes Dewey's "neglect of the politics necessary for contemporary publics to solve their intellectual problems and to build a new state and his refusal to speculate on the forms this state might take" (1991:316). "Decentralizing power would also, of course, raise difficulties of the sort Dewey fudged in merely asserting the easy interdependence of local communities with the Great Community" (317). Westbrook finds little in Dewey's further political writings to change this judgment: "Dewey never returned in any systematic fashion to these unanswered questions" (318). In *Liberalism and Social Action*, "his thinking remained bedeviled by the lack of a clear program of action" (439). In the end, however, Westbrook portrays Dewey as inspirational: "We could do worse than turn to Dewey for a full measure of the wisdom we will need to work our way out of the wilderness of the present" (552).

Chapter 1

1. Campbell 1995; Rockefeller 1991; Ryan 1995; Shusterman 1994a, 1994b; West 1989; Westbrook 1991.
2. Barber 1984; Dryzek 1990; Green 1985; Mansbridge 1983; Pateman 1970; Pitkin and Shumer 1982; and others.
3. Bellah et al. 1985; Sandel 1996.
4. The concept "reflectively settled practices" is explained in Chapter 2, under "Justification."

Chapter 2

1. Social scientists have taken much of their understanding of science, not from the study of natural science practice, but second hand from positivist philosophy of science. Resorting to postempiricist language to rationalize its failings, as rational choice theory does, does not change the positivist underpinnings of that approach (J. Friedman 1996).
2. Hacking's incisive understanding of Dewey's orientation is delivered in one pregnant sentence: "My own view, that realism is more a matter of intervention in the world, than of representing it in words and thought, surely owes much to Dewey" (1983:62). Hacking proceeds to elaborate his own view, with examples from the recent history of science, but does not explicate, or even cite, any of Dewey's texts.
3. The principle source for the following account is Roller and Roller (1954)—the source for Kuhn's (1970) remarks on scientific revolution in the field of electricity. Heilbron (1982) is an additional source.
4. Conduction does occur in nature, as when lightning travels from a roof to the ground, but this was not yet known in Gray's time. Indeed, it was necessary to see it in the laboratory before its brief, sudden, and perplexing natural occurrence could be understood.

5. This is not to say that Franklin's theory was accepted immediately or unanimously. There were still anomalous electrical effects that it failed to account for, and there were rival scientific factions which criticized Franklin on this account (Heilbron 1982). It was only in the next generation that fully unified accounts of electrical repulsion as well as attraction were achieved. This underscores the importance of the criterion of unification, and the central role of replication, discourse, and criticism within scientific communities, as discussed below.

6. Maxwell's laws are highly settled theoretical achievements and are constantly being employed by scientists. This does not mean that they encounter no anomalies and require no correction or revision. It was actually asymmetries in Maxwell's theory that inspired the work that led Einstein to relativity theory. Another anomalous condition, the spectrum of electromagnetic radiation in a cavity, or "black body," led to Planck's quantum hypothesis. Relativity theory and quantum mechanics have become, in their turn, highly settled knowledge, constantly being employed in pursuit of further discoveries, but are not without their own anomalies.

7. One condition for ideal speech mentioned by Benhabib is not fulfilled, and its absence foreshadows a critique of Dewey's account of the scientific community, considered below. This condition is that, "all must have equal chances . . . to express their feelings, wishes, and intentions" (Benhabib 1986:285). Such subjective states are not considered relevant in scientific discourse.

8. With regard to today's "big science," Ravetz (1971) pays tribute to the norms and organization of the scientific community, even as he describes the threats to it from the trends of massive growth, bureaucratization, and bitter struggle for survival and success.

9. Feynman, in his introductory physics lectures, presents the principle of superposition as a vivid example of the tractability of major phenomena in physics. An electrical field, for example, can be determined by superimposing the effects of each electron acting separately, without having to worry about interaction effects and consequent nonlinearity (Feynman, Leighton and Sands 1963–1966).

10. There is, to be sure, discussion of scientific values like scope, fruitfulness, accuracy, and unification, if not broader human values. But this more limited discourse does not require the same skills and knowledge as discussion of human values. Both scientific and ethical inquiry require a certain sensitivity, or feel, or intuition, but in the former, it is a feel for physical processes, and in the latter, it is an appreciation of the emotions and motivations of persons (E:268–270).

11. This awareness of responsibility sets up a greater potential conflict than Dewey acknowledges. As a physicist, should one pursue fascinating questions about the fundamental structure of matter which have no direct, and no foreseeable indirect consequence for human life? Or should one, for example, study the depletion of the ozone layer, or global warming, or nu-

clear proliferation? The latter are not scientifically fundamental issues, not "rich," or "ripe," from a scientific viewpoint—but with vast and fateful consequences for life on this planet. Should one judge that the problem is less one of research than of advocacy, and switch to grassroots education and organizing for environmental protection—changing one's entire career? Physicist Joseph Rotblat, winner of the Nobel Peace Prize, made approximately that decision (Rotblat 1985), but few other physicists have done so. Dewey would not presume that there is a single right answer in this dilemma. Not every individual scientist—given the individual's particular capabilities, present opportunities and responsibilities, life history, and other idiosyncrasies—should come to the same decision. It is sufficient to suggest that, if genuinely faced, this would be an agonizing dilemma for many scientists. In his discussion of social science, Dewey raises similar questions. There he argues that questions of human values are intrinsic to the successful pursuit of social inquiry. They are inescapable, even for those who seek to address value issues only from their professional stance. That claim is taken up in the next chapter, on social science.

Chapter 3

1. Elliott 1991; Merrifield 1989; Sanford 1970; Schon 1983, 1991; Whyte 1991.

2. Bowman and Stone 1996; Dahl 1985; Gewirth 1996; Krimerman and Lindenfeld 1992; Morrison 1995; Schweikart 1980.

3. The discussion now moves from interpretation to critique, and then to the place of values in social science. Further issues about interpretation are taken up below in relation to the agenda of today's philosophy of social science.

Chapter 4

1. This example is chosen, principally, because Gilligan (1982), whose approach to deliberation has notable resemblances to Dewey's, devotes several chapters to it, based on interviews with women who struggled with such decisions. My discussions with abortion counselors about the process of deliberation are also drawn upon. This issue has been widely discussed by ethicists, but with emphasis on reasoning from principles in order to justify a particular position. The goal here is to focus on the process, irrespective of the outcome. Bringing up this case risks evoking deep, passionately held convictions not amenable to discussion. My intention, however, is not to challenge those core beliefs and values, but to look at a broader context of which they are a part, and examine a process of deliberation in which they are included. A second risk is repeating here what has happened in national

political discourse, eclipsing crucial issues of distributive justice and social class with a narrow focus on "social" issues. Full Deweyan inquiry into abortion politics, however, reveals class issues intrinsic to the abortion controversy, as Luker has shown (1984), and as discussed in the next chapter.

2. In general, the outcomes of full deliberation are choices which we recognize as moral. Dewey's account passes the test of verisimilitude. In the normative ethics section of the next chapter, I further discuss substantive ethical principles which emerge from deliberation as dramatic rehearsal, and decision as conflict-resolution. Dewey, however, makes a stronger claim: what we generally recognize as moral is precisely the outcome of the deliberation and decision processes he has reconstructed. That is, the ethic of a culture is nothing more, nor less, than its reflectively settled practices and the principles that may be drawn from them.

References

Works by John Dewey

1882–1898. *John Dewey: The Early Works, 1882–1898.* Ed. J. Boydston.
  5 vols. 1967–1972. Carbondale, IL: Southern Illinois University Press
1899–1924. *John Dewey: The Middle Works, 1899–1924.* Ed. J. Boydston.
  15 vols. 1976–1983. Carbondale, IL: Southern Illinois University Press.
1908. With J. Tufts. *Ethics.* MW5.
1909. *Moral Principles in Education.* MW4:265–291.
1910. "The Influence of Darwin on Philosophy." MW4:3–14.
1915a. *Democracy and Education.* New York: Macmillan.
1915b. With E. Dewey. *Schools of Tomorrow.* New York: E. P. Dutton & Co.
1916. *Essays in Experimental Logic.* Chicago: University of Chicago Press.
1920. *Reconstruction in Philosophy.* New York: Henry Holt & Co. 2d ed.
  Boston: Beacon Press, 1948.
1922. *Human Nature and Conduct.* New York: Henry Holt & Co. New
  York: Modern Library, 1930.
1925–1953. *John Dewey: The Later Works, 1925–1953.* Ed. J. Boydston.
  17 vols. 1981–1992. Carbondale, IL: Southern Illinois University Press.
1925. "The Development of American Pragmatism." LW2:3–21.
1926. "Philosophy and Civilization." LW3:3–10.
1927a. "Anthropology and Ethics." LW3:11–24.
1927b. *The Public and Its Problems.* New York: Henry Holt & Co.
1928a. "Philosophies of Freedom." LW3:92–114.
1928b. "Progressive Education and the Science of Education." LW3.
1929a. *The Quest for Certainty.* New York: G. P. Putnam's Sons.
1929b. *Experience and Nature.* New York: W. W. Norton & Co. (orig. ed.
  1925).

1929c. "Sources of a Science of Education." LW5:1–40.

1930a. *Individualism Old and New.* New York: Minton, Balch & Co.

1930b. "Three Independent Factors in Morals." LW5.

1931a. "Science and Society." LW6:53–63.

1931b. "Social Science and Social Control." LW6:64–68.

1932. With J. Tufts. *Ethics.* Rev. ed. LW7.

1933. *How We Think.* Rev. ed. Boston: D. C. Heath & Co.

1934a. *Art as Experience.* New York: Minton, Balch & Co.

1934b. *A Common Faith.* New Haven: Yale University Press.

1935. *Liberalism and Social Action.* New York: G. P. Putnam's Sons.

1936. "Authority and Social Change." LW11:130–145.

1937a. "Democracy and Educational Administration." LW11:217–225.

1937b. "The Unity of the Human Being." LW13:322–337.

l938a. *Experience and Education.* London: MacMillan.

1938b. *Logic: The Theory of Inquiry.* New York: Henry Holt & Co.

1939a. "Creative Democracy—The Task Before Us." LW14:224–230.

1939b. "Democratic Ends Need Democratic Methods for their Realization." LW14:367–368.

1939c. "The Economic Basis of the New Society." LW13:309–322.

1939d. "Experience, Knowledge and Values: A Rejoinder." LW14:3–90.

1939e. *Freedom and Culture.* New York: G. P. Putnam's Sons.

1939f. *Theory of Valuation.* Chicago: University of Chicago Press.

1941. "The Basic Values and Loyalties of Democracy." LW14:275–277.

1944. "The Challenge to Liberal Thought." LW15:261–275.

1946. *Problems of Men.* New York: Philosophical Library.

1947. "Liberating the Social Scientist." LW15:224–238.

1948. "Introduction: Reconstruction as Seen Twenty-Five Years Later." In *Reconstruction in Philosophy.* 2d ed. Boston: Beacon Press.

1950. "John Dewey Responds." LW17:84–87.

Works by Other Authors

Adams, F. 1975. *Unearthing Seeds of Fire: The Idea of Highlander.* Winston-Salem: John F. Blair.

Agassi, J. 1971. *Faraday as a Natural Philosopher.* Chicago: University of Chicago Press.

Alexander, T. M. 1987. *John Dewey's Theory of Art, Experience and Nature: The Horizons of Feeling.* New York: State University of New York Press.

———. 1995. "John Dewey and the Roots of Democratic Imagination." In *Recovering Pragmatism's Voice: The Classical Tradition, Rorty, and the Philosophy of Communication,* ed. L. Langsdorf and A. R. Smith, 131–154. Albany: State University of New York Press.

Alexander, J., B. Giesen, R. Munch and N. Smelser, eds. 1987. *The Micro-Macro Link*. Berkeley: University of California Press.

Alperovitz, G. 1996. "The Reconstruction of Community Meaning." *Tikkun* 11; 3:13–16, 79.

Alperovitz, G. and G. Faux. 1984. *Rebuilding America: A Blueprint for the New Economy*. New York: Pantheon.

Arbogast, M. 1994. "Building on Common Ground: Opponents in the Abortion Controversy Join Forces." *The Witness* (April 1994).

Avery, M., B. Streibel, B. Auvine and L. Weiss. 1981. *Building United Judgment: A Handbook for Consensus Decision Making*. Madison: Center for Conflict Resolution.

Baier, A. 1991. *A Progress of Sentiments: Reflections on Hume's Treatise*. Cambridge: Harvard University Press.

Barber, B. 1984. *Strong Democracy*. Berkeley: University of California Press.

———. 1995. *Jihad Versus MacWorld*. New York: Times Books.

Becker, T. and R. Scarce. 1986. "Teledemocracy Emergent: State of the American Art and Science," In *Progress in Communication Sciences*, Volume VIII, ed. B. Dervin and M. Voigt. Norwood, NJ: ABLEX Publishing Corporation.

Belenky, M., B. Clinchy, N. Goldberger and J. Tarule. 1986. *Women's Ways of Knowing: The Development of Self, Voice, and Mind*. New York: Basic Books.

Bell, D. and I. Kristol, eds. 1981. *The Crisis in Economic Theory*. New York: Basic Books.

Bellah, R., R. Madsen, W. Sullivan, A. Swidler and S. Tipton. 1985. *Habits of the Heart*. Berkeley: University of California Press.

———. 1991. *The Good Society*. New York: Knopf.

Benello, C. G. 1992. *From The Ground Up: Essays on Grassroots and Workplace Democracy*. Ed. L. Krimerman, F. Lindenfeld, C. Corty, and J. Benello. Boston: South End Press.

Benhabib, S. 1986. *Critique, Norm, and Utopia: A Study of the Foundations of Critical Theory*. New York: Columbia University Press.

———. 1992. "Autonomy, Modernity, and Community: Communitarianism and Critical Social Theory in Dialogue." In *Cultural-Political Interventions in the Unfinished Project of Enlightenment*, ed. A. Honneth et al., 39–59. Cambridge: M.I.T. Press.

———. 1996. "Toward a Deliberative Model of Democratic Legitimacy." In *Democracy and Difference: Contesting the Boundaries of the Political*, ed. S. Benhabib, 67–94. Princeton: Princeton University Press.

———, ed. 1996. *Democracy and Difference: Contesting the Boundaries of the Political*. Princeton: Princeton University Press.

Bernstein, P. 1976. *Workplace Democratization: Its Internal Dynamics*. New Brunswick, NJ: Transaction Books.

Bernstein, R. J., ed. 1960. *Dewey on Experience, Nature, and Freedom.* New York: Bobbs Merrill.

———. 1966. *John Dewey.* New York: Washington Square Press.

———. 1971. *Praxis and Action: Contemporary Philosophies of Human Activity.* Philadelphia: University of Pennsylvania Press.

Bledstein, B. J. 1976. *The Culture of Professionalism: The Middle Class and the Development of Higher Education in America.* New York: Norton.

———. 1983. *Beyond Objectivism and Relativism.* Philadelphia: University of Pennsylvania Press.

Blum, L. A. 1994. *Moral Perception and Particularity.* Cambridge: Cambridge University Press.

Boggs, C. 1995. *The Socialist Tradition.* New York: Routledge.

Boguslaw, R. 1965. *The New Utopians: A Study of System Design and Social Change.* Englewood Cliffs, NJ: Prentice Hall.

Bohman, J. 1990. "Communication, Ideology, and Democratic Theory." *American Political Science Review* 84:93–109.

———. 1991. *New Philosophy of Social Science.* Cambridge: M.I.T. Press.

———. 1999. "Democracy as Inquiry, Inquiry as Democratic: Pragmatism, Social Science, and the Cognitive Division of Labor." *American Journal of Political Science* 43; 2 (April 1999):590–607.

Boisvert, R. 1988. *Dewey's Metaphysics.* New York: Fordham University Press.

Bourne, R. 1917. "Twilight of Idols." In Bourne *War and the Intellectuals: Collected Essays, 1915–1919,* ed. C. Resek, 3–14. New York: Harper and Row 1964.

Bowles, S. and H. Gintis. 1986. *Democracy and Capitalism: Property, Community, and the Contradictions of Modern Social Thought.* New York: Basic Books.

Bowman, E. A. and B. Stone. 1996. *Worker Ownership on the Mondragon Model: Prospects for Global Workplace Democracy An Occasional Paper.* Stillwater, PA: GEO.

Boyte, H. 1989. *Commonwealth: A Return to Citizen Politics.* New York: Free Press.

Boyte, H. and F. Riessman, eds. 1986. *The New Populism: The Politics of Empowerment.* Philadelphia: Temple University Press.

Bruner, J. 1966. "Some Elements of Discovery." In *Learning by Discovery: A Critical Appraisal,* ed. L. Shulman and E. Keislar, 101–113. Chicago: Rand McNally.

Burton, J. 1987. *Resolving Deep-Rooted Conflict: A Handbook.* Lanham, MD: University Press of America.

Bush, P. 1997. "Team Up with Parents, Say School Reformers in 20 States." *Doing Democracy* 4; 2:7.

Bush, R. A. B. 1989. "Efficiency and Protection, or Empowerment and Recognition?: The Mediator's Role and Ethical Standards in Mediation." *Florida Law Review* 41; 2:253–286.

Cahn, S. M., ed. 1977. *New Studies in the Philosophy of John Dewey.* Hanover, NH: University Press of New England.

Calhoun, C., ed. 1992. *Habermas and the Public Sphere.* Cambridge: MIT Press.

Campbell, D. and J. Stanley. 1963. *Experimental and Quasi-Experimental Designs for Research.* Chicago: Rand McNally.

Campbell, J. 1995. *Understanding John Dewey: Nature and Cooperative Intelligence.* Chicago: Open Court.

———. 1998. "Dewey's Conception of Community." In *Reading Dewey: Interpretations for a Postmodern Generation,* ed. L. Hickman, 23–42. Bloomington: Indiana University Press.

Capra, F. and C. Spretnak (in collaboration with R. Lutz). 1984. *Green Politics.* New York: Dutton.

Carter, S. L. 1993. *The Culture of Disbelief: How American Law and Politics Trivialize Religious Devotion.* New York: Basic Books.

Charity, A. 1995. *Doing Public Journalism.* New York: Guilford.

Clemens, E. S. 1997. *The People's Lobby: Organizational Innovation and the Rise of Interest Group Politics in the United States, 1890–1925.* Chicago: University of Chicago Press.

Cohen, J. 1996. "Procedure and Substance in Deliberative Democracy." In *Democracy and Difference: Contesting the Boundaries of the Political,* ed. S. Benhabib, 95–119. Princeton: Princeton University Press.

Colburn, B. and J. Rogers. 1996. "What's Next? Beyond the Election," *Nation* (November 18, 1996): 11–18.

Comer, J. P. 1988a. "Educating Poor Minority Children," *Scientific American* 259; 5:42–48.

———. 1988b. *Maggie's American Dream.* New York: New American Library.

———. 1993. *School Power: Implications of an Intervention Project.* 2d ed. New York: Free Press.

Comer, J. P., N. M. Haynes, E. T. Joyner and M. Ben-Avie, eds. 1996. *Rallying the Whole Village: The Comer Process for Reforming Education.* New York: Teachers College Press.

Connolly, W. E. 1991. *Identity and Difference: Democratic Negotiations of Political Paradox.* Ithaca: Cornell University Press.

Co-op America Quarterly. Washington, DC: Co-op America.

Cork, J. 1950. "John Dewey and Karl Marx." In *John Dewey: Philosopher of Science and Freedom,* ed. S. Hook, 331–350. New York: The Dial Press.

Cuoto, R. 1992. "What's Political About Self-Help?" *Social Policy* 23; 2:39–43.

Dahl, R. 1985. *A Preface to Economic Democracy.* Cambridge: Polity Press.

Daly, H. and J. B Cobb, Jr. 1994. *For the Common Good: Redirecting the Economy Toward Community, the Environoment, and a Sustainable Future.* 2d ed. Boston: Beacon Press.

Damico, A. J. 1978. *Individuality and Community: The Social and Political Thought of John Dewey.* Gainesville: University Presses of Florida.

Davis, A. 1989. "In Theory: An Interview with Mary Parker Follett." *Negotiation Journal.*

Dean, J. W. 1981. "The Dissolution of the Keynsian Consensus." In *The Crisis in Economic Theory,* ed. D. Bell and I. Kristol, 19–35. New York: Basic Books.

Delgado, G. 1986. *Organizing the Movement: The Roots and Growth of Acorn.* Philadelphia: Temple University Press.

Deming, B. 1984. *We Are All Part of One Another: A Barbara Deming Reader.* Ed. J. Meyerding. Philadelphia: New Society Publishers.

Diggins, J. 1994. *The Promise of Pragmatism: Modernism and the Crisis of Knowledge and Authority.* Chicago: University of Chicago Press.

Doing Democracy. Brattleboro, VT: Center for Living Democracy.

Dreyfus, H. L. and S. E. Dreyfus. 1986. *Mind Over Machine: The Power of Human Intuition, and Expertise in the Era of the Computer.* New York: Free Press.

———. 1990. "What is Morality?: A Phenomenological Account of the Development of Ethical Expertise." In *Universalism vs. Communitarianism: Contemporary Debates in Ethics,* ed. D. Rasmussen, 237–264. Cambridge: M.I.T. Press.

Dryzek, J. S. 1990. *Discursive Democracy: Politics, Policy, and Political Science.* Cambridge: Cambridge University Press.

Edel, L. and E. Flower. 1985. "Introduction." In *John Dewey: The Later Works, 1925–1953,* Volume 7, ed. J. Boydston, vii–xxxv. Carbondale: Southern Illinois University Press.

Edelman, M. 1964. *The Symbolic Uses of Politics.* Urbana: University of Illinois Press.

Edwards, C., L. Gandini and G. Forman. 1993. *The Hundred Languages of Children: The Reggio Emilia Approach to Early Childhood Education.* Norwood, NJ: Ablex Publishing Corporation.

Ehrenreich, B. 1989. *Fear of Falling: The Inner Life of the Middle Class.* New York: Pantheon Books.

Elliott, J. 1991. *Action Research for Educational Change.* Milton Keynes: Open University Press.

Emery, F. and E. Trist. 1973. *Towards a Social Ecology: Contextual Appreciations of the Future in the Present.* London: Plenum Publishing.

Erikson, E. 1993. *Young Man Luther: A Study in Psychoanalysis and History.* New York: Norton.

Esping-Anderson, G. 1985. *Politics Against Markets: The Social Democratic Road to Power.* Princeton: Princeton University Press.

Evans, S. 1979. *Personal Politics: The Roots of Women's Liberation in the Civil Rights Movement and the New Left.* New York: Vintage Books.

Ezekiel, R. 1995. *The Racist Mind: Portraits of Neo-Nazis and Klansmen.* New York: Viking.

Fay, B. 1996. *Contemporary Philosophy of Social Science.* Oxford: Blackwell.

Feyerabend, P. 1970. "Consolations for the Specialist." In *Criticism and the Growth of Knowledge,* ed. I. Lakatos and A. Musgrave, 197–230. Cambridge: Cambridge University Press.

Festenstein, M. 1997. *Pragmatism and Political Theory: From Dewey to Rorty.* Chicago: University of Chicago Press.

Feynman, R., R. B. Leighton and M. Sands. 1963–1965. *The Feynman Lectures on Physics.* Reading, MA: Addison Wesley.

Fischer, F. 1990. *Technocracy and the Politics of Expertise.* Newbury Park, CA: Sage Publications.

Fisher, R. and W. Ury. 1981. *Getting to Yes: Negotiating Agreement Without Giving In.* Boston: Houghton Mifflin.

Fishkin, J. 1991. *Democracy and Deliberation: New Directions for Democratic Reform.* New Haven: Yale University Press.

———. 1996. *The Voice of the People.* New Haven: Yale University Press.

Fitch, R. 1996. "In Bologna, Small is Beautiful." *Nation,* May 13, 1996:18–21.

Flacks, R. 1988. *Making History: The Radical Tradition in American Life.* New York: Columbia University Press.

Flanagan, O. 1991. *Varieties of Moral Personality: Ethics and Psychological Realism.* Cambridge: Harvard University Press.

Follett, M. P. 1924. *Creative Experience.* New York: Longmans, Green & Co.

———. 1942. *Dynamic Administration: The Collected Papers of Mary Parker Follett.* Ed. H. Metcalf and L. Urwick. New York: Harper.

Forester, J. 1993. *Critical Theory, Public Policy, and Planning Practice.* Albany: State University of New York Press.

Foster, L. and P. Herzog, eds. 1994. *Defending Diversity: Contemporary Philosophical Perspectives on Pluralism and Multiculturalism.* Amherst: University of Massachusetts Press.

Franke, R. and B. Chasin. 1989. *Kerala: Radical Reform as Development in an Indian State.* San Francisco: The Institute for Food and Development Policy.

Frankel, C. 1977. "John Dewey's Political Philosophy." In *New Studies in the Philosophy of John Dewey,* ed. S. Cahn, 3–44. Hanover, NH: University Press of New England.

Friedman, J., ed. 1996. *The Rational Choice Controversy: Economic Models of Politics Reconsidered.* New Haven: Yale University Press.

Friedman, M. 1953. "Methodology of Positive Economics." In *Essays in Positive Economics,* 3–43. Chicago: University of Chicago Press.

Fromm, E. 1947. *Man for Himself: An Inquiry into the Psychology of Ethics.* New York: Rinehart.

Gadamer, H.-G. 1975. *Truth and Method.* Translation edited by G. Barden and J. Cumming. New York: Seabury Press.

Galbraith, J. K. 1958. *The Affluent Society.* Boston: Houghton Mifflin.

Galston, W. A. 1994. "Review of *Democratic Community: NOMOS XXXV.*" *American Political Science Review* 88; 3:732–733.

GEO: Grassroots Economic Organizing Newsletter. Stillwater, PA: GEO.

Gewirth, A. 1996. *The Community of Rights.* Chicago: University of Chicago Press.

Gilligan, C. 1982. *In a Different Voice: Psychological Theory and Women's Development.* Cambridge: Harvard University Press.

Ginsburg, F. 1998. "Rescuing the Nation." In *Abortion Wars: A Half Century of Struggle, 1950–2000,* ed. R. Solinger, 227–250. Berkeley: University of California Press.

Girvetz, H. K. 1973. *Beyond Right and Wrong: A Study in Moral Theory.* New York: Free Press.

Gitlin, T. 1995. *The Twilight of Common Dreams: Why America is Wracked by Culture Wars.* New York: Henry Holt and Co.

Gold-Steinberg, S. and A. Stewart. 1998. "Psychologies of Abortion: Implications of a Changing Context." In *Abortion Wars: A Half Century of Struggle, 1950–2000,* ed. R. Solinger, 356–373. Berkeley: University of California Press.

Gordon, D. 1972. *Theories of Poverty and Underemployment: Orthodox, Radical, and Dual Labor Market Perspectives.* Lexington, MA: D. C. Heath.

Gorney, C. 1998. *Articles of Faith: A Frontline History of the Abortion Wars.* New York: Simon and Schuster.

Gouinlock, J. 1972. *John Dewey's Philosophy of Value.* New York: Humanities Press.

Green, P. 1985. *Retrieving Democracy: In Search of Civic Equality.* Totowa, NJ: Rowman & Allanheld.

Griffin, C. W., M. J. Wirth and A. G. Wirth. 1986. *Beyond Acceptance: Parents of Lesbians and Gays Talk About Their Experiences.* New York: St. Martin's Press

Gueron, J. 1986. *Work Initiatives for Welfare Recipients.* New York: Manpower Demonstration Research Corporation.

Guignon, C. B. 1991. "Pragmatism or Hermeneutics? Epistemology after Foundationalism." In *The Interpretive Turn: Philosophy, Science, and Culture,* ed. D. Hiley, J. Bohman, and R. Shusterman, 81–101. Ithaca: Cornell University Press.

Gutmann, A. and D. Thompson. 1996. *Democracy and Disagreement: Why Moral Conflict Cannot be Avoided in Politics, and What Should be Done About It.* Cambridge: Harvard University Press.

Habermas, J. 1971. *Knowledge and Human Interests.* Translated by J. J. Shapiro. Boston: Beacon Press.

———. 1979. *Communication and the Evolution of Society.* Translated by T. McCarthy. Boston: Beacon Press.

———. 1992. *Postmetaphysical Thinking: Philosophical Essays.* Translated by W. M. Hohengarten. Cambridge: M.I.T. Press.

———. 1993. *Moral Consciousness and Communicative Action.* Translated by C. Lenhardt and S. W. Nicholson. Cambridge: M.I.T. Press

————. 1996. *Between Facts and Norms: Contributions to a Discourse Theory of Law and Democracy*. Translated by W. Rehg (orig. German ed. 1992). Cambridge: M.I.T. Press.

Hacking, I. 1983. *Representing and Intervening: Introductory Topics in the Philosophy of Natural Science*. Cambridge: Cambridge University Press.

Hadamard, J. 1986. *Essay on the Psychology of Invention in the Mathematical Field*. Princeton: Princeton University Press.

Hall, A. R. 1959. "The Scholar and the Craftsman in the Scientific Revolution." In *Critical Problems in the History of Science*, ed. M. Clagett, 3–29. Madison: University of Wisconsin Press.

Hampshire, S. 1971. *Freedom of Mind*. Princeton: Princeton University Press.

Hanson, N. R. 1958. *Patterns of Discovery: An Inquiry into the Conceptual Foundations of Science*. Cambridge: Cambridge University Press.

Hawken, P. 1993. *The Ecology of Commerce: A Declaration of Sustainability*. New York: HarperCollins.

Hegel, G. W. F. 1977. *Phenomenology of Spirit*. Translated by A. V. Miller. Oxford: Oxford University Press.

Heilbron, J. L. 1982. *Elements of Early Modern Physics*. Berkeley: University of California Press.

Heisenberg, W. 1983. *Tradition in Science*. New York: Seabury Press.

Held, V. 1993. *Feminist Morality: Transforming Culture, Society, and Politics*. Chicago: University of Chicago Press.

Hempel, C. 1965. *Aspects of Scientific Explanation*. New York: Free Press.

Hesse, M. 1980. *Revolutions and Reconstructions in the Philosophy of Science*. Bloomington: Indiana University Press.

Hickman, L. A. 1990. *John Dewey's Pragmatic Technology*. Bloomington: Indiana University Press.

————, ed. 1998. *Reading Dewey: Interpretations for a Postmodern Generation*. Bloomington: Indiana University Press.

Hiley, D. R., J. M. Bohman and R. Shusterman. 1991. *The Interpretive Turn: Philosophy, Science, and Culture*. Ithaca: Cornell University Press.

Hirschman, A. O. 1970. *Exit, Voice, and Loyalty: Responses to Decline in Firms, Organizations, and States*. Cambridge: Harvard University Press.

Hochschild, J. L. 1993. "Disjunction and Ambivalence in Citizen's Political Attitudes." In *Reconsidering the Democratic Public*, ed. G. Marcus and R. Hanson, 187–210. University Park: Pennsylvania State University Press.

Hollinger, D. 1991. "A Radical Democrat." Review of Westbrook 1991. *Atlantic* 268; 5, November:152–155.

Honneth, A., T. McCarthy, C. Offe and A. Wellmer, eds. 1992a. *Cultural-Political Interventions in the Unfinished Project of Enlightenment*. Translated by B. Fultner. Cambridge: M.I.T. Press.

————. 1992b. *Philosophical Interventions in the Unfinished Project of Enlightenment*. Translated by W. Rehg. Cambridge: M.I.T. Press.

Hook, S., ed. 1950. *John Dewey: Philosopher of Science and Freedom.*
New York: The Dial Press.
———. 1974. *Pragmatism and the Tragic Sense of Life.* New York: Basic
Books.
In Context: A Journal of Hope, Sustainability, and Change. Bainbridge
Island, WA: Context Institute.
Isaac, J. C. 1999. "The Algebra Project and Democracy." *Dissent* 46; 1,
Winter:72–79.
Jacksteit, M. and A. Kaufmann. 1995. *Finding Common Ground in the
Abortion Conflict: A Manual.* Washington, DC: Common Ground Net-
work for Life and Choice.
———. 1996. "Introduction." In *Common Ground on Teen Pregnancy:
A Pro-Choice, Pro-Life Conversation: Network Papers No. 2,* ed. M. Jack-
steit, 1–3. Washington, DC: Common Ground Network for Life and
Choice.
Joas, H. 1993. *Pragmatism and Social Theory.* Chicago: University of Chi-
cago Press.
Johnson, M. 1993. *Moral Imagination: Implications of Cognitive Science for
Ethics.* Chicago: University of Chicago Press.
Jonsen, A. R. and S. Toulmin. 1988. *The Abuse of Casuistry: A History of
Moral Reasoning.* Berkeley: University of California Press.
Kaplan, L. 1998. "Beyond Safe and Legal: The Lessons of Jane." In *Abortion
Wars: A Half Century of Struggle, 1950–2000,* ed. R. Solinger, 33–41.
Berkeley: University of California Press.
Kasmir, S. 1996. *The Myth of Mondragon: Cooperatives, Politics, and Work-
ing Class Life in a Basque Town.* Albany: State University of New York
Press.
Katz, L. G. and B. Cesarone, eds. 1994. *Reflections on the Reggio Emilia Ap-
proach.* Urbana: ERIC Clearinghouse on Elementary and Early Childhood
Education.
Katzenstein, P. J. 1984. *Corporatism and Change: Austria, Switzerland, and
the Politics of Industry.* Ithaca: Cornell University Press.
Kaufman-Osborn, T. 1991. *Politics/Sense/Experience: A Pragmatic Inquiry
into the Promise of Democracy.* Ithaca: Cornell University Press.
Kazin, M. 1995. *The Populist Persuasion: An American History.* New York:
Basic Books.
———. 1996. "Alternative Politics." *Dissent* 43; 1, Winter:22–26.
Kekes, J. 1989. *Moral Tradition and Individuality.* Princeton: Princeton Uni-
versity Press.
———. 1993. *The Morality of Pluralism.* Princeton: Princeton University
Press.
Kelly, J. R. 1994. "A Dispatch from the Abortion Wars: Reflections on 'Com-
mon Ground.'" *America* 171; 7:8–13.
Key, V. O. 1966. *The Responsible Electorate: Rationality in Presidential
Voting, 1936–1960.* Cambridge: Harvard University Press.

King, Rev. M. L., Jr. 1986. *A Testament of Hope: The Sermons, Writings and Speeches of Martin Luther King, Jr.*, ed. J. M. Washington. New York: HarperCollins Publishers.

Klatch, R. 1987. *Women of the New Right*. Philadelphia: Temple University Press.

Klawans, S. 1996. "Two Ollies—True North." *The Nation* 263; 2, July 8, 1996:35–36.

Kloppenberg, J. T. 1986. *Uncertain Victory: Social Democracy and Progressivism in European and American Thought, 1870–1920*. New York: Oxford University Press.

Knight, J. and J. Johnson. 1994. "Aggregation and Deliberation: On the Possibility of Democratic Legitimacy." *Political Theory* 22; 2:277–296.

Knorr-Cetina, K. and A. Cicourel, eds. 1981. *Advances in Social Theory and Methodology: Toward an Integration of Micro and Micro-sociologies*. London: Routledge & Kegan Paul.

Kohlberg, L. 1981. *The Philosophy of Moral Development*. San Francisco: Harper and Row.

Krimerman, L. and F. Lindenfeld. 1992. *When Workers Decide: Workplace Democracy Takes Root in North America*. Philadelphia: New Society Publishers.

Kuhn, T. 1970. *The Structure of Scientific Revolutions*. 2d ed. Chicago: University of Chicago Press.

———. 1977. "Objectivity, Value Judgment, and Theory Choice." In *The Essential Tension: Selected Studies in Scientific Tradition and Change*, 320–339. Chicago: University of Chicago Press.

Laclau, E. and C. Mouffe. 1985. *Hegemony and Socialist Strategy: Toward a Radical Democratic Politics*. London: Verso.

Lakatos, I. 1970. "Falsification and the Methodology of Scientific Research Programmes." In *Criticism and the Growth of Knowledge*, ed. I. Lakatos and A. Musgrave, 91–96. Cambridge: Cambridge University Press.

Lakatos, I. and A. Musgrave, eds. 1970. *Criticism and the Growth of Knowledge*. Cambridge: Cambridge University Press.

Lakoff, G. 1996. *Moral Politics: What Conservatives Know that Liberals Don't*. Chicago: University of Chicago Press.

Lantieri, L. and J. Patti. 1996. *Waging Peace in Our Schools*. Boston: Beacon Press.

Lappé, F. and P. M. DuBois. 1994. *The Quickening of America: Rebuilding Our Nation, Remaking Our Lives*. San Francisco: Jossey Bass.

Lasch, C. 1979. *The Culture of Narcissism: American Life in An Age of Diminishing Expectations*. New York: W. W. Norton & Co.

Laue, J. and G. Cormick. 1978. "The Ethics of Intervention in Community Disputes." In *The Ethics of Social Intervention*, ed. G. Bermant, H. Kelman, and D. Warwick, 205–232. New York: Wiley.

Lawson, R. A. 1971. *The Failure of Independent Liberalism: 1930–1941*. New York: G. P. Putnam's Sons.

Lerner, M. 1986. *Surplus Powerlessness: The Psychodynamics of Everyday Life and the Psychology of Individual and Social Transformation.* Oakland, CA: The Institute for Labor and Mental Health.

———. 1996. *The Politics of Meaning: Restoring Hope and Possibility in an Age of Cynicism.* Reading, MA: Addison-Wesley.

Lind, M. 1995. *The Next American Nation: The New Nationalism and the Fourth American Revolution.* New York: Free Press.

Lindblom, C. E. 1990. *Inquiry and Change: The Troubled Attempt to Understand and Shape Society.* New Haven: Yale University Press.

Living Democracy. Brattleboro, VT: Center for Living Democracy.

Loevinger, J. 1976. *Ego Development.* San Francisco: Jossey Bass.

Luker, K. 1984. *Abortion and the Poltics of Motherhood.* Berkeley: University of California Press.

Luskin, R. C., J. S. Fishkin, R. Jowell and R. Gray. 1996. "Considered Opinions: Deliberative Polling in the U. K." Paper presented to the Annual Scientific Meeting of the International Society for Political Psychology, Vancouver, B.C., June 30, 1966.

MacIntyre, A. 1988. *Whose Justice? Which Rationality?* Notre Dame, IN: Notre Dame University Press.

Maffetone, S. 1998. "Political Liberalism, Abortion, and the Limits of Public Reason." Paper presented to University Seminar in Social & Political Thought, Columbia University, January 22, 1998.

Manicas, P. 1989. "Pragmatic Philosophy and the Charge of Scientism." *Transactions of the Charles Peirce Society* 23:179–222.

Mansbridge, J. 1983. *Beyond Adversary Democracy.* 2d ed. Chicago: University of Chicago Press.

———. 1993. "Self-Interest and Political Transformation." In *Reconsidering the Democratic Public,* ed. G. Marcus and R. Hanson, 91–109. University Park, PA: Pennsylvania State University Press.

———. 1996. "Using Power/Fighting Power: The Polity." In *Democracy and Difference: Contesting the Boundaries of the Political,* ed. S. Benhabib, 46–66. Princeton: Princeton University Press.

Marcus, G. E. and R. L. Hanson, eds. 1993. *Reconsidering the Democratic Public.* University Park, PA: Pennsylvania State University Press.

Marrow, A. 1969. *The Practical Theorist.* New York: Basic Books.

Marsh, J. 1995. *Critique, Action, and Liberation.* Albany: State University of New York Press.

Maslow, A. 1954. *Motivation and Personality.* New York: Harper.

May, R. 1953. *Man's Search for Himself.* New York: Norton.

McCamant, K. and C. Durrett. 1994. *Cohousing: A Contemporary Approach to Housing Ourselves.* 2d ed. Berkeley: Ten Speed Press.

McCarthy, T. 1992. "Philosophy and Social Practice: Avoiding the Ethnocentric Predicament." In *Philosophical Interventions in the Unfinished Project of Enlightenment,* ed. A. Honneth et al., 241–260. Cambridge: M.I.T. Press.

Medoff, P. and H. Sklar. 1994. *Streets of Hope: The Fall and Rise of an Ur-ban Neighborhood.* Boston: South End Press.

Meeker-Lowry, S. 1988. *Economics as If the Earth Really Mattered: A Cata-lyst Guide to Socially Conscious Investing.* Philadelphia: New Society Publishers.

Meier, D. 1995. *The Power of Their Ideas: Lessons for America from a Small School in Harlem.* Boston: Beacon Press.

Memmi, A. 1965. *The Colonizer and the Colonized.* Boston: Beacon Press.

Merrifield, J. 1989. *Putting the Scientists in their Place: Participatory Re-search in Environmental and Occupational Health.* New Market, TN: Highlander Center.

Milbrath, L. M. 1989. *Envisioning a Sustainable Society: Learning Our Way Out.* Albany: State University of New York Press.

Miller, J. 1991. "The Common Faith." Review of Westbrook 1991. *Nation* 253; 12, October 14, 1991:450–454.

Moon, J. D. 1993a. *Constructing Community: Moral Pluralism and Tragic Conflicts.* Princeton: Princeton University Press.

———. 1993b. "Theory, Citizenship, and Democracy." In *Reconsidering the Democratic Public,* ed. G. Marcus and R. Hanson, 211–222. University Park, PA: Pennsylvania State University Press.

Moore, C. 1996. *The Mediation Process: Practical Strategies for Resolving Conflict.* 2d ed. San Francisco: Jossey Bass.

Morgan, G. ed. 1983. *Beyond Method: Strategies for Social Research.* Bev-erly Hills: Sage Publications.

Morris, D. and I. Shapiro, eds. 1993. *John Dewey: The Political Writings.* Indianapolis: Hackett Publishing Company.

Morrison, R. 1995. *Ecological Democracy.* Boston: South End Press.

Nagel, E. 1961. *The Structure of Science: Problems in the Logic of Scientific Explanation.* New York: Harcourt Brace & World.

New Options. Washington, DC: New Options Inc.

Niebuhr, H. R. 1963. *The Responsible Self.* New York: Harper and Row.

Nino, C. S. 1996. *The Constitution of Deliberative Democracy.* New Haven: Yale University Press.

Noddings, N. 1984. *Caring: A Feminine Approach to Ethics and Moral Edu-cation.* Berkeley: University of California Press.

Norton, D. L. 1991. *Developmental Democracy: A Politics of Virtue.* Berke-ley: University of California Press.

Nussbaum, M. 1990. *Love's Knowledge: Essays on Philosophy and Litera-ture.* Oxford: Oxford University Press.

———. 1996. "Compassion: The Basic Social Emotion." In *The Communi-tarian Challenge to Liberalism,* ed. E. Paul, F. Miller, Jr., and J. Paul, 27–58. Cambridge: Cambridge University Press.

Osborne, D. 1990. *Laboratories of Democracy: A New Breed of Governors Creates Models of National Growth.* Boston: Harvard Business School Press.

Ostrom, E. 1990. *Governing the Commons: The Evolution of Institutions for Collective Action.* Cambridge: Cambridge University Press.

Page, B. I. and R. Y. Shapiro. 1993. "The Rational Public and Democracy." In *Reconsidering the Democratic Public,* ed. G. Marcus and R. Hanson, 35–64. University Park, PA: Pennsylvania State University Press.

Pateman, C. 1970. *Participation and Democratic Theory.* Cambridge: Cambridge University Press.

Pettit, P. 1993. "Consequentialism." In *A Companion to Ethics,* ed. P. Singer, 230–240. Oxford: Blackwell.

Pitkin, H. F. 1981. "Justice: On Relating Private and Public." *Political Theory* 9; 3:327–352.

Pitkin, H. F. and S. Shumer. 1982. "On Participation." *Democracy* 2; 4: 43–54.

Pogrebin, L. C. 1991. *Deborah, Golda, and Me: Being Female and Jewish in America.* New York: Doubleday.

Poincare, H. 1952. *Science and Hypothesis.* New York: Dover.

Polanyi, M. 1962. *Personal Knowledge: Towards a Post-Critical Philosophy.* New York: Harper & Row.

———. 1966. *The Tacit Dimension.* Garden City, NY: Doubleday.

Polya, G. 1954. *Induction and Analogy In Mathematics.* Princeton: Princeton University Press.

Popkin, S. 1991. *The Reasoning Voter: Communication and Persuasion In Presidential Campaigns.* Chicago: University of Chicago Press.

Popper, K. 1959. *The Logic of Scientific Discovery.* (Original German ed. 1934). London: Hutchinson and Co.

———. 1965. "Unity of Method in the Natural and Social Sciences." Reprinted in *Philosophical Problems of the Social Sciences,* ed. D. Braybrooke, 32–41. London: MacMillan.

Prychitko, D. L., ed. 1998. *Why Economists Disagree: An Introduction to Alternative Schools of Thought.* Albany: State University of New York Press.

Putnam, H. 1984. *Meaning and the Moral Sciences.* London: Routledge & Kegan Paul.

———. 1992. "A Reconsideration of Deweyan Democracy." In *Renewing Philosophy,* 180–200. Cambridge: Harvard University Press.

Putnam, R. 1993. *Making Democracy Work: Civic Traditions in Modern Italy.* Princeton: Princeton University Press.

Putnam, R. A. 1997. "Some of Life's Ideals." In *The Cambridge Companion to William James,* ed. R. A. Putnam, 282–289. Cambridge: Cambridge University Press.

Quine, W. V. 1961. "Two Dogmas of Empiricism." In *From a Logical Point of View: Nine Logico-Philosophical Essays.* 2d ed., 20–46. New York: Harper and Row.

Quine, W. V. and J. S. Ullian. 1970. *The Web of Belief.* New York: Random House.

Rachels, J. 1977. "John Dewey and the Truth about Ethics." In *New Studies in the Philosophy of John Dewey*, ed. S. Cahn, 149–171. Hanover, NH: University Press of New England.

Rasmussen, D., ed. 1990. *Universalism Vs. Communitarianism: Contemporary Debates in Ethics*. Cambridge: M.I.T. Press

Ratner, S. 1989. "Introduction." In *John Dewey: The Later Works, 1925–1953*, Volume 6, ed. J. Boydston, xi–xxiii. Carbondale IL: Southern Illinois University Press.

Ravetz, J. 1971. *Scientific Knowledge and Its Social Problems*. New York: Oxford University Press.

Rawls, J. 1971. *A Theory of Justice*. Cambridge: Harvard University Press.

———. 1993. *Political Liberalism*. New York: Columbia University Press.

Reagon, B. J. 1983. "Coalition Politics, Turning the Century." In *Home Girls, A Black Feminist Anthology*, ed. B. Smith. Latham, NY: Kitchen Table Women of Color Press.

Rensenbrink, J. 1992. *The Greens and the Politics of Transformation*. San Pedro, CA: R. & E. Miles.

Riecken, H. and R. Boruch, eds. 1974. *Social Experimentation: A Method for Planning and Evaluating Social Intervention*. New York: Academic Press.

Riessman, F. 1992. "The Politics of Self Help." *Social Policy* 23; 2:28–31.

Risen, J. and J. L. Thomas. 1998. *Wrath of Angels: The American Abortion War*. New York: Basic Books.

Rivlin, A. 1971. *Systematic Thinking for Social Action*. Washington, DC: Brookings Institution.

Rockefeller, S. C. 1991. *John Dewey: Religious Faith and Democratic Humanism*. New York: Columbia University Press.

Roemer, J. 1994. *A Future For Socialism*. Cambridge: Harvard University Press.

Rogers, C. 1951. "Dealing with Breakdowns in Communication: Interpersonal and Intergroup." Reprinted in C. Rogers *On Becoming a Person: A Therapist's View of Psychotherapy*, 329–337. Boston: Houghton Mifflin.

———. 1961. *On Becoming a Person: A Therapist's View of Psychotherapy*. Boston: Houghton Mifflin.

Rogers, J. 1996. "Why We Need an Independent Politics, and How to Build It." *Dissent* 43; 2, Spring:91–94.

Rogin, M. 1983. "In Defense of the New Left." *Democracy* 3; 4, Fall:106–116.

Roller, D. and D. H. D. Roller. 1954. *The Development of the Concept of Electric Charge: Electricity from the Greeks to Coulomb*. Cambridge: Harvard University Press.

Rorty, R. 1979. *Philosophy and the Mirror of Nature*. Princeton: Princeton University Press.

———. 1982. *Consequences of Pragmatism: Essays, 1972–1980*. Minneapolis: University of Minnesota Press.

———. 1995. "Response to James Gouinlock." In *Rorty and Pragmatism:*

The Philosopher Responds to His Critics, ed. H. J. Saatkamp, Jr., 91–99. Nashville: Vanderbilt University Press.

Rose, M. 1995. *Possible Lives: The Promise of Public Education in America.* Boston: Houghton Mifflin.

Rosen, J. 1996. *Getting the Connections Right: Public Journalism and the Troubles in the Press.* New York: Twentieth Century Fund.

Rosenberg, A. 1988. *Philosophy of Social Science.* Boulder: Westview Press.

Rosenthal, S. B. 1986. *Speculative Pragmatism.* LaSalle, IL: Open Court.

Ross, D. 1991. *The Origins of American Social Science.* Cambridge: Cambridge University Press.

Rotblat, J. 1985. "Leaving the Bomb Project." *Bulletin of the Atomic Scientists* 41; 7, August: 16–19.

Rouse, J. 1987. *Knowledge and Power: Toward a Political Philosophy of Science.* Ithaca: Cornell University Press.

Rubin, L. B. 1976. *Worlds of Pain: Life in the Working Class Family.* New York: Basic Books.

Ruddick, S. 1989. *Maternal Thinking: Toward a Politics of Peace.* Boston: Beacon Press.

Ryan, A. 1992. "The Legacy of John Dewey." Review of Westbrook 1991. *Dissent* 39; 2: 273–278.

———. 1993. "The Liberal Community." In *Democratic Community: Nomos XXXV*, ed. J. W. Chapman and I. Shapiro, 91–114. New York: New York University Press.

———. 1995. *John Dewey and the High Tide of American Liberalism.* New York: Norton.

Ryle, G. 1949. *The Concept of Mind.* New York: Barnes and Noble.

Saint, S., and J. Lawson. 1994. *Rules for Reaching Consensus: A Modern Approach to Decision Making.* Amsterdam: Pfeiffer.

Sandel, M. 1996. *Democracy's Discontents: America in Search of a Public Philosophy.* Cambridge: Harvard University Press.

Sanford, N. 1970. "What Happened to Action Research?" *Journal of Social Issues* Autumn, 26: 3–23.

Sarason, S. B. 1996. *Revisiting "The Culture of the School and the Problem of Change."* New York: Teachers College Press.

Schon, D. 1983. *The Reflective Practitioner: How Professionals Think In Action.* New York: Basic Books.

———, ed. 1991. *The Reflective Turn: Case Studies in and on Educational Practice.* New York: Teachers College Press.

Schwartz, E. A. 1991. "The Radicalism of a Liberal." Review of Westbrook 1991. *New York Times Book Review*, September 22, 1991: 48–49.

Schweikart, D. 1980. *Capitalism or Worker Control?.* New York: Praeger.

Schwerin, E. 1995. *Mediation, Citizen Empowerment, and Transformational Politics.* Westport, CT: Praeger.

Shapere, D. 1971. "Scientific Theories and Their Domains." In *The Structure of Scientific Theories*, ed. F. Suppe. 518–565. Urbana: University of Illinois Press.

Shulman, G. 1983. "The Pastoral Idyll of Democracy." *Democracy* 3; 4: 43–84.

Shusterman, R. 1994a. "Dewey on Experience: Foundation or Reconstruction." *The Philosophical Forum* XXVI:2, Winter 1994:127–148.

———. 1994b. "Pragmatism and Liberalism: Between Dewey and Rorty." *Political Theory* 22; 3:391–413.

———. 1997. *Practicing Philosophy: Pragmatism and the Philosophical Life.* New York: Routledge.

Silver, M. 1994. "Irreconcilable Moral Disagreement." In *Defending Diversity: Contemporary Philosophical Perspectives on Pluralism and Multiculturalism,* ed. L. Foster and P. Herzog, 39–58. Amherst: University of Massachusetts Press.

Simmons, L. 1994. *Organizing in Hard Times: Labor and Neighborhoods in Hartford.* Philadelphia: Temple University Press.

Singer, P. 1993. *Practical Ethics.* 2d ed. Cambridge: Cambridge University Press.

Sizer, T. 1992. *Horace's School: Redesigning the American High School.* Boston: Houghton Mifflin.

Sleeper, R. W. 1986. *The Necessity of Pragmatism: John Dewey's Conception of Philosophy.* New Haven: Yale University Press.

Smiley, M. 1990. "Pragmatic Inquiry and Social Conflict: A Critical Reconstruction of Dewey's Model of Democracy." *Praxis International* 9; 4:365–380.

Solinger, R., ed. 1998. *Abortion Wars: A Half Century of Struggle, 1950–2000.* Berkeley: University of California Press

Stiefel, M. and M. Wolfe. 1994. *A Voice for the Excluded. Popular Participation in Development: Utopia or Necessity.* London: Zed Books.

Strong, T. B. and F. A. Sposito. 1995. "Habermas's Significant Other." In *The Cambridge Companion to Habermas,* ed. S. White, 263–288. Cambridge: Cambridge University Press.

Students for a Democratic Society. 1962. *The Port Huron Statement.* New York: Students for a Democratic Society. (Reprinted in *The New Radicals: A Report with Documents,* ed. P. Jacobs and S. Landau, 150–162. New York: Random House).

Susskind, L. and J. Cruikshank. 1987. *Breaking the Impasse: Consensual Approaches to Resolving Public Disputes.* New York: Basic Books.

Sutton, F. X., S. Harris, C. Kaysen and J. Tobin. 1961. *The American Business Creed.* 2d ed. New York: Schocken Books.

Taylor, C. 1977. "What is Human Agency." In *The Self,* ed. T. Mischel, 103–135. Oxford: Blackwell.

———. 1985. "Interpretation and the Sciences of Man." In *Philosophical Papers II: Philosophy and the Human Sciences,* 15–57. Cambridge: Cambridge University Press.

———. 1989. *Sources of the Self.* Cambridge: Harvard University Press.

Tiles, J. E. 1988. *Dewey.* London: Routledge.

Toulmin, S. 1970. "Does the Distinction between Normal and Revolution-

ary Science Hold Water?" In *Criticism and the Growth of Knowledge*,
ed. I. Lakatos and A. Musgrave, 39–47. Cambridge: Cambridge University
Press.

Tronto, J. C. 1994. *Moral Boundaries: A Political Argument for an Ethic of
Care*. New York: Routledge.

Ury, W. L, J. M. Brett and S. B. Goldberg. 1988. *Getting Disputes Resolved:
Designing Systems to Cut the Costs of Conflict*. San Francisco: Jossey
Bass.

Vanek, J. 1970. *The General Theory of Labor Managed Market Economies*.
Ithaca: Cornell University Press.

Wachtel, P. L. 1989. *The Poverty of Affluence: A Psychological Portrait of
the American Way of Life*. Philadelphia: New Society Publishers.

Walker, M. U. 1998. *Moral Understandings: A Feminist Study in Ethics*.
New York: Routledge.

Walton, R. E., J. Cutcher-Gershenfeld and R. B. McKersie. 1984. *Strategic
Negotiations: A Theory of Change in Labor-Management Relations*.
Boston: Harvard Business School Press.

Walzer, M. 1983. *Spheres of Justice: A Defense of Pluralism and Equality*.
New York: Basic Books.

———. 1996. "Minority Rites." *Dissent* Summer: 53–55.

Warren, M. 1992. "Democratic Theory and Self-Transformation." *American
Political Science Review* 86:8–23.

———. 1995. "The Self in Discursive Democracy." In *The Cambridge Companion to Habermas*, ed. S. White, 167–200. Cambridge: Cambridge University Press.

———. 1996. "What Should We Expect from More Democracy?: Radically
Democratic Responses to Politics." *Political Theory* 24; 2:241–270.

Webne-Behrman, H. 1996. "Seeking Common Ground on Teen Pregnancy:
A Facilitator's Perspective." In *Common Ground on Teen Pregnancy:
A Pro-Choice, Pro-Life Conversation, Network Papers No. 2*, ed. M. Jack-
steit, 19–22. Washington, DC: Common Ground Network for Life and
Choice.

Weisman, A. 1998. *Gaviotas: A Village to Reinvent the World*. White River
Junction, VT: Chelsea Green.

West, C. 1989. *The American Evasion of Philosophy: A Genealogy of Pragmatism*. Madison: University of Wisconsin Press.

Westbrook, R. 1991. *John Dewey and American Democracy*. Ithaca: Cornell
University Press.

White, S. K., ed. 1995. *The Cambridge Companion to Habermas*. Cambridge: Cambridge University Press.

Whyte, W. F., ed. 1991. *Participatory Action Research*. Newbury Park, CA:
Sage Publications.

Whyte, W. F. and K. K. Whyte. 1991. *Making Mondragon: The Growth and
Dynamics of the Worker Cooperative Complex*. 2d ed. Ithaca: ILR Press.

Williams, B. 1973. "Ethical Consistency." In *Problems of the Self*, 166–186.
Cambridge: Cambridge University Press.

Winch, P. 1958. *The Idea of a Social Science.* London: Routledge & Kegan Paul.

Woliver, L. R. 1996. "Rhetoric and Symbols in American Abortion Politics." In *Abortion Politics: Public Policy in Cross Cultural Perspective,* ed. M. Githens and D. McBride Stetson, 5–28. New York: Routledge.

Wong, D. B. 1994. "Coping with Moral Conflict and Ambiguity." In *Defending Diversity: Contemporary Philosophical Perspectives on Pluralism and Multiculturalism,* ed. L. Foster and P. Herzog, 13–38. Amherst: University of Massachusetts Press.

Wood, G. H. 1992. *Schools that Work: America's Most Innovative Public Education Programs.* New York: Plume. Penguin Books.

Woolpert, S., C. Slaton and E. Schwerin, eds. 1998. *Transformational Politics: Theory, Study, and Practice.* Albany: State University of New York Press.

Wuthnow, R. 1994. *Sharing the Journey: Support Groups and America's New Quest for Community.* New York: Free Press.

Wypljewski, J. 1997. "A Stirring in the Land." *Nation* September 8/15: 17–25.

Yankelovich, D. 1991. *Coming to Public Judgment: Making Democracy Work in a Complex World.* Syracuse: Syracuse University Press.

Yes! A Journal of Positive Futures. Bainbridge Island, WA: Positive Futures Network.

Young, I. M. 1996. "Communication and the Other: Beyond Deliberative Democracy." In *Democracy and Difference: Contesting the Boundaries of the Political,* ed. S. Benhabib, 120–135. Princeton: Princeton University Press.

———. 1997. "The Complexities of Coalition." *Dissent* 44; 1, Winter: 64–69.

Yunus, M. 1997. "The End of Poverty." *Yes: A Journal of Positive Futures* I; 1, Winter: 12–16.

Index